PE

Noel 'Razor' Smith was born in London in 1960. He has fifty-eight criminal convictions and has spent the greater portion of his adult life in prison. While in prison he taught himself to read and write, gaining an Honours Diploma from the London School of Journalism and an A Level in Law. He has received a number of Koestler awards for his writing and has contributed articles to the *Independent*, the *Guardian*, *Punch*, the *Big Issue*, the *New Statesman* and the *New Law Journal*. Smith is currently serving a life sentence for armed robbery. His first book, *A Few Kind Words and a Loaded Gun*, was published by Penguin in 2004.

Raiders

The True Stories of Britain's Most
Daring and Dangerous Bank Robbers

RAZOR SMITH

PENGUIN BOOKS

PENGUIN BOOKS

Published by the Penguin Group
Penguin Books Ltd, 80 Strand, London WC2R ORL, England
Penguin Group (USA) Inc., 375 Hudson Street, New York, New York 10014, USA
Penguin Group (Canada), 90 Eglinton Avenue East, Suite 700, Toronto, Ontario, Canada M4P 2Y3
(a division of Pearson Penguin Canada Inc.)
Penguin Ireland, 25 St Stephen's Green, Dublin 2, Ireland
(a division of Penguin Books Ltd)
Penguin Group (Australia), 250 Camberwell Road, Camberwell, Victoria 3124, Australia
(a division of Pearson Australia Group Pty Ltd)
Penguin Books India Pvt Ltd, 11 Community Centre, Panchsheel Park, New Delhi – 110 017, India
Penguin Group (NZ), 67 Apollo Drive, Rosedale, North Shore 0632, New Zealand
(a division of Pearson New Zealand Ltd)
Penguin Books (South Africa) (Pty) Ltd, 24 Sturdee Avenue, Rosebank, Johannesburg 2196, South Africa

Penguin Books Ltd, Registered Offices: 80 Strand, London WC2R ORL, England

www.penguin.com

First published 2007
1

Set in 11.75/13.5 pt Monotype Garamond
Typeset by Rowland Phototypesetting Ltd, Bury St Edmunds, Suffolk
Printed in England by Clays Ltd, St Ives plc

ISBN 978–0–141–03227–6

For my brother, Mick – and all the other angels with dirty faces who wanted to be Jimmy Cagney but grew up to be Pat O'Brien. Spit in their eye, Rocky!

Acknowledgements

Thanks are due to my friend and agent, Will, and to Tony, Jon and all the team at Penguin for their hard work on my behalf. To my family, as ever, my children and grandchildren – may you walk in sunshine always. To Jemma, for everything. And to all the outlaws, in-laws, diamond geezers and straight shooters: Alan Ward, Johnny Shelley, Steve Montgomery, Tel Currie, Terry Smith, Roy Shaw, Chaz Bronson, Frannie Pope, Charlie Tozer, Tony Argent, Billy Cockram, Mitchell Wright, Freddie Lunn, Ray Bishop, Nicky Wood, Greg Crabtree, Jason Pickles, Marvin Baker, Vic Dark, Daren Newland, Mark Aldridge, Nolan Watts, Davie Bruce, Alec Begg, Will Beck, Steve Bunker, Andy Nolan and the Bible Code Sundays, and to my pals in New Zealand, Liam Carpenter and Rocky – to name but a few. Our situation does not require victory, it only forbids surrender. Stay lucky!

Contents

Preface

The legend goes that when infamous American outlaw Jesse James first proposed robbing Union banks by walking through the front door armed and during business hours Cole Younger said, 'Hell, Jesse, ain't nobody robbed a bank like that before!' To which the innovative young Mr James is reputed to have replied, 'Sure, but carts didn't have wheels until someone thought of 'em.' Events were to prove Jesse's pioneering modus operandi very successful indeed as the James/Younger gang went on to rob the modern equivalent of $5 million in their four-year career as bank robbers. And the guns-through-the-front-door technique that worked so well back in the 1860s is still being used by bank robbers all over the world to this day.

Jesse James, first of the modern bank robbers, went down in history as a folk hero and is still revered and idolized, mainly due to the efforts of Hollywood and the American hunger for a history of any kind. America loves its bank robbers, from John Dillinger and Willie Sutton to Bonnie and Clyde (though the latter duo were not strictly 'bank' robbers, more spree-killers who nicked a few quid at gunpoint along the way). American outlaws have inspired many books, articles, films and documentaries, which examine their lives and exploits in great detail and it has to be said that not one of them seems to have come out of it in too bad a light.

For some reason, the public, on the whole, seems to have a sort of sneaking admiration for the bank robber. As long as he does not use unnecessary violence on the innocent and gets away with a nice haul from what are basically seen as faceless big-business institutions, then some citizens seem willing to give him a bye. From my own experience, the British public is not that different in outlook to its American cousins when it comes to its home-grown blaggers. I would lay odds that if a survey were done asking the British public to list in order of importance the crimes that frighten them and affect their everyday lives, bank robbery would come pretty far down that list. But put those same people on a jury and let them hear bank staff and customers describe their bowel-emptying terror during a robbery and suddenly they realize that the reality is not some Hollywood caper with handsome and witty actors playing a part but a terrifying and traumatizing ordeal for those involved. Bank robbery is one of those crimes which, when viewed from a distance, would seem to be fairly impersonal and 'victimless'. But it's not.

Yet still we make folk heroes of our robbers, and it has been happening for a long time. Think Robin Hood and Dick Turpin: if the James/Younger gang originated the walk-in bank robbery, then Hood and Turpin set the template for modern-day cash-in-transit robbers, who are, in effect, contemporary highwaymen. In the twentieth century the Great Train Robbers immediately spring to mind, with their 'daring' 1963 £2 million mail-train robbery. The train robbers and latterly John 'Public Enemy Number One' McVicar have achieved iconic status in Britain, with books written by them and about them and in each case a successful film. The British have a tradition of producing the kind of criminals who can plan and execute a daring blag, and in the last fifty-odd years we've had some big ones: the Eastcastle Street Post-Office Job (£238,000 cash; 1953), the Great Train Robbery (£2.6 million cash; 1963), the Wembley Bank Robbery (£138,000 cash; 1969), the Security Express Robbery (£6 million cash; 1983), the Brinks Mat Gold-Bullion Robbery (£26 million gold bullion; 1983), the Knightsbridge Safety-Deposit Robbery (£60 million cash plus drugs and diamonds; 1987), the Millennium Dome Diamond Robbery

(£200 million in diamonds; 2000), the Northern Bank Robbery in Belfast (£26.5 million cash; 2005), and the Tonbridge Security-Depot Robbery (£25 million cash; 2006). For the sake of accuracy, it should be said that the Knightsbridge job was planned and carried out by an Italian leading a multinational crew and the Millennium Dome job was only an attempt and the robbers were captured on the scene. But there's no doubt about it, we do love a good heist. By rights, we shouldn't admire these men, because when it comes right down to it they are no more than parasites too greedy and lazy to work for a living. So why, when we hear that they've pulled one off, no matter how much we outwardly tut and shake our heads in disgust, is there still some small part of us that gives a tiny cheer and thumbs its little nose at conventionality? I guess there's a bit of the rebel in all of us.

For the men who do these things, choosing to commit armed robbery for a living is not something to take lightly. Apart from the obvious minus that when they get nicked, as they inevitably do, they are looking at a very hefty prison sentence (the average sentence for bank robbery with no one physically injured and no shots fired is fifteen years and up), they also have to take into account that they are offering themselves up to specialist armed police squads, some of whom have less than savoury reputations for shooting first and asking questions later – too late. There is also the chance that, carrying a firearm, they might kill someone, through panic and desperation or even by accident, and that means a minimum of thirty years in prison. So it's not a career that anyone would want to stroll into for the experience. It is a very serious business, and I should know. For nearly thirty years I was an armed robber, not one of the household names, though some of my exploits did occasionally attract headlines in local papers. I was a career criminal, a 'working' robber, active almost every week when I was not in prison. Over the years, both inside and out, though mainly in, I met and associated with a lot of armed robbers and, invariably, we exchanged information and stories. In my experience robbers are a different breed to most other criminals – they are flashier, louder, more rebellious and more willing to take risks. They also, I believe, have a better sense of humour and an eye for the absurd. Gather a team of robbers together in any drinking club or prison exercise yard and pretty soon you'll be hearing their stories, sometimes terrifying, often boastful and arrogant, occasionally sad, mostly hilarious, but always interesting. The stories here are true, and most have been verified through court depositions, media reports and third-party witnesses. The majority were passed to me by word of mouth from those involved and have been written from memory. Only the names and some details have been changed. This has been done to protect the guilty, as well as the innocent.

Personally, I no longer class myself as a criminal. That was something I did in a past life before I found a long and painful rehabilitation. In the parlance of my previous associates in 'the heavy mob', I am what is known as a 'rusty gun'. And to tell you the truth, I don't miss the old days that much – being coshed, stabbed, shot at and locked up in prison for decades has lost whatever appeal it once had for me. In the following pages I hope you will be able to see that life as a serious career criminal, far from being glamorous and full of glory, is actually a very sad existence with only the grim and unappealing prospect of incarceration or, in some cases, death. Nobody gets away with it – not for long anyway. The men whose stories I tell in the following pages have paid, or are paying even as you read, for their crimes.

I do not condone any crime not committed out of real poverty or desperation, but I am a sucker for a good story. So if you've ever wondered what it's like to go to work wearing a ski-mask and carrying a sawn-off shotgun, to walk out of a bank with enough money to retire on, or to be shot at by armed police officers, then wonder no more – just read on.

Noel 'Razor' Smith
In Prison
2006

1. Tough Tony Takes a Beating

Tough Tony was a man who was very close to me for a very long time. He was a south London robber who had been at the game for many years and looked out of his element when not waving a gun in someone's face or stalking the landing of a top-security prison. By his own estimate, Tough Tony had been involved in over two hundred armed raids since his teens and had served a total of twenty-three years in prison for some of them. Tony was very proud of the fact that he had never fired a shot on any of his robberies, nor ever had to physically assault anybody. He used to say that if a robber had to resort to actual physical violence then he might as well get out of the game and become a football hooligan. I always thought this lack of ruthlessness on his part was probably the reason why he was still a bread-and-butter robber and had not been invited on to any of the major robbery teams despite his criminal pedigree and experience.

But he was good at what he did. It was said that if Tough Tony couldn't rob it, then it wasn't worth two-bob, and if he could, then he would. He was the sort of geezer who was up for anything at the drop of a hat. You only had to turn up at his gaff and offer a bit of work and he would be sitting in the get-away motor with his shotgun on his lap before you'd finished the last word of your sentence. Tony loved to rob, and over the years he told me many stories about the things that happened while he was 'working'. The story I have included here, which he told me on the exercise yard at HMP Whitemoor in 2001, is one of the best. And here's how it played out.

It was January 1993 and Tough Tony was not long out of jail, having just served ten years of a fifteen-year sentence for the armed robbery of a post-office security van. Money was pretty tight but he had managed to scrape together enough to buy a double-barrelled sawn-off twelve-bore shotgun, two cartridges for the gun and a cheap Mk5 Ford Cortina – the essential starting pack for any ambitious blagger looking to get back into the game and earn a nice few quid. He'd teamed up with an old pal, a sulphate dealer known as Whizzy, who was also feeling the pinch and didn't mind doing a bit of driving but drew the line at actually handling a firearm or putting the cosh about. Whizzy was a pacifist and hated violence – except when it was being done for money and to other people – but he was mustard as a wheelman.

Tough Tony was an 'old skool' crook, particularly when it came to his crime partners – the get-away driver got 50 per cent of whatever was robbed. After all, Tony figured, and not wrongly in my opinion, the get-away driver was putting himself on offer for at least a seven-stretch if things went King Kong. And seven years in jail is no walk in the park for anyone. Some robbery firms put their drivers on as little as 10 per cent of the take, which can be a nice payday if you're blagging a couple of mil, but on a standard bit of work this kind of financial disparity can lead to animosity. The last thing you want is to leg it away from the work with alarms going off and armed Old Bill on their way only to find that your wheelman has copped the hump with you and gone for a cuppa. So Tough Tony kept his confederates keen and paid the cost to be the boss.

Whizzy had never driven on a robbery before and Tough Tony was a bit rusty himself from his decade of incarceration so he decided to start with something a bit simple. He picked out a small branch of one of the high street banks, figuring that the till money would come to around five grand, which would be enough for another couple of cheap get-away cars and to get by on while they recce'd a better bit of work. This particular brand of bank was one that Tough Tony had never robbed before, through no particular reason other than he had just never got around to them. He knew that walk-in bank robberies were basically the same no matter the marque of the bank, with only minor refinements needed. The trouble was that Tony had been away at the Greybar Hotel for a long time and bank robberies in London had trebled in number since he was last on the street. The result of this was that some of the household-name banks were taking a tough line on walk-in robberies. Unknown to their customers, certain banks developed a policy of protecting the money at all costs. The cashiers were to drop to the floor in the event of a robbery and keep out of sight. They were behind bullet-proof screens, and if the robber couldn't see them he could hardly shoot them, let alone get them to hand over the cash. The money and the staff would be perfectly safe, but the suits who devised this plan either gave no thought to, or didn't give a fuck about, their 'valuable' customers, who would be left in the banking hall at the mercy of angry and frustrated men carrying, in many cases, loaded firearms.

A lot of walk-in robbers found out that the only way to get the cashiers out of their hidey-holes was to grab hold of a customer, put the gun up to their head and threaten loudly to execute them unless the money was handed over. This usually worked. But the suits at one well-known high street bank had decided that they would not hand over another penny to robbers, even if they turned every one of their banking halls into a slaughterhouse. Of course, they never made this public but hoped the robbers would eventually get the message and leave them alone. It was one of these banks that Tough Tony chose as his warm-up.

Feeling a little bit nervous, Tough Tony climbed out of the

get-away car and leant back in to tell Whizzy that he shouldn't be long and he was not to move the car from this spot. He straightened his shoulders and shifted the weight of the sawn-off in his waistband underneath his overcoat. As he headed across the pavement he pulled his flat cap low over his face and glanced about for anything suspicious. At the doorway of the bank he unbuttoned his overcoat, got his hand on the butt of the sawn-off and took a deep breath. Tough Tony hit the quiet banking hall like that old cartoon of Tas the Tasmanian devil, shouting at everyone to 'Stand still!' and pointing the shotgun threateningly at anyone who did not instantly obey. There were five or six customers in the bank and Tony knew he had to deal with them first and quickly. Snarling, growling and firing dire threats liberally sprinkled with obscenities, Tony herded the cowed customers to the back wall of the bank, well away from the entrance, and turned his attention to the staff. But when he looked behind the jump it was as deserted as the *Marie Celeste*. Tony, having dealt with most things while engaged in robbery over the years, gave the screen a thump with the butt of his shotgun. 'Get up, you slags, and start handing over the money or I'll start shooting these customers!' He heard a collective gasp from the line of white-faced customers but turned his face towards them and gave a panto-mime wink as if to say, 'Only kidding!' – though I don't suppose this did too much to calm their terror. The cashiers made no move to get off the floor and Tony redoubled his threats. 'If you don't get up here and hand over the money by the count of three, I'll shoot two of these people! I fucking mean it!' When you are in a bluff situation – and Tough Tony was bluffing because he would no more shoot an innocent customer than he would stick his head in an electric cheese-grater – the most foolish thing you can do is impose a time limit on your bluff. Because when that time limit runs out you have to either shit or get off the pot.

'One!' As Tough Tony began his count the only other sounds in the banking hall were the sobbing and praying of the poor customers. 'Two!' Tony stood at the counter and watched for movement behind the jump, but there was nothing. Surely, he thought, they wouldn't leave their customers to be shot over a measly bit of till money that was fully insured anyway? He hesitated, then – 'Three!' Nothing. Tough Tony couldn't believe it. This was outrageous! He was severely pissed off at not getting the money, but more so by the idea that the cashiers would callously leave their customers at the mercy of an armed and threatening man. Like most of the robbers I have met, Tough Tony cared not a jot about justice but got the raving hump over injustice. He gave the bullet-proof screen another bash with his gun butt and was tempted to fire a shot into it but didn't want to waste a cartridge. 'You fucking bunch of cowardly wankers!' he shouted in frustration through one of the till-wells. 'I'll be waiting outside for you cunts one of these dark nights! Mugs!' He started to leave but then turned to the customers, who were still lined up against the back wall, gibbering wrecks each and every one. Tough Tony shrugged. 'Sorry about that,' he said. 'But if I was you I'd change my bank, because if I wasn't such a nice fella you could all be dead now.' Then he was gone, out the door and into the get-away car.

Even years later I could hear the bewilderment in Tough Tony's voice as he spoke about the bank that wouldn't pay out. He just couldn't get his mind around the concept of big business being willing and able to sacrifice lives for a few quid. Despite threatening people with a gun for a living, Tony had never shot anybody and was adamant that he never would. 'I'm there for the money,' he would say. 'If I wanted to shoot people I would have joined the police force.'

His first attempt to get back into the game having turned into a bit of a farce, Tough Tony's confidence had taken a bit of a knock. But he wasn't ready to give up and go straight just yet. Besides, he wasn't fit for any other line of work and had been a criminal since before he had left school. His next idea was to play it safe and hit a bank that he had robbed in the past. This is not that unusual among robbers. I know people like to say that lightning never strikes twice in the same place and that criminals never return to the scene of the crime, but that's just not true in either case. When you've had a nice touch from some jug you always keep it in mind to rob again at some stage in the future when things are a bit desperate. Some robbers take this to extremes: another old mate of mine, now deceased, called Little Andy, had his own personal building society which he would rob whenever he was short of cash and couldn't be bothered working too hard. It got so that when they saw him coming they would put the money up on the counter and not get too involved. He robbed the same premises nine times in fourteen months, and in the end they closed the branch down and sold the building to an estate agent for offices. Anyway, after parking the get-away car up for a couple of days in order for the heat to die down a bit, Tough Tony and Whizzy headed for a bank in Thornton Heath.

This time everything went according to plan and Tough Tony walked out of the bank with £7,500, which was a much-needed boost to his confidence as well as his finances. Now that they had a few quid in the bank, so to speak, Tough Tony and Whizzy could devote their time to searching for a suitable target that would give them a big enough prize to get off the breadline. Tough Tony had a penchant for security vans, cash-in-transit being his preferred kind of robbery. Mostly he went for 'pony-bags', which are the small boxes carried across the pavement to the bank by a lone security guard. They are called pony-bags by the criminal fraternity because in criminal parlance a pony is twenty-five, and the bags were insured to contain a maximum of £25,000. Sometimes, to save time, a security guard would, against company policy, take a chance on walking more than one bag across at once, and it was these little lapses that pony-bag robbers lived for. Tough Tony was now on the look-out for a careless guard. He chose Croydon town centre as his hunting ground because of the many advantages it offered the enterprising blagger. The actual shopping centre, a wide road with every kind of bank and retail outlet, was closed to motorized traffic other than emergency services and security vans. Every day the vans of several different cash-in-transit companies would pull into this wide thoroughfare and spend hours making pick-ups from the scores of busy premises. It was so crowded with shoppers and pedestrians that it was easy to blend in and get a good nut at the security guards' routines. Plus, there were a couple of dozen routes out of the centre by foot, motorbike or car. On the minus side, there was the fact that because so much money passed across the pavement every day there were often 'spotters' from the security firms, plain-clothes employees who would plot up and watch for anyone suspicious and be in direct contact with the police. But Tough Tony had been lucky in Croydon in the past and he was determined that he would be again.

For a couple of days Tough Tony mooched around the main shopping thoroughfare, eating soggy burgers, drinking exotically named coffee and generally keeping a sharp but seemingly innocent eye on the comings and goings of the vans and guards. Perhaps because of the spotters, all the guards on the main drag seemed to be very conscientious in their work and stuck to the limit of one pony-bag on the pavement at a time. So Tony decided to expand his circle and check out the sidestreets. It was while he was loitering on one of these sidestreets pretending to read a copy of the *Sun* while keeping his eyes peeled that he stumbled across a coup so mouth-wateringly delicious that he almost took a bite out of it there and then. A large white security van pulled up at the kerb of a wide expanse of pavement in front of a small row of premises that included a bank and a well-known travel agency. The first thing Tony noticed was that the driver of the van looked about seventeen years old and, instead of checking the surrounding area for suspicious characters and suspect vehicles, as he was supposed to, he seemed more interested in finding the right angle in his wing mirror to check his hair and squeeze a couple of his spots. Tough Tony couldn't believe how lax about security this youth seemed, but it was great for him and he lapped it up like a saucer of cream.

Next, the door of the van opened and a woman in the livery of the security company stepped out on to the pavement. The female guard was no higher than five foot two and weighed in at a good sixteen stone. Years later, as he was telling me about this, Tough Tony swore that he still had a bruise on his foot where his jaw dropped when he saw her. The female guard waddled around to the cash chute on the side of the van and gave a signal knock on the side. The small steel door flew up to reveal a large security box. From where he was standing Tony could see that this was the holy of holies for the lone or small-team security-van robber – a ton-box. The ton-box has added security devices, such as exploding dye-packs and a screamer alarm (though there are ways in which robbers can neutralize these), so it is insured for up to £100,000 going across the pavement. For Tough Tony this was like an angel had flown down from heaven and sprinkled stardust all over his mooey!

As Tony watched in astonishment the female guard struggled across the wide expanse of pavement with the box. If he'd had his gun on him he would have been very tempted to go and take the box right then. In fact, he seriously contemplated just going and slapping the guard and taking it, but his car was parked over a mile away and he guessed he might look

8

a bit suspicious running through Croydon shopping centre with a screaming, smoking security box. So Tony swallowed. He made a mental note of the time and location and vowed to return the next week as the box finally disappeared through the door of the travel agency.

When Tough Tony described the job he had found, Whizzy was a bit dubious. He couldn't believe that an easy bit of work like this was presenting itself on the streets of the robbery capital of Britain and suggested that it might be a set-up, a ready-eye by Old Bill in the hope of ambushing a couple of blaggers. To be fair to Whizzy, the Flying Squad, who dealt only in armed robbery in London, had previous for sitting on jobs of this kind, knowing the work would be viewed as a peach by any blagger worth his salt. But Tough Tony was a veteran of the game and could usually smell the Flying Squad from half a mile away and upwind and he was sure they had not been in the area. It was standard to check the surrounding streets, and Tony had been meticulous about this. In the normal course of events, he would have had a radio scanner, usually a top-of-the-range Bearcat, in order to pick up messages over the police wavebands that would give him a clue whether they were near by, but he hadn't yet got around to buying one. But Tony trusted his instincts, and his instincts said this was a goer. In order to put Whizzy's mind at ease, Tough Tony agreed that the two of them should go and take another look at the work the following week, before they actually tackled it.

The very next week the lads took up their positions and watched the exact same routine again – the spotty geek driver, the dumpling box-carrier, the near-empty street. It was all perfect. After the van had gone Tough Tony and Whizzy spent over an hour checking out every vantage point from which the Squad could keep a ready-eye and launch an ambush but the whole area was cleaner than a lifeboat captain's whistle. On the drive back into south London they decided it would go the following week and they would spend the next couple of days making a plan of action.

The plan that Tough Tony came up with was simple. The short sideroad in which the van stopped was a one-way street and a no-parking zone for ordinary traffic, so Whizzy would park the get-away car half up on the pavement with the hazard lights flashing. He would set up one of those plastic 'Emergency Warning' triangles behind the car and have the bonnet up as though it had just conked out and he was working on it. Being only twenty-five feet away from the work, Whizzy would have a perfect view of when it went down and that would be his signal to close the bonnet and get ready for the off in the driver's seat of the get-away motor. Meanwhile, Tough Tony, dressed in his long overcoat and with his flat cap again pulled low over his eyes, would be standing looking at the offers in the window of the travel agency. Under his coat Tony would have his faithful sawn-off shotgun, with a strong piece of string tied to the butt and looped around his neck so that it could hang unseen but be within reach when needed. He would wait for the dumpling with the box to get to within a couple of feet of him and then whip the gun up and demand the box. If all went to plan, and there was no reason to think it wouldn't, then Tony would be in the get-away car neutralizing the security devices in the box in less than a minute, and within four minutes he and Whizzy would be half a mile away transferring the money to the change-over car, which was parked up in the car park of a block of flats. They went through the plan several times looking for flaws and then they just had to wait for the day of the job.

On the morning of the robbery the lads were up early and raring to go. They knew that by the end of the day they would be considerably richer if all went well, and that's enough to add a bounce to anyone's step. Tony drove the change-over car, a ten-year-old but tidy-looking Volkswagen Golf with three months' tax on the window, up to the car park, tailed in another Mk5 Cortina by Whizzy. Once the Golf was in place Tony took the happy-bag containing the sawn-off and the tool he would need to neutralize the cash box and climbed into the Mk5 with Whizzy. On the way to the work Tony looped the gun round his neck by its lanyard and prepared himself with a couple of deep-breathing exercises. Going on a robbery is no casual affair for anyone except the most stone-faced, nerveless bastards, and most robbers approach it in the same way as an athlete would approach a world-record attempt. You have to loosen your body and then psych yourself up in order to give your best performance. You need to attain a state of total concentration and single-mindedness even as the adrenaline is coursing through your body, churning your stomach and turning your muscles to lead. The big difference between the two professions is that if an athlete comes second he won't end up shot by the police or serving the next ten-stretch in prison.

At the appointed hour, after a quick cup of coffee in a nearby cafe, Whizzy had the Mk5 up on the pavement with the bonnet up and Tough Tony was trying to make himself inconspicuous with his bogus window-shopping. Ten o'clock, the hour when the van had appeared in the preceding two weeks, came and went with no sign. Tony knew you had to allow for traffic delays, but at 10.10 he was starting to get nervous. He couldn't go on walking up and down this small parade of shops and businesses indefinitely. Sooner or later someone would start to wonder what his game was. Under his heavy overcoat, and despite the cold January weather, he was starting to sweat like a vicar in a brothel. Then a gimlet-eyed traffic warden turned into the street and made a beeline for the Mk5. Whizzy, covering his panic well, told the warden that he thought his engine had overheated and that the AA were already en route. The warden accepted his story and strolled on looking for easier meat, and both Tough Tony and Whizzy mopped their sweaty foreheads and raised eyebrows at each other from a distance.

At 10.17 Tony was just about ready to walk away from the work and try again the following week when the big white security van hove into view. Tony was relieved to see the familiar sight of the careless spotty geek of a driver and gave Whizzy an almost imperceptible nod as he unbuttoned his overcoat and got ready. Whizzy casually put the bonnet of the Mk5 down and walked to the driver's door. The passenger door of the security van opened but, instead of the female dumpling, a monster climbed out. Tony described it as looking like a six foot four inch albino silverback gorilla in a guard's suit. The geezer was huge, with shoulders as wide as most people are long and arms hanging almost to his knees. He adjusted the chin strap of his helmet with hands as big as frying pans and fingers like bunches of bananas and scowled around the street like he was daring someone even to look at him sideways. Tough Tony swallowed hard and felt a sinking feeling in his stomach. The humungous security guard stamped up to the side of the van where the hatch was situated and Tough Tony later swore that when he banged his fist on the reinforced metal of the van he left a dent. The box came sliding out and the guard lifted it like it was made of paper and set out striding across the pavement to where Tough Tony was standing.

There was no way Tough Tony was going to leave the work now that everything was on site. He had been surprised and a bit shaken by the sight of the guard, but size meant nothing when you had an equalizer in the form of a sawn-off double-barrelled twelve-gauge. Tony had seen some very hard men hang their heads and take a back seat when faced with the threat of a sawn-off and he was guessing that this creature would be no different. When the guard got to within three feet of him Tough Tony spun around and whipped the shotgun up so that it was pointing at his midriff. 'Drop the fucking box!' he yelled menacingly. But instead of stopping in his tracks like a normal man faced with such a sight, the big guard never even broke his stride. Instead he swung the metal cash box upwards with such force that it hit the tip of the barrels of Tough Tony's shotgun and knocked it clean out of his hands. If the gun had not been looped around his neck on a length of string it might have ended up on the roof of the building behind him. As it was, the gun flew into the air, reaching the top of its arc, and then ended up swinging around and hitting Tough Tony square in the back, the string cutting deep into his neck and leaving a friction burn that was still visible three months later. One minute Tough Tony had the gun in his hands and the next he was standing there with nothing. The guard dropped the box and smiled at Tony, but it was the kind of smile that spoke of pain for its recipient, and Tough Tony went cold. For a second neither man moved, and then Tough Tony scrabbled behind his back trying to get his hand on the shotgun. He wasn't quick enough and the guard hit him in the side of the head with a fist the size of a Christmas ham.

Now Tough Tony didn't get his nickname for nothing. He'd been a pretty good fist-fighter in his day and a lot of people said he was a bit warm at the old glove game, so he could take a punch. Which was lucky for him because the dig he got from the guard would have felled a donkey. It knocked Tony backwards up against the window of the travel agency and trapped the shotgun firmly between his back and the glass. The guard wrapped one big hand tightly around Tony's throat and drew his fist back to punch him again with the other. By this time Tony was in a panic, but he managed to flail out and catch the guard in the eye with a loose finger, which made him automatically release his grip on Tony's throat and cover his injured eye. But the finger-in-the-eye coup wasn't going to stop this geezer for too long and Tony knew his only hope was to get hold of the shotgun. He had never shot anyone in his life, but if he could get his hands on the gun this fella was going to be the first. Unfortunately for Tony but fortunately for the guard, the gun had become entangled in the folds of his overcoat and he couldn't quite get a grip on it. The guard, seeing what Tony was up to, threw another massive punch and caught him on the cheekbone. This time Tough Tony went down. He hit the hard pavement with a thump that knocked all the breath out of him and the guard dropped on top of him and began throwing punches at his face.

While all this was going on, Whizzy was sitting in the car watching the action in the rear-view mirror. Every time Tough Tony got a dig Whizzy would wince in sympathy, but there was no way he was going to leave the safety of the car and get involved. Fisticuffs was not Whizzy's forte – he much preferred to iron out any differences with a game of Monopoly. He could see that the guard was getting the better of Tony and knew that it was reaching the stage where he was going to have to do something or they could both end up nicked. So after a moment's contemplation, during which Tough Tony took a big right-hander that split his eyebrow and almost finished him off, Whizzy swung the passenger door of the Mk5 open and threw the stick into reverse. Looking back over his shoulder at the mêlée on the pavement, he gunned the engine and took his foot off the clutch.

Tough Tony may not have actually been in hell but he was certainly standing in the doorway of it. The guard was beating the shit out of him and actually laughing as he was doing it, and the pain as each granite fist pounded his tender flesh was almost excruciating. Tony was still desperately clinging to the thought that if he could reach the gun everything would be sweet, so now his left arm was trapped under his body seeking for cold metal and warm wood. He told me later that he was glad he hadn't got his finger to the triggers because he was in

14

such a state that he probably would have pulled them just to take the guard's attention off his poor face. If he had pulled even one of the double-barrel's triggers while it was underneath him and tangled in his coat, he might have shot himself. As it was, he was near to passing out and still couldn't reach the gun. He took a hard punch that split the other eyebrow and made him see yet more stars and the warm blood filled his eye socket, leaving him half blind. He didn't just lie there and take it, he struggled and thrashed his head about trying to dodge the blows, but he was growing weaker by the second, and it got to the stage where he knew he could take no more punishment. He was going under. Even his good eye was starting to blur at the edges. And then, suddenly, the guard was gone. It was as though he had just flown away.

Whizzy had reversed the Mk5 up on to the pavement at high speed and either through luck or fantastically good judgement had hit the security guard with the open passenger door, causing him to be launched from the prostrate and bleeding figure of Tough Tony. The guard did three full somersaults through the air and hit the hard pavement ten feet away. Whizzy didn't stop to think, he just leant over and grabbed Tough Tony by the collar of his overcoat and dragged his head and shoulders up on to the door sill. 'Get in!' he screamed, and without waiting to see if his confederate was capable of following this order, he rammed the stick into second gear, gunned the engine and took off, leaving an inch of rubber on the pavement. Tough Tony was in bits and as weak as a kitten but he managed to cling on to the car for the first twenty feet, his body and legs dragging along the pavement. 'Help me!' he managed to croak, and Whizzy, seeing that Tony was not in the passenger seat, jammed on the anchors.

By this time, the street had all but come to a standstill as pedestrians and motorists alike had stopped to watch the real-life action movie unfolding before them. The cash box was lying on its side on the pavement emitting a high-pitched screech and sending up a cloud of foul-smelling red signal smoke. The driver of the security van had activated his alarm as soon as he noticed something going on and all the lights on the van were flashing in unison as a very loud recording of a mechanical-sounding voice informed everyone within a large radius, 'We are being robbed! Please notify the police immediately!', over and over like a robotic parrot. Parts of the otherwise pristine pavement were stained with splashes of Tough Tony's blood and burnt rubber from the Mk5's tyres, and the guard was lying on his back with his feet in the gutter.

Whizzy reached over and pulled Tony further into the car. He flopped into the passenger seat and managed to mumble, 'Go! Go!' through bloody and mangled lips. Whizzy put his foot down again but released the clutch too quickly and the Mk5 jumped forward, then stalled. As Whizzy quickly reached for the ignition key, he saw something in his rear-view mirror that almost made him shit his pants. 'Oh fuck!' he said in a trembling voice. 'He's fucking coming!' The guard had been stunned by the impact of the Mk5's passenger door and made dizzy by his tumbling flight but he wasn't badly injured and had got back on to his feet as Whizzy was pulling Tough Tony into the car. He shook his huge head and then took off running towards the Mk5. Someone had tried to rob him and the fun wasn't over just yet.

Inside the car Tough Tony was moaning in agony and bleeding all over himself while Whizzy frantically keyed the motor. At last the engine burst into life and the Mk5 shot out into the road and away from the fast-approaching security guard. They left him clutching no more than a cloud of exhaust fumes, and Whizzy breathed a sigh of relief. When they had put a couple of streets between the scene of the crime and themselves Whizzy relaxed and turned to the ruin of what was once Tough Tony's face and said, in all seriousness, 'Did you get the money?' Tough Tony told me that if he'd had the strength at that moment he would have got Whizzy in a headlock and rammed his head off the windscreen several times. But all he could do was moan and bleed some more.

Tough Tony spent the next week in bed. When he finally did venture out his face was still sporting the colours of the rainbow. The day's excitement had been a bit too much for Whizzy and he decided that armed robbery was not really his game, so he retired and went back to small-scale drug deals. Tough Tony never forgot the loyalty he had shown by rescuing him from the giant guard and whenever he's out of jail and has a nice touch he always bungs Whizzy a nice few quid. In time, Tough Tony went back to work and eventually joined a little crew who were having it off by robbing night deliveries to cash-machines. These days he's serving seven years for sawing the barrels off a shotgun, a serious criminal offence, believe it or not, and for being in possession of the gun with intent. I don't think Tough Tony will ever change his ways – he's invested too much of his life into what he is – but stranger things have happened. Just look at me. At one stage of my life I was Tough Tony in so many ways.

2. Big Bad Bob, the Water-Pistol Bandit, and How He Hit the Big One

Big Bad Bob was a Scotsman and in his mid-forties when I first met him on D wing of Wandsworth prison in 1989. He already had a long criminal career behind him and was serving nine years for armed robbery committed in his native Scotland. How Bob came to be in an English prison as far south as Wandsworth was a story typical of his untrustworthiness and low cunning. Soon after getting his nine-stretch he was transferred to one of the newer Scottish jails, HMP Schotts, in Lanarkshire. The regime was a bit lax then as most of the screws were brand-new on the job. Bob's father was pretty ill at the time so, despite having served only a year of his sentence, he applied for a compassionate parole in order to visit him at home. Bob, like a lot of criminals who eventually gravitate to armed robbery, was a pretty personable man, and it was said that he could charm the birds from the trees, though I must admit I always viewed him as the stereotypical dour Scotsman. Perhaps that's because I never had anything he wanted bad enough to bother turning the charm on. Anyway, Bob was granted a few hours' parole, during which he was to be escorted by two young and inexperienced screws, handcuffed to one of them at all times. On the journey to his dad's house Bob was the life and soul of the sweatbox, cracking jokes, telling stories and generally geeing the two trainee turnkeys up. So by the time they landed at the house, the dim uniformed twosome thought Bob was a great fella and not at all as bad as some of the neds they had to deal with on a daily basis back at the jail. All was going well until Bob, as per his plan, suddenly had an attack of diarrhoea and confessed a desperate need to use the toilet. The screws, not wanting to appear insensitive to the needs of their new best friend, decided it would be OK to take the handcuffs off as long as Bob gave his word of honour that he wouldn't try and have it on his toes. Big Bad Bob, the expression of a newly whelped spaniel on his villainous features, swore on a stack of holy bibles ten feet high that he would not try to leg it, and the screws took him at his word. Needless to say, five minutes after the cuffs were removed Bob was on his way to England as fast as his legs would carry him.

Once he arrived in London Big Bad Bob got to work plying his trade as an armed robber. He had a pretty clever MO when it came to blagging, and it was one that was to work a treat in the Smoke. As he worked alone and never used a real gun, a water-pistol being his 'weapon' of choice, Bob usually targeted small financial establishments where there were only one or two cashiers to deal with. In his native Scotland it had been building societies, but in London he noticed there were several small bureaux de change where tourists could swap their traveller's cheques and native currency for the coins and notes of the realm. These premises usually had no more than two cashiers so Bob decided to give one a try. His robberies were never very financially rewarding and Bob would be quite happy to get two or three grand from his graft, enough to get him a decent hotel for a couple of weeks, a mid-range prostitute to service his needs and a few wee drams of an evening. All-in-all Bob was a pretty simple man and lived each day as it came.

He would find a small bureau de change he liked the look of and then have a good mooch around the area to check his get-away routes and any police presence. Bob couldn't drive so he always made his get-away on foot, or by public transport if the opportunity presented itself. One thing that was essential for the operation was that there was a public telephone near by. Don't forget, this was in the 1980s when mobile phones were playthings of only the richest yuppies and cocaine dealers and public phone-booths were the only telecommunications option available to the poor on the move. He would note down the phone number of his target branch and check the interior and cashiers by walking past several times. He'd then phone and ask to speak to the manager, knowing the gaff was no more than a hole in the wall and that the manager probably doubled as the cashier and trebled as the cleaner. He would then urgently introduce himself as Detective Inspector William Shatner of the Flying Squad and breathlessly explain that his squad had been following a very dangerous serial robber known as the Cashier Killer. They had him under surveillance right at this moment and it appeared that he was about to target their premises. He told them in no uncertain terms to remain calm, to hand over all the cash. The Squad would be waiting to pounce and arrest the robber the minute he left their premises. He would end the call by warning the manager to do nothing to alert this dangerous robber to the plan, such as pressing any alarm or CCTV buttons. 'This man is a stone killer,' he would tell them. 'He will start shooting at the slightest provocation!'

Getting Bob's call out of the blue would usually throw the manager into confusion, and Bob's plan would capitalize on this. A couple of minutes later, in would come Big Bad Bob, dressed in a heavy overcoat and with a flat cap pulled low over his eyes. He would stroll into the gaff, pull his water-pistol, which, when you are expecting a gun, would be gun-like enough to pass muster in the eyes of a terrified cashier, and growl, 'Give me all the money!' Bob later told me that on a couple of occasions the cashier would be wearing a smug expression below the immediate fear on their face, because they thought that the police were waiting outside to capture him and return their money. They would load the notes from their till into Bob's plastic bag and pass it over without a murmur. Bob was smart enough to know that if there was even a suspicion that he had used a real gun on these robberies then not only would the police double their efforts to find him but, when he was eventually captured, as he knew he would be, then that suspicion could add at least five years to his sentence. So Bob wanted no one to be in any doubt about the veracity of his 'firearm'. To this end, his final act on each job was to squirt his water-pistol on the window outside in full view of the watching cashiers. Then he would hurry away with his bag of ill-gotten, leaving the people in the bank waiting for a police operation that was never going to happen. In time the penny would drop and they would be on the blower to Old Bill, but by then Bob would be ensconced in his hotel, supping champagne and checking the prices of the local call-girls.

For a few months Bob worked this plan all over London, with moderate financial success. He was nicking enough dosh to live a very comfortable life for a man who should have been eating porridge in the confines of a Scottish nick, and loving it. Then one afternoon, quite by accident, Bob stumbled into the robber's holy grail. All robbers, and all types of thief really, hope for the Big One, the bit of work that will provide a windfall beyond their wildest dreams. The hope is always there that one day they may steal enough, if not to retire on then certainly to make up for all the times in their career when they ended up with the contents of a gas meter or were left wearing the paper hat. Most criminals go through their careers never even getting a sniff of the Big One, but some, the lucky or clever few, find out that sometimes crime does pay. So it was with Big Bad Bob.

For Bob, the robbing of small bureaux de change by telephone and water-pistol had become routine and he never deviated from his original plan. He had neither the wherewithal nor the inclination to up his game. For a man working alone and with minimum resources, Bob thought he was doing very well. Of course he had ambitions, but they didn't usually extend further than a better class of hotel and getting enough dosh together to hire two prostitutes to put on a lesbian show for him. The thing about committing these kinds of walk-in robberies is that you never know what you are going to get. The average bank starts the day with a £2,000 float in each till, so if you rob a bank early in the morning and there are three tills open, you can almost guarantee a £6,000 payout. But rob the same bank at lunch-time, after they have had a morning of paying out, and you might get as little as £600. But then, if you come in just before closing time, when the local shop-keepers have spent the afternoon banking their takings, you could walk out with £20,000. Unless you have inside infor-mation and are going after a specific prize, it's a case of cock your gun and take your choice on walk-in bank robberies.

On this particular afternoon Bob had selected his target and made his phone call. What he didn't know was that he was about to get a taste of the Big One. The branch he had chosen was expecting some heavy business due to the start of the tourist season and its central location, and ten minutes before Bob made his phone call they had received a delivery of English and foreign currency – dollars, deutschmarks and yen – from their security carriers: £90,000 worth. When Bob phoned this prize had not yet gone into the time-locked vault and was sitting under the counter in cloth money-bags. Bob walked in with his bag, water-pistol in hand and a Cashier Killer sneer on his features, and nearly fainted with excitement when, instead of the usual couple of bundles of banknotes, he was handed four heavy cloth bags. The cashier, following Detective Inspector Shatner's orders to a T, handed over 'all the money'. Big Bad Bob, now breathless with excitement and giddy with the weight of money in his grasp, left at a gallop, forgetting to fire his water-pistol at the window.

When he got back to his flop and emptied the bags over the dusty carpet, the sight of so many bundles of brightly coloured banknotes gave him an erection the like of which he hadn't had since he was a teenager. Big Bad Bob had hit the big time and now he would be able to afford that lesbian show, and much, much more. After staring at and touching the money for a couple of hours Bob packed it into a holdall, threw in his few belongings and got a taxi to one of the best hotels in London's Kensington. Booking himself into one of their mid-price suites – well, no matter how much money he had, he was still a Scotsman – he ordered a bottle of chilled champagne and a steak sandwich. Bob was in heaven and it didn't take him long to get on the blower and order up a couple of fallen angels to provide his entertainment.

That month, Bob barely left his suite, ordering whatever he needed via the room's phone and venturing out only to change up wads of his foreign currency in some of the very banks he had targeted for future robberies. Bob's philosophy was to live for today and enjoy it. When the money ran out he knew he would have to go back to work but he would cross that counter when he came to it. Unfortunately for Big Bad Bob, the hotel he was staying at had two ex-coppers working as hotel detectives, or glorified security guards, whose job it was to be on the look-out for suspicious characters who might want to rip the hotel off or steal from the guests' rooms and such. And these two yard dogs, with their years of experience at spotting a 'wrong 'un', had got Bob squarely in their sights. Something about this reclusive jock who rarely ventured from his suite, paid for everything in cash and had a stream of top-class brasses tending to his nightly needs got the radar of these ex-Old Bill pinging like an Atari 500. They kept a close eye on him and didn't really like what they were seeing, so they took a photograph of him from their CCTV system and sent it to their former police colleagues to see if anything was known.

When the police received Bob's picture from hotel security they almost creamed their blue-serge pants. Not only was he on their computer as a prison escapee but on one of his bureau robberies he had been captured on the security cameras and was known to the Flying Squad as the Water-Pistol Bandit. In Kensington police station, in the early hours, a squad of armed police officers was assembled for a briefing. So while Big Bad Bob was lying in his luxury hotel bed in the arms of a couple of exhausted ladies of the night and dreaming of his next big score, the Flying Squad was half a mile away studying his photograph and loading their Smith & Wesson Model 10 revolvers in anticipation. As Bob had failed to squirt off his water-pistol on his last job, the police, as they always do, had to work on the assumption that there was a possibility that Bob could now be in possession of a real gun. This gave them the right to shoot him dead if he made any suspicious-looking movements when they burst in on him. And in the case of armed police with their fingers on the trigger, a suspicious-looking move could be something as simple and innocuous as blinking at the wrong moment.

In the event, the police entered the hotel quietly at a few minutes after 6 a.m., and the hotel detectives let them into Bob's suite with their passkeys. When Bob was awakened by a kick in the thigh and opened his eyes to see the barrels of seven cocked revolvers pointing at his face, he knew the gig was up. The police cuffed him with plastic ties and took a few victory photos of themselves standing over their downed prey for the scrapbook before searching the room. They found his water-pistol, still fully loaded and dripping a puddle in a drawer, and the remains of his prize – £900 sterling, £1,250 in deutsch-marks, a couple of thousand in dollars and yen. That was all that was left of the ninety-large he had skedaddled with less than five weeks earlier. Bob had done his best to follow the robber's creed to the letter: if you steal money then you had better fucking well spend it, and fast, because if you get caught with it they'll only take it back.

After being charged with four counts of armed robbery and possession of an imitation firearm with intent, Bob was remanded to await trial. This was where I met him, at Wandsworth jail. But, for Bob, even being in prison did not mean the game was over. He put his cunning little mind to work and came up with a plan to get himself back on the street. Now that he'd had a taste of the good life, he was more determined than ever to get out and get it again. Keeping Bob in jail was like trying to keep a yokel down on the farm once he'd seen the lights of gay Paree. Très difficult. Using his legendary charm, Bob managed to wangle himself a job in the central kitchen, where he palled up with an Essex outlaw named Terry the Trip doing a twelve-stretch for possession of Class A drugs with intent to distribute. Terry had been at Wandsworth for a while and was awaiting a transfer to Parkhurst prison, on the Isle of Wight, but in the meantime he had worked his way up from lowly spud-peeler to number one baker in the kitchen. Bob spotted the possibilities offered by Terry's position and turned the charm on this drug-dealing dough-kneader until pretty soon Bob and Terry were going two-of-toast. Terry, like any normal person facing twelve years in prison, was amenable to Bob's suggestion that an escape might be in the offing, so Bob explained his plan.

As the top baker, it was Terry's job to make all the bread and rolls for a prison with a population of two thousand cons, so the principal officer-in-charge of the kitchen would start his shift at 5 a.m. and come and unlock Terry's cell at five thirty, when the rest of the jail was still asleep and there was only a skeleton staff of night-patrol officers on duty. He would escort Terry to the kitchen and they would set about baking the bread for the breakfast meal served at eight thirty. After a lot of good-natured badgering by Terry, whom he trusted, the kitchen PO decided to give Bob a trial as Terry's assistant. Bob had told the PO that on the out he had been a master baker and that he was eager to work so, knowing that with two inmates doing the job he could put his feet up and read his paper in the morning, the PO took Bob on. He sent a memo to security telling them of his move, but in a jail as big as Wandsworth paperwork has a tendency to get lost on a regular basis. I suppose that if security had been aware of Bob's move to early morning kitchen duty they may have suspected that he might be up to no good, given his pedigree. But no one said a dicky bird.

Over the next couple of weeks, while the kitchen PO dozed in his office, Bob and Terry utilized their early mornings to gather together the materials for a ladder. Using various lengths of wood ripped from cell furniture and the five-foot wooden paddles used in the kitchen to stir the massive steel cauldrons for cooking porridge, stew and curry, they managed to fashion a makeshift ladder that would bring them within six feet of the top of the perimeter wall. Then, when all the components of their escape kit were stashed in various places around the large kitchen, they made their move. The PO picked them up from their cells one morning, as usual, and took them down to the kitchen as the prison slept. But once inside the kitchen, they attacked and overpowered the PO. Using string to bind his hands behind his back, they took his keys and gagged him with sticking-tape before locking him in the big freezer. Unfortunately, the PO weighed about eighteen stone and as they were manhandling him into the walk-in freezer, he fell from their grasp and broke his thumb. (Injuring a screw on an escape would mean they were both guaranteed a good kicking in the punishment block over and above the one they would get anyway. It also meant that they could now be charged in an outside court or, at the very least, be up before the Board of Visitors and lose unlimited remission for causing 'gross personal violence to an officer'.)

They quickly assembled their ladder and, using the PO's

keys, they made their way through several locked gates until they were under the lowest part of the perimeter wall. But when they put their ladder up and started their ascent, the shortcomings of their woodwork skills became apparent and the ladder snapped in half under their weight. Bob, being a definite belt-and-braces man, had anticipated just such an eventuality and had brought along a length of rope made from plaited prison sheets and a grapple of sorts made from parts of a tubular cell chair. He launched the grapple towards the top of the wall several times but it failed to catch. He was undaunted and told me later that he had been prepared to stand there throwing it for however long it took.

Unluckily for the would-be jail breakers, the nearest wing to their section of wall was G wing, which housed all those prisoners who were kept on protection for various reasons, such as being sex offenders, debtors and informers. If the lads had tried their escape alongside any of the other wings and had been spotted by a con, it was almost a 100 per cent certainty that the alarm would not have been raised. As it was, some hobbit on G wing happened to be up and about and saw the escape in progress from his cell window. Probably drooling at the thought of the amount of brownie points it would give him with the screws, the snitch pressed his cell bell and informed the night-patrol screw what was happening. Within minutes of the alarm being raised, Bob and Terry were trying to ward off truncheon blows from the hastily assembled heavy mob while being dragged feet first to the punishment block. But the beating they got on the way to solitary was to pale into insignificance when the main body of the staff came on duty and discovered their kitchen colleague trussed up like an oven-ready chicken inside the freezer. Covered in frost and with a broken thumb that had swollen up to the size of a Cumberland sausage, he was a pretty sorry spectacle, and let's just say that for the rest of that long day Bob and Terry took so many right-handers they were almost begging for a left.

Bob and Terry were charged with attempted escape and assaulting a prison officer and stayed in the punishment block for the next six months. They each lost 180 days' remission in front of the Board of Visitors and got regular slappings from the block screws just to keep them on their toes. While in the chokey at Wandsworth, Bob collapsed one day, and after being rushed to the prison hospital wing he was diagnosed as having an irregular heartbeat and told that his heart was so bad that he could drop dead at any minute. They don't believe in sugar-coating anything in jail and maybe they were hoping that the shock of this news alone would be enough to finish Bob off. After all, he was becoming a fucking nuisance to the prison system.

The second significant thing that happened to Bob during this period was that he was taken up to the Old Bailey to be sentenced for the bureaux de change robberies he had committed while at large from his nine-stretch. Bob pleaded guilty to four counts of armed robbery, and the judge, probably having heard about Bob's dodgy heart, decided he needed another heavy shock to sort him out. Before passing sentence the judge slagged Bob for about fifteen minutes, comparing him to Rob Roy for bringing his marauding to England's green and pleasant land. There was the usual guff and stock phrases beloved by judges everywhere, danger to the public, blah, blah, blah, never in all my years, blah blah blah, horsewhipped through the streets, blah blah, blah. And if the old boy had had a black cloth handy there's no doubt he would have draped it over his silly wig. Then the judge sentenced Bob to five years' imprisonment on each charge, to run consecutively with each other, making twenty years, but the killer was when he ordered this sentence to run consecutively with his first sentence of nine years, making a total of twenty-nine years' imprisonment in all! How Bob's ticker didn't just give up the ghost there and then is a cause of wonder to me. I mean, you expect a lump of bird when you stick your hands up to armed robbery, but the Krays only got twelve months more than Bob and they murdered a couple of people.

I saw Big Bad Bob when he came back from court that day. He looked like a broken man as he was hustled towards the punishment block by six grim-faced screws. His sentence meant he automatically became a category A prisoner, unable to leave his cell without at least three screws and a guard dog in attendance. His every move would be recorded in his category A book, kept by the senior officer, and this is why being category A is called being 'on the book' by prisoners. Apart from being category A, Bob was also category E, meaning he was an escapee and had to wear a prison uniform with a broad yellow stripe on it so he could be easily identified at all times. I managed to give him a wave and shouted for him to keep his chin up. For a couple of days Big Bad Bob's harsh sentencing was the talk of the wing, and then, as is the way in prison, he was all but forgotten, demoted to being just another semi-legend who would get a mention whenever yard talk turned to the subject of using sledgehammers to crack nuts.

It would be many years before I met up with Big Bad Bob again, but I kept my ears open for mentions of him. Prisoners love to talk and, let's face it, it's one of the few things we can do a lot of over the years – that and count bricks – so I heard a few things. The word on the grapevine was that he'd had his sentence reduced by the appeal court to a more manageable eighteen years. The next I heard, about ten years later, was that Bob was back to his old ways. He had got his head down and started studying for a degree in criminology, while also turning on his legendary charm. Eventually he passed his degree and asked for a few hours' parole to go to London and collect it at the Open University ceremony. Because the governor and staff of the nick he was then at had seen only the personable side of Bob, he was granted this parole, but he had to give his word of honour that he would not let anyone down. Bob agreed. But the memory of the day he hit the Big One was still fresh in Big Bad Bob's mind, and he knew he had the makings of one last run left in him. So Bob went to London, but he slipped his guard and never did make it to the degree ceremony. Instead, he hit three more banks, only by this time his telephone routine was old hat and he chose the desperado route by queuing up and handing a note to the cashier saying that he had a gun and wanted all the money. It wasn't long before Bob was recaptured and, this time, the judge gave him a life sentence under the Two Strikes Act.

That should have been the end of Big Bad Bob – most men would never be able to get another lick of the ice-cream after smearing it over their clothes so many times – but Bob was a trier and God loves a trier. I next ran into him on the yard in Whitemoor top-security jail in Cambridgeshire and he did not seem at all down in the mouth, considering he had more bird wrapped around him than the avian fancier of Alcatraz. He told me that he had finally seen the light and that he had volunteered for HMP Grendon, a therapeutic prison in Buckinghamshire. He figured that a course of intensive group therapy might help him to understand himself better, and I was impressed at this new Bob. But then he had to ruin it all by rubbing his hands together and adding, 'And if that doesn't work for me, I've heard the wall is easy to climb!'

Bob went off to Grendon, and I joined him there two years later. At Grendon Bob flourished and put all his charm to work in an all-out offensive, and after four years of constant understated manipulation he was finally granted category D status and sent to Ford open prison in Sussex. I really believed that Bob had changed, as did a lot of other people, and now that he was in an open jail there was no need for escape, as he would probably be released on life licence within two years anyway.

Bob did well in open conditions for almost three months. He was given a privilege job, working in a charity shop in the local town, and was allowed out of prison almost every day. But then, I can only assume, Bob started thinking about the Big One again. And passing banks, post offices and building societies on his way to work every day was like blowing a bugle into the ear of a senile old war horse. One day, when he was working in the shop with a young female assistant, Bob made his move. Locking the girl in a back office, he filled a bag with clothes, nicked the few quid out of the till and headed off in search of the wild side of life once more. Pretty soon a man fitting Bob's description began to pop up all over the place – usually in banks while they were being robbed. He became such a nuisance that he featured on BBC's *Crimewatch UK* programme, and once his mugshot had been flashed on millions of television screens, Big Bad Bob's days of wine and roses could be counted on the fingers of a one-handed leper. But it was his bad heart that led to his capture. Now in his sixties and having put a lot of strain on an old ticker that had never been in the best of shape, Bob finally succumbed to a heart attack. He was rushed to hospital, and it was while he was on the operating table with his chest wide open for a heart bypass that his slumbering features were recognized by the surgeon, an avid *Crimewatch UK* viewer. When Bob came around from his successful operation he found himself hand-cuffed to his hospital bed and guarded by eager and vigilant police officers.

For Big Bad Bob, the Water-Pistol Bandit, the gig truly was up. In the words of some old song or other this time they put him so far back into jail they'll have to pump oxygen to him. Why, when he was on the verge of getting out legally, did Bob decide to fuck it all up and do a runner with the charity-shop cash, which amounted to £30? Only Bob can answer that one, and these days he's kind of incommunicado. But having been to some of the places that Bob has been, I can guess. He got himself on that fast-spinning roundabout of crime and imprisonment and didn't have the sense or even the desire to get off again. Bob had had a taste of what he thought was the high life when he'd hit the Big One and the thought that he could do that again haunted him for the next eighteen years. He had nothing else – no home, no family – and his only friends were in prison. So I can imagine him, sixty-four years old, standing at the counter of that charity shop and wondering what the fuck he was going to do when he did get out for good. Sit in some grotty bedsit on a pittance of a pension and watch the rest of his life slip away? But the alternative? Run free, hit a few banks, live some life? He must have calculated that even when he got caught it wouldn't be so bad: prison was his home and he knew he could survive it for however long he had left.

And then there's the fact that Bob had a lot of confidence in his ability to work the system. Maybe right now he's cracking a few jokes with some prison governor, working his way in close, biding his time, until – Bang! Wherever he is, I'd lay odds that Big Bad Bob, in his head at least, will be planning a comeback. It's in his nature.

3. Wild Wayne

Wild Wayne was from north London and a bit of an impulsive character. Back in the late eighties he was heavily into the acid-house scene. Going to raves, taking vast amounts of Ecstasy and dancing all night like a zombie was what he really enjoyed doing, and he wasn't averse to resorting to a bit of thievery in order to fund his lifestyle. He wasn't really a career criminal and also did a bit of straight work when he could get it, labouring or stacking shelves in supermarkets, but Wayne had ambitions beyond his abilities and was certain he was going to strike it lucky sooner or later. He didn't want very much – just more money than he could carry and the admiring glances of a pretty woman. I don't think Wayne had any Chinese mates and I'm not sure he knew this, but the Chinese have a saying: be careful what you wish for because you just might get it. Now maybe Wayne would have heeded this warning, had he heard it, and maybe not, but subsequent events were to prove that it could have been tailor-made for him. Here's how it all went down.

One summer's morning in 1990 Wild Wayne was making his way home from an all-night rave and just coming down from his Ecstasy buzz. He had been up for twenty-seven hours, without sleep, but wasn't feeling too bad, only a little light-headed. It was around seven and the sun was already shining brightly over the Holloway Road. As Wayne sat on the pavement with his back against a wall, sipping Lucozade and just watching this part of London slowly come to life, he idly wondered how he might be able to earn himself a few quid that week. He was flat broke and there was another rave being held the coming weekend that he really wanted to go to. Raving wasn't cheap: a single decent Ecstasy tablet would set him back a minimum of £15 in those far-off days when what you were getting was almost pure MDMA and not a pot-luck of various different chemicals. Then there were incidentals such as transport and expensive bottled water to prevent dehydration while dancing non-stop for twelve hours at a time. Wayne glanced across the road and noticed a bank almost opposite where he was sitting. This got him wondering how much money was just sitting in that dull grey building doing nothing while he didn't have a pot to piss in or a window to throw it out of. He thought about what it might be like to just walk into that bank and walk back out with the money. That would really be something! Just as he was thinking these idle thoughts, he noticed a man in a suit and carrying a briefcase approaching the door of the bank.

In the slightly unsteady gait of the man in the suit Wayne thought he recognized a fellow traveller, someone who might be suffering the effects of a late night spent in the throes of intoxication or substance abuse. As he watched with interest, the suited man searched his pockets in a distracted manner for a good couple of minutes before coming up with a heavy ring of keys. The man took a white hanky from his pocket and mopped his sweaty brow before apparently gathering his wits about him enough to tackle the door. Very interested and amused now, Wayne stood up and took a few steps towards the kerb on his side of the road in order to get a better view. The suited man took a while to find the key he was looking for and when he went to insert it he fumbled the ring and the keys fell to the pavement at his feet. On the other side of the road Wayne chuckled out loud. And then, like an unexpected whack on the back of the head with a Louisville Slugger, an idea burst into Wayne's mind. Without hesitating or stopping to think further, Wayne jogged out into the road, dodging the sporadic traffic as he made his way across to the bank.

By the time Wayne had traversed the traffic on the Holloway Road and reached the pavement on the other side the suited man had his key in the lock and was pushing the door to the bank open. With a quick glance around for any witnesses, Wayne came up behind him. Clamping his arm tightly around the man's throat, he pushed him into the dimly lit foyer of the deserted bank and kicked the door closed behind them. 'I've got a knife and if you don't co-operate I'll cut your fucking throat! Understand?' Wayne hissed in the suited man's ear. The man, completely taken by surprise, could only grunt his assent and nod his head slightly. For Wayne this was all moving very fast and he could scarcely believe he was actually inside the bank. Now he would have to improvise. Keeping his arm around the man's neck so that he could not see his face or that Wayne had no knife, he pushed him further into the bank. 'Listen very carefully,' he said forcefully. 'We've been watching you for weeks. My partner is on the roof of one of the shops across the road and at this very minute he has your head in the sights of a high-powered rifle. Understand?' The man nodded again. 'All we want is the money and then we'll be gone. If you try any fucking tricks you'll be shot. Now, I'm going to put my knife away, because you're going to behave, aren't you?' The man nodded a third time. So Wayne made a move as though he was putting a knife in his waistband and took his arm off the man's neck.

The man, now very shaken by his experience, stood there for a moment with his eyes on the floor and his briefcase still clutched in his hand. Then he whispered, 'Can I go to the toilet? I think I'm going to be sick.' Wayne had been right about the man and told me later that he could still smell the alcohol on him from a heavy night's partying. The man showed Wayne where the staff toilets were and then threw up his ring into the bowl. While the man was talking to God on the big white telephone Wayne was figuring out his strategy. He assumed that the man must be a big cheese in the bank, which was why he had the keys and was the first one in, so Wayne would simply wait for his vomiting to stop and then get him to open the vault. He would grab the money, tie the man up and be on his way before any more staff arrived. His heart began to race at the thought of the money. Wayne had never seen more than £500 all together in one place in his life but now he was going to be rich! He wondered how much would be in the vault – £20,000? £30,000? £50,000?! That was about as high as Wayne could force himself to go, and he started to get impatient to get his hands on the money. Finally the man retched his last and emerged from the toilet whey-faced and wiping dribble from his lips. 'OK,' said Wayne firmly. 'Down to business. Where's the vault?'

The man, still quite unsteady on his feet, led Wayne through the back of the bank and down three stone steps to a large barred gate, behind which was a formidably thick steel vault door that looked just like something out of a film. Wayne could almost smell the crisp new banknotes that were stacked behind the door, and he couldn't help rubbing his hands together in glee. 'Right,' he said. 'Get it open.'

His sickly-looking hostage stared at him in confusion. 'What?' he asked.

Wayne, having got this far against all odds, wasn't going to stand for any stalling. 'Don't fuck me about,' he growled. 'Open the vault or you'll cop an unfortunate one, I'm telling you!'

The man added fear to his already pathetic-looking features and Wayne's heart sank as he realized it was genuine. 'I don't have the keys to the vault!' he whimpered. 'They're kept by the security manager and the head cashier! I just open up the premises. Besides, the vault's on a time-lock and can't be opened until 9.15!'

Wayne glanced at his Casio – it was only 8.10. 'Fuck it!' he spat in frustration. But then his brain started ticking quicker than any clock. The man was still whimpering quietly. Wayne glared at him. 'Shut the fuck up, will you, I'm trying to think.' There was silence in the antechamber of the vault for a couple of minutes as Wayne weighed up his situation.

Months later on the exercise yard in Wormwood Scrubs Wayne told me that he spent those minutes of silence looking at almost every angle but the factor that swayed him to carry on was that he had the element of surprise on his side. He was already inside the bank, and no one knew this except himself and the sick man. He said, 'I did some quick calculations and thought, Fuck it, I'm here now and it would be a shame to get this close to the cash and not have it.' Wild Wayne, petty thief, cheesy quaver and dreamer, was not giving up without a fight. He took his hostage into the small staff kitchen and got him to make them both a cup of coffee while he picked the man's brains. The bank was quite a large one, and if all the staff turned up for work that day there would be seventeen of them. This was a lot of people to try and control, particularly when he did not have a weapon. Spotting a bread knife in the sink, Wayne seized it. It was a pretty cheap and flimsy affair but he figured it would be better than nothing. The sick man didn't notice Wayne slipping the blade into his waistband and carried on explaining the bank's routine. The staff arrivals would be staggered over a period from eight thirty to nine o'clock, which was good news for Wayne. The last thing he wanted was seventeen people turning up at once. Hoping for a place to put the rest of his would-be hostages, Wayne found out that there was a lockable room at the back of the bank known as the 'book room' and sick man had the key. Just as they were finishing their coffee there came three rings on the bank's doorbell, the signal used by bank employees to let sick man know they were staff and not some dodgy blagger trying to get in. That morning they were to find their security signal redundant, as the dodgy blagger was already inside. Wayne warned the sick man that if he tried to alert the rest of the staff in any way the accomplice with the sniper's rifle would turn his head into trifle without a moment's hesitation and led him into the enclosed foyer of the bank.

Wayne waited in the shadows behind the door as sick man opened it for the arriving staff. There were three of them, all too busy bantering with each other even to acknowledge the sickly look on their colleague's face as they walked into the dim interior of the bank. Once the door had been shut Wayne stepped from the shadows and put the long blade of the bread knife up to sick man's throat and whistled loudly to attract the attention of the new arrivals. When they saw what confronted them the words died on their lips and the colour drained from their faces. 'Tell them!' Wayne snarled, believing what he had to say would have more impact coming from the mouth of someone they knew. Sick man quickly stuttered his way through the details about the sniper and how Wayne's gang was highly professional and there only for the money and no one would get hurt if they co-operated. When he was finished Wayne gave them the evil eye and pushed sick man forward. 'Let's go,' he snarled. 'I'm locking you into the book room.' And they went, as meek as lambs and as silent as a school full of deaf mutes.

With the first three members of staff safely locked up, Wayne started to feel better about his plan. He was buoyant and happy but didn't know whether that was the residue of Ecstasy in his system or real optimism. He warned sick man to point out the holders of the vault keys as soon as they appeared and took him back to the front door to wait for the next lot. The next to arrive was the head cashier, a very good-looking woman in her thirties, who didn't bat an eyelid when confronted by the knife-wielding Wayne. In fact, her only concern seemed to be for sick man, who by now looked like one of the walking dead from a video-nasty zombie flick. She ordered Wayne to get sick man some water and let him sit down for a while. Wayne explained to her that he needed sick man to let the rest of the staff in, and she said she would do that herself if he let sick man rest. Wayne thought about it for a moment – it could be a trap, maybe the sight of the head cashier at the door would be a signal that all was not well in the premises? But, as he confessed later, Wayne liked the look of this woman – who from this point on will be known as Jane – and was growing tired of sick man's groaning and whimpering. Wayne agreed to let Jane take over door duties and locked sick man in the book room with the others.

For the next twenty minutes all went according to plan and another twelve staff were admitted to the bank in twos and threes and locked into the book room. Jane seemed unruffled by what was happening and even chatted away to Wayne as he went about his business. Despite the situation, Wayne found himself warming to this calm, beautiful woman, and a couple of times he even forgot that they were predator and victim. The only person who had still not arrived at the bank by nine was the second vault-key holder and Wayne was starting to get worried. Jane reassured him that the man they were waiting for sometimes turned up a bit late because he lived on the outskirts of London and traffic was a problem. But the thing that kept running through Wayne's mind was that the second key holder was a security officer and the one person likely to spot something suspicious. As they waited, Jane engaged Wayne in conversation. She asked him why he was doing this, and Wayne shrugged and told her that he had just kind of walked into it. She asked him if he was going to hurt any of the bank staff and got him to promise that he wouldn't. Wayne, his tough-guy image slipping, promised he wouldn't hurt anyone, and in reality he probably wouldn't.

By 9.10 Wayne had been inside the bank for almost one and a half hours and still hadn't seen a penny, and the previous night's Ecstasy buzz was definitely wearing off. He started to feel edgy, unable to keep still for long, walking in tight circles and urging the last man to turn up so he could get the cash and go. Finally, at 9.14 there came three rings on the bell and Jane opened the door to admit the security manager. As the man entered he was apologizing for being late and bemoaning the state of traffic on the roads, and Wayne knew he suspected nothing. As the door closed Wayne grabbed Jane from behind in the by now familiar routine and put the blade to her throat. He felt bad about doing it, but this was the final piece of his plan and he needed to put on a good show for the security manager. The man immediately assessed the situation and agreed to co-operate. Wayne's heart sang – this was it, he was almost rich.

Wayne marched Jane and the manager back to the vault and watched as they used their two-piece twelve-inch keys to open the security locks. Once it was unlocked, the manager swung the thick steel door open and Wayne got a warm feeling in the pit of his stomach at the sight of so many bundles of banknotes sitting there on the shelves. Grinning like a moron who's just taken an overdose of happy pills, he stood and looked at the prize for a minute. Then it was back to the plan. He couldn't afford to have the security manager loose in case he tried anything. Wayne didn't trust anyone with 'security' in their title – to him it smacked of ex-SAS or someone of that ilk – so Wayne marched him across to the book room and locked him in with the rest of the hostages. He kept Jane with him, trusting her not to try anything silly. He even had the impression that she quite liked him. In other circumstances, he mused, they might have had a chance together. What Wayne didn't know was that he was probably suffering from a phenomenon known as Stockholm Syndrome, in reverse, where hostages seem to bond with their captors in what might be considered life-threatening and desperate situations. But quite apart from not having any friends of the Chinese persuasion, Wayne knew sweet fuck-all about psychology either.

Once inside the vault, Wayne became breathless with excitement as he ran his fingers over the piles of cash. Most of the money was in £5,000 packets, wrapped tightly in clear plastic bags and neatly piled. He looked around for something to carry it in and could find nothing, so he went out into the banking hall to look for a bag of some sort. He found a leather sports bag, abandoned by one of the staff on their way to captivity in the book room, and quickly emptied its contents on one of the counters before hurrying back into the vault to refill it with cash. In less than a minute the sports bag was full to the brim with packets of money and there was still more left on the shelves. Looking at the overflowing bag on the floor, Wayne was suddenly overcome with pure greed. Why should I leave any of this money behind? he thought to himself. It's all mine – what's the point of half-robbing a bank? Fuck it, I'm having it all! He hurried out of the vault and into the staff kitchen, where he found a pile of black plastic bin liners. They were very thin but if he doubled them up they should hold a bit of weight. Back in the vault, Jane stood watching him load the bin liners with money. She didn't say anything, but Wayne could feel a wave of mild disapproval coming from her. He didn't care, greed was upon him and he was determined to sack the vault. It turned out that there was a total of £189,000 in that bank vault, a lot of it in £10 and £20 notes, and by the time he was ready to go, Wild Wayne had every penny of it bagged.

It was now 9.35, but Wayne wasn't too worried as the bank wasn't due to open for business until ten. He got Jane to help him carry the bags out to the foyer and stack them in a corner. The get-away was going to be a bit iffy, but it just so happened

41

that Wayne knew the phone number of one of those dodgy backstreet mini-cab firms who didn't ask questions. He got on the phone and ordered a cab to pick him up from the bank and was told that the driver would be with him in twenty minutes. He knew he was cutting it a bit fine, but once the cab was at the door, he would quickly load the bags and be on his way. Who was going to say anything, even if they saw him? The only people who knew he had robbed the bank were safely locked up in the book room. Wayne looked down at the bags – he had made it! He thought he might slip down to Dover and catch a ferry to France, for a start. There was bound to be a hue and cry over this, and pretty soon the police would know who had done it because his fingerprints were everywhere in the bank and he hadn't worn a mask. Still, they would have to fucking catch him, and that wouldn't be easy when he could afford to go anywhere in the world.

As he settled down to wait for his get-away cab, Wayne remembered that he had a small piece of hash that he kept to take the edge off his Ecstasy comedowns, so he decided to celebrate the almost perfect crime with a spliff. He built his smoke expertly while sitting on the bags that contained his ill-gotten fortune and sparked up. The effects of the hashish were calming, and Wayne felt good. Not one to bogart a joint, despite his many other faults, Wayne offered a toke to Jane. She refused, obviously, and began to ask more probing questions. What would his family think when they found out what he'd done? What about his girlfriend? Surely such a nice-looking lad had a girlfriend? Maybe it was the euphoria of getting the money, or the effects of the hash, but Wayne became convinced that Jane really fancied him. He was just on the verge of asking her if she wanted to come with him to Europe when there was one long loud ring on the doorbell. Wayne didn't like the sound of it; it seemed insistent and somehow authoritarian to him. Jane was calmly looking at him.

'It could be your car,' she said simply, and Wayne's heart slowed from its wild gallop. He went to his usual spot behind the door and got her to open it. Looking through the crack at the hinges of the door, Wayne's world fell from a great height and shattered into many pieces, like an ice sculpture hitting a marble floor. Standing at the door of the bank were two uniformed police officers, and they didn't look as though they had come to cash a cheque.

What Wayne didn't know was that one of the security features of the bank was a silent-alarm button situated inside the vault, and when he had been looking for bags in which to transport the cash, the ever-resourceful Jane had taken the opportunity to press the button. Several times. In addition to the silent-alarm button there was a prearranged signal with the police: if they turned up at the bank in response to the alarm and saw that the blinds on the small window next to the main entrance remained down, then there was an intruder inside. And the blinds were now definitely down. Unfortunately, in the two weeks preceding Wayne's opportunistic entry, the silent alarm had been playing up and had gone off for no apparent reason on several occasions, and the uniformed officers who were now responding to the alarm knew this. What they didn't know about, because they hadn't bothered to avail themselves of the information, was the extra signal of the window blind. So it was in tired resignation that they turned up on the doorstep of the bank that morning, having already made up their minds it was another false alarm.

When Jane opened the door and saw the police, she figured that her ordeal was finally over. But instead of rushing inside, batons drawn, they showed no sense of urgency whatsoever. The first words out of the copper's mouth were 'We know it's another false alarm but we have to check. Is everything OK?' Jane, aware that Wayne was only two steps away with the knife now back in his hand, put on a bright voice. 'Yes, Constable,

43

everything is just super!' But as she spoke the twitching of her mouth and the wink of her eye belied the words on her lips. Sadly, her facial pantomime was in vain, as one of the coppers was staring at the passing traffic and scratching his balls while the other was concentrating on putting her reply into his notebook. Having received the verbal response they expected, the cops gave her a cheery 'Good morning' and climbed back into their patrol car. You can only imagine the frustration Jane must have been feeling as she reluctantly closed the door on her one chance of salvation. I should imagine the words 'Keystone' and 'cops' couldn't have been far from her mind.

The cops continued their patrol but called in their findings to the station via their radio. It was just by chance that whoever was in charge back there was fully in the picture about the security signals and asked them if they had checked whether the window blind was up or down. With a sigh of frustration – after all, they had joined the force to catch criminals, not to investigate faulty alarms – the driver turned the patrol car around and headed back to the bank to check that the blinds were up.

Back inside the bank, Wayne now figured he had it made in the shade, the gods were obviously smiling on him and all the signs were good that he was going to be spending the next six months sunning himself on the French Riviera and drinking smuttily named cocktails from umbrella-laden glasses. The cops turning up and then fucking off again was the cherry on the cake. Not only had he pulled off a major robbery, but he had also managed to leave Old Bill wearing the paper hat as well – what a touch! He celebrated with another joint and wished the cab would hurry up.

When the patrol car pulled up outside the bank on the now-busy Holloway Road and the cops saw that the blinds were down, their suspicions finally began to be aroused. Not only were the blinds down, but it was five minutes after ten and there was no sign of movement from within the building.

44

They decided to investigate further and rang the bell again. The absolutely reckless stupidity of this move was breathtaking. Suppose there was actually a heavily armed and desperate gang of robbers inside the bank? What were they two cops going to do, put them under arrest? Once again Jane opened the door, but this time they were looking genuinely interested. 'Just routine, for our report,' the first copper opened. We need to know if you've reported the malfunction of your alarm system to the security company yet?' As he spoke, his colleague kept to one side of the door and mouthed the words, 'Are you all right?' Jane, realizing that the penny had finally dropped, shook her head slightly and frowned as she answered the first copper in a calm and confident voice. That was all they needed, so they said their goodbyes and left.

Inside, Wayne was no longer happy. He knew that the cops coming back couldn't bode well, even if their enquiry did seem innocuous. He cursed the amount of time the mini-cab was taking to reach him and decided to phone them again. This time he got the stock reply: 'Yeah, the driver's only five minutes away from you now.' After putting the phone down, Wayne contemplated just walking out with as much as he could carry and making his way on foot until he could find transport, but then greed kicked in again and he dismissed the idea. Instead, he sat back down on the bags to wait, puffing on his spliff and eyeing the gorgeous Jane.

Outside, the two police officers had driven their car about twenty-five feet away, where they couldn't be spotted by any-one inside the premises, and had radioed in an urgent alarm call. Within minutes of their call being received, the Flying Squad, PT17, the Tactical Firearms Squad, the uniformed branch and a team of hostage negotiators were on their way to the bank, lights flashing and sirens wailing. They blocked off both ends of Holloway Road and set up observation posts and firing positions for the police marksmen on the roofs of the surrounding buildings. The police had no idea what they would be up against, but whatever it was, they would be ready.

The first inkling Wayne had that something might be going seriously wrong was when he noticed that he could no longer hear any traffic. He nipped over to the main window, lifted a corner of the blind to get a look and was surprised to see that the road was deserted. It was as though a giant hand had come down and scooped up every car, bus and pedestrian on the Holloway Road. Through his hash-induced haze, Wayne felt the icy fingers of panic creeping into his mind. Squinting he concentrated his gaze and suddenly saw a flash of reflected light and the hint of a blue-chequered cap in one of the open windows of the building across the street and his buzz became well and truly naused. He looked further down the street and saw a man in plain clothes carrying a handgun at port-arms and looking towards the bank. He quickly let the blind down and stepped back from the window. 'Shit!' was all he could think of to say. Just then a phone behind the counter jangled into life and Wayne almost shrieked in panic.

On the other end of the phone was a top police hostage negotiator. As soon as he introduced himself, Wayne realized his dreams of *la dolce vita* were a non-starter. He was trapped like a tick in a horse blanket, but he was determined to at least hang it out until he'd smoked the last of his hash. Wayne knew that as soon as he stepped outside he would be on his way to a long prison sentence, so he decided to try and make the most of the short time he had left as a relatively free man. He emptied the bags of money over the floor and rolled in the blanket of currency, he lit his spliffs with £50 notes and made towers from bundles of legal tender. When he grew tired of this, he had himself a little kick-around with £15,000 in £5 notes lashed together as a ball. At lunch-time, having a severe attack of the munchies, he got on the blower to the police negotiator and ordered up a meal for himself and the hostages.

The police turned to a local fast-food outlet, and a copper in shirtsleeves, to show he wasn't armed, delivered a selection of pizzas and soft drinks to the door. Wayne got Jane to bring the meal inside and deliver it to the by now hot and exhausted employees in the book room. In between amusing himself and talking tough to the police negotiator on the phone, Wayne tried to charm Jane into giving him her phone number. He also asked for her address so he could write to her from prison. Jane played along with him to keep him sweet, but all she really wanted was out of the bank that had become her own prison.

For ten hours Wayne remained in the bank with his hostages while outside armed police, the media and the public strained their eyes trying to catch a sight of him. Then, when his hash had run out and he had grown bored of it all, he decided it was time to give up. He told the negotiator that he was letting Jane leave first, then he would throw his weapon out and come himself. Before he let Jane walk from the bank he demanded a kiss from her, and she obliged with a peck on the cheek. Satisfied with this, Wayne wistfully watched her walk to freedom, then he had an idea. He took a wad of £50 notes from one of the packages and, folding them as thin as he could, he slipped them between the cheeks of his arse, where he hoped they would remain unfound despite searches. He figured it was his money anyway and he might as well get out with something. Besides, he was bound to need a bit of cash in prison. Then he opened the door of the bank and threw his knife on to the pavement before stepping out into the sunlight with his hands held high and a stoned grin on his face. The press photographers caught every second of it, and these pictures led on the front pages of most of the tabloids the next morning.

Within seconds of his surrender, Wayne was lying face-down on the Holloway Road with his hands plasti-cuffed behind his back and a score of armed coppers pointing their guns at his head. As they put him into the police car for a swift ride to the station, one of the watching reporters shouted, 'Why did you do it?', and Wayne, his grin still in place, shrugged. 'It was just a joke!' he said. And then he was gone.

For a while Wayne was a bit of a celebrity among the cons in the Scrubs. I met him when I heard through the grapevine that he was looking to change up some £50 notes for more manageable denominations and he was willing to take seventy pence for each pound. I was happy to do the bit of business and not ask too many questions, but Wayne turned out to be a pretty effusive character and told his story well. Twelve months after being nicked outside the bank Wayne appeared at the Old Bailey and pleaded guilty to robbery and false imprisonment. He had no previous convictions, and the prosecution accepted that this had not been a planned bit of work, more an impulsive action by a man of previous good character. The judge took this into account and sentenced Wayne to seven years' imprisonment. I heard he took it well.

It seemed that circumstances had conspired to give Wayne a taste of the very things he had wished for – more money than he could carry and a pretty girl – but he found himself unable to grasp either. In the time that I knew him, his biggest regret was not having just left the bank with most of the money when he had the chance, but he admitted greed had got the better of him. As far as I know, Wild Wayne completed his sentence, got out and has never been in trouble since. And the lesson I learned from all this? Listen to the Chinese, sometimes they talk a lot of sense. And if a mini-cab firm tells you that your cab will be there in five minutes – don't fucking believe them.

4. Steve the Saint

Steve the Saint has been a good pal of mine for over twenty years, though we only ever seem to meet up in prison – which, I suppose, says bundles about what abject failures we have been as criminals. He was called 'the Saint' because he had a tattoo of a stick-man with a halo on his hand, the old Simon Templar logo from the sixties TV show. Plus, he had the patience of a real saint. I first saw him on the exercise yard of HMP Pentonville back in the eighties, when he was chasing a big black fella with a table leg in his hand and murder in his eyes. The black fella, whose nickname was Diablo, was one of those bodybuilder types who tend to think they can throw their weight around and bully people just because they've chemically enhanced their muscle mass and have a good line in scowls. At the time, Diablo had set himself up as some kind of strong-arm man on the remand wing and was bullying the weaker prisoners out of their canteen. Steve the Saint, who had been a pretty good boxer in his day and didn't take any shit from anyone, was not one of Diablo's carefully chosen victims, but one of his frailer friends was, so Steve, in the best tradition of the Magnificent Seven, gathered Diablo's victims together and led them in an ambush. They smuggled various weapons, such as wooden legs ripped from their cell tables and PP9 batteries in socks, out on to the exercise yard one morning and laid a trap for Diablo. On the yard at Pentonville there is a small one-storey building that houses three urinals and a toilet for the use of prisoners during exercise. It is, like most prison toilets, a dismal affair that reeks of piss and is never cleaned, and mostly it was used as a hidey-hole where the hardcore junkies took their gear, away from the gimlet eyes of the screws. The toilets were so foul that most of the screws wouldn't go near them without a gas mask and protective clothing. So Steve the Saint gathered his little crew of Mexican villagers in there and got one of them to go and whisper in Diablo's ear that there was a lucrative deal involving four ounces of snout going down in the khazi. Diablo took the bait, and when he walked into the stench-filled building he was set upon by a crowd of his victims, led by the club-wielding Steve the Saint. Diablo took one hell of a beating but managed to break free and leg it across the exercise yard to where the screws were standing guard, pursued by the howling, tool-waving mob. I had only been in the 'Ville for a couple of days and didn't know what was going on, so I watched with interest as Diablo reached the screws and started begging them to protect him. Of course, the screws knew all about Diablo's bullying – they had seen it all before – and also knew that it wouldn't be long before he got what he deserved. No one likes a bully, not even other bullies, so the screws decided to cock a deaf 'un and pretend they could see or hear nothing untoward. They simply turned away from the begging, crying Diablo as though he wasn't there, and this was the green light for Steve the Saint to continue the punishment beating. And he took full advantage, laying into Diablo with his makeshift club until the bully was a whimpering, broken wreck. After this kind of public humiliation, Diablo's strong-arming days were over in the 'Ville, and he would have to request protection and a ship-out. Job done.

A couple of days after the turn-out on the yard I was introduced to Steve the Saint by a mutual friend, and I found him to be a very interesting character. He was six foot one and athletic in build, with a broken nose and the biggest hands I'd ever seen on a man. The broken nose and the myriad tattoos he sported on his neck, knuckles and forearms made him look like a typical thug, but he was soft-spoken, very friendly and articulate. Over the years I was to find that not only was Steve the Saint an excellent and erudite raconteur but was probably the most knowledgeable man, particularly when it came to British history, I had ever met. He was also one of those anomalies you come across now and again – a lower-working-class man from the socialist stronghold of the Old Kent Road housing estates who would, if given the chance, vote Conservative, loved Maggie Thatcher and Winston Churchill and was a very serious royalist. I was the opposite to Steve the Saint in my views and this led to many a protracted argument over the next two decades. But all of our arguments were pretty good-natured and it was lucky that we both had a sense of humour that allowed us to banter with each other over politics and royalty. I got to like Steve very quickly and we would play kaluki together, a card game a bit like rummy popular in prison, and later, in HMP Whitemoor, Scrabble. We were both very competitive and neither of us could stand to lose to the other, so there was always an edge to our games.

At the time I met Steve the Saint I was on remand for GBH and possession of a semi-automatic firearm, and he was on remand for a series of post-office robberies. In 1982 the *News of the World* ran a centre-page spread called 'Cop a Robber' in which they would publish stills from security cameras of the commission of various armed robberies and invite anyone who recognized the robbers to phone in and claim a reward. One of the pictures that appeared was of a fresh-faced Steve the Saint, pre-broken hooter, wearing a big pair of sunglasses and carrying a pump-action shotgun and robbing a Bermondsey post office. The newspaper gave all the pictured blaggers nick-names, and the one they chose for Steve was 'the Choirboy'. Maybe it was the graininess of the picture or the angle it was taken from, but nobody recognized the thug-like Steve as 'the Choirboy', so the phones remained silent on him. But a few years later he was captured anyway, for another job, and they pinned the earlier Choirboy jobs on him as well.

When he left school Steve had been offered a job by a south London face who was big in the porn industry and tried to give a bit of a helping hand to some of the tearaway kids on the manor. It was also very handy having a front man with very few or no criminal convictions, in case things went Pete Tong and someone had to get their collar felt. The first job offered was managing a tiny pornographic cinema in Soho, and the money was fantastic so Steve agreed to take it. Soho in the seventies was much more seedy and villain-controlled than it is now, and Steve learnt the business from the old masters. Every month a CID man from the Vice Squad would turn up and be given a package of used banknotes in order to keep things sweet. Steve told me that it was common knowledge at the time that you couldn't operate in Soho without the co-operation of bent Old Bill, and they had to be bunged an earner or you could find yourself getting raided every five minutes.

The first gaff that Steve was put in to manage was a hardcore gay cinema and he was shocked by some of the things he saw there. It was his job to go in on the night shift and give the gaff a tidy-up before opening up at 10 p.m. Then he would sit in the little kiosk until 6 a.m. and sell tickets to the punters who rolled up throughout the night. It could have been a very boring job as the only two people working there were Steve and the projectionist and the latter never came out until the end of his shift, but the characters who turned up at the kiosk were a constant source of wonder and amusement. Steve told me there was one man of about seventy who used to turn up every Friday night in full schoolboy outfit of short grey trousers, blazer, cap and satchel, his wizened, toothless face stretched into a leer as he purchased his ticket. There were also a lot of other bizarre characters – fat men dressed in

Lederhosen, skinny men in full Nazi uniform with Hitler moustaches, others in frocks with feather boas around their pudgy, stubble-shadowed necks, and many more.

At the end of his first shift Steve found that pornographic films were not the only attraction of the darkened cinema for the bizarre clientele. At close of play Steve had to enter the cinema, switch on the main lights and clear the punters out to make ready for the next shift. He told me that the first time he switched the lights on he thought the ten or so men there were fighting on the floor below the screen, they all seemed to be tangled up in a bundle of flesh. But when he looked closer he could see that they were in various states of sexual congress. Steve was shocked rigid by what he saw and immediately switched the lights off again. But then he got paranoid and imagined some of the punters breaking off from the naked, sweating, fisting mass and creeping towards him, so he turned the lights back on. The punters, it seemed, had no shame at all about what they were up to and slowly disentangled themselves, got dressed and left, chatting away to each other as though walking out of a night at a legitimate theatre. After that first night Steve came to take such things in his stride. His routine was to switch the main lights on and off in quick succession as a signal to the punters that festivities were at an end, and then go and sit in his kiosk and wait for them to troop out.

After six months in the gay cinema Steve got a transfer to one of the porn bookshops further up the street and was happy dealing with the dirty-raincoat and fetish brigade there for the next couple of years. Then things began to change around Soho. There was a big investigation into corruption in the Vice Squad, with several senior detectives taking early retirement 'on medical grounds', which is police-speak for getting out with your pension intact before you get nicked, and a new mob came in who weren't prepared to be bent. The shop that Steve was working in was one of the first targets of the newly purified Vice Squad and it contained so many violations of its licence that it was immediately closed down, along with many others. Steve found himself unemployed. He drifted into a bit of cannabis-dealing and then chequebook and card fraud, which was very big at the time, before buying a gun and trying a bit of the heavy. This was when he became known as the Choirboy.

Subsequently, Steve the Saint appeared at the Old Bailey and was given eight years' imprisonment for his post-office blags and possession of a firearm. I was found not guilty of GBH at Inner London Crown Court but pleaded guilty to possession of a firearm without a licence and was given three years, the maximum for this charge at the time. Steve and I went our separate ways, he to Parkhurst and me to Wandsworth. It would be a good few years before we met up again, but we kept in touch via messages through third parties moving between jails. In Parkhurst Steve settled down to do his bird and got on with nearly everyone. In the eighties and nineties HMP Parkhurst was one of the few jails that wouldn't take sex offenders, at the insistence of the prisoners themselves. A well-known face and armed robber had been stabbed to death in the main kitchen by a violent paedophile in an argument over something trivial, and the inmates of Parkhurst, a top-security prison holding some of the most violent and notorious prisoners in the system, set out to seriously assault all sex offenders in the jail. After several stabbings, coshings and scaldings the authorities decided it might be prudent to ship all sex offenders out to other jails and stop sending them to Parkhurst. So, because there was now no one to look down on and plot up on, the cons in Parkhurst became eager for action and began to take out their frustrations on the screws and each other. It was said that Parkhurst was run by the cons and, as a result, it was not a jail for the faint-hearted. Someone only had to whisper that so-and-so was a suspected grass or had been seen talking to the screws in a friendly manner and so-and-so would find himself being eyed up as a target for the dozens of desperate violent criminals eager for a bit of excitement to smash the boredom and sameness of every single day in an island prison.

Steve the Saint wasn't averse to a bit of violence himself but he was also one of those men who feel deep empathy with other people. He hated to hear about or witness injustice to others, particularly the weak. One incident at Parkhurst that stuck with him, which he was to relate to me years later, was a case of mistaken identity that almost led to the killing of an innocent man. Every Thursday the National Draft (which was what the transfer of prisoners all over the country to different prisons was called before it was privatized and given to outside contractors) delivered three or four new arrivals to Parkhurst. The prisoners in the jail, knowing that new arrivals were on their way, would slip down to the wing office and check the list of names to see if any of the new bods were old friends, or enemies. One day a name – Burdet – seemed to ring a bell with a particularly spiteful prisoner who took great pleasure in putting it on other cons because he had a secret dodgy past himself, and he racked his brain in an effort to recall where he had heard it before. At last it came to him: there had been a serial rapist from Portsmouth with the same name. Putting these facts together, this individual was able to 'deduce' that the authorities were trying to pull a fast one by slipping a sex case on to the wing, and that would never be accepted by the cons. He made it his business to tell all the hard, action-loving faces on the wing about his discovery, getting them alert for the violence that was to come. Of course, he made sure to embellish his story by saying he remembered the case well and that one of the screws had let it slip that this geezer was definitely the one.

The new receptions turned up on the wing, and Burdet proved to be a quiet, nondescript man who didn't know anyone in the jail. This was further proof of his sex-case status, if any were needed, because a normal con would at least have someone who could vouch for him. The con who had started the witch hunt came to Steve the Saint and asked him if he wanted to take part in the violence to come, but Steve declined, saying that perhaps they should be sure about the new fella before any action was taken. Everyone looked at him like he was a right lemon and told him that they were sure already. Steve shrugged and went back to his game of cards. That evening the unsuspecting Burdet wandered around what he thought would be his new home for the next few years. Far from being a serial rapist, he was a first offender who had received seven years for the manslaughter of one of his friends during a drunken pub fight, which is why he didn't know anyone in Parkhurst. As he walked around the wing, he became aware that he was getting some evil looks and the cold-shoulder treatment from other cons, but with no experience of prison to fall back on, he assumed that this was normal for new guys and once he'd been there a while they would get to know him. He had been asked only one question, by a stone-faced bloke at the hot-plate as he collected his evening meal: 'Where are you from?' Burdet smiled and said the word that sealed his fate: 'Portsmouth.' And that was it. Behind the scenes, the action merchants, filled with what they considered righteous anger, got tooled up. Later in the evening, when the trap had been laid, someone slipped up to Burdet and told him he was wanted in the television room. Not stopping to wonder who could possibly want him, Burdet climbed the stairs and walked straight into the beating of his life. Eight or nine cons laid into the unsuspecting Burdet with everything from batteries in socks to home-made clubs. It was a terrible hiding, and within seconds he was unconscious and being kicked all over.

Eventually the avenging angels of B wing considered he'd had enough and dispersed to change their clothes and dump their weapons. Then a couple of faces who hadn't taken part in the actual beating dragged the broken and bloody body from the TV room and down the stairs to the wing office. They dumped the unconscious man in the doorway in front of the screws, telling them, 'We found this rapist upstairs, better call an ambulance for him.' The message was loud and clear: you've been sussed trying to put an undercover sex case among us, but we don't fool easy. The screws quickly got on the blower to the medics.

Burdet died twice on the way to the local hospital, and it was only the CPR skills of the medical team that revived him and kept him breathing. He had a broken jaw, a fractured skull and a blood clot on the brain, among other things, but he survived. It was a few days later that the real story came out about Burdet, and it turned out that the real serial rapist – a fella called Burnette from Plymouth – was serving his sentence in HMP Long Lartin. The mood on the wing was sombre, and the near-murder of the innocent Burdet made Steve decide that he never wanted to come back to prison again. He was finished with crime, and when he got out he would be going straight. But the best-laid plans of mice and cons . . .

Once he had finished his sentence Steve the Saint headed back to the Old Kent Road and settled down. He was determined never to go back to armed robbery but found that life was not going to be easy for an ex-con. What little straight work he could get was low-paid and soul-destroying for someone who had been used to spending like a sailor on three-day shore leave, but Steve persevered. After a while he met a nice girl and they fell deeply in love. Carol was from a good family and had never had much to do with anyone like Steve before, so he kept much of his past a secret from her. She didn't know that he had worked in the porn business, been the Choirboy or done a sentence in Parkhurst. She just saw him as a bit of a rough diamond. After a while they moved in together, to Steve's council flat on the Aylesbury estate, and were very happy. But Steve found work hard to get, and he gradually got involved in a bit of small-time cannabis-dealing in order to pay the rent and put food on the table. Then Steve met an old mate of his who was doing really well in the skunk business. At that time, skunk, a particularly potent form of cannabis plant, was fairly new to England and was commanding big money from the discerning weed-smokers of this country. Most of it was imported from Holland, but a few enterprising growers found that, with the right equipment and conditions, they could grow it here and still get the big money for it. Steve's pal, Fergie, was one such grower who was having it large on the proceeds and he helped Steve out with a few quid when he was on his arse. Steve asked if he could join Fergie's 'cartel' for a while in order to get back on his feet but that was a no-go as Fergie had partners who weren't hiring. They wanted to keep the profits to themselves for as long as possible. But Fergie, feeling sorry for his old mate, agreed to help Steve set up his own skunk farm in his council flat if Steve could put up the money for all the equipment and paraphernalia he would need to start off with. The start-up gear would come to just under £3,000, but the trouble was that Steve didn't have two half-pennies to rub together, let alone three grand. He decided to think about it.

By now he and Carol had been living together for over a year and were still bang in love, so Steve decided it was time to tell her about his murky past. He sat her down one evening and laid it all out for her, holding nothing back. When he had finished she had tears in her eyes but grabbed him in an embrace and told him it didn't matter, any of it. As long as they were together she didn't care what had happened in the past. Steve was relieved at this, because he really did love her and didn't know what he would do if she wasn't in his life. Now that he had given up his past, he decided to broach his thoughts on the future. He told Carol all about the idea of starting a skunk farm, how much money they could earn, how low the risk of being caught was and how much of a difference it would make to their quality of life. Carol asked if it would be a long-term thing. Of course not, said Steve, it would be a one-off. Just enough to earn a big profit to keep them going until something better, more legit, came along. For a couple of days they discussed it and finally Carol was won over. Once she had agreed to the idea in principle, Steve dropped his next bombshell: they would need three grand to start it up. They each put forward ideas for how they might get this money, but none was viable and they both knew it. Then Steve brought up the one sure way by which he could get hold of that sort of cash: he suggested he rob a bank.

Carol was horrified at Steve's suggestion, but he did his best to reassure her. He explained it like this: he had been a pretty successful armed robber in the past and knew the mechanics intimately, plus, the chances of him being caught on one last job must be millions to one. He would be in and out in three minutes with the cash, the cash they needed to start changing their lives! He would wear a mask and nobody would ever know it was him. He knew what he was doing, he was a professional. It took almost a week, but finally Carol was worn down by his persistence and agreed that they should try it. Steve didn't particularly want to rob a bank, but he knew deep down that nobody was going to give him and Carol a hand-out. If they wanted a better life, then they would have to go out and take it. So he began to put his rudimentary plan into action.

First, he went to one of his old contacts to try and get a gun. He wanted a handgun, preferably a revolver, because it would be easier to conceal, but when his contact found out that Steve didn't have the £300 fee for the cheapest handgun, he offered him the only gun he had available to the more cheapskate customers – an ancient, single-barrel, hammer-cock sixteen-bore shotgun that looked like it was only being held together by the gaffer tape around its pockmarked stock. Most armourers have a lend-lease policy whereby you can take a gun for a decent deposit and return it after the bit of work you want it for, the deposit being non-refundable. If you have to shoot anybody with the gun, you will normally have to pay the full price and buy the gun outright. The ammunition is also on hire and that also has to be paid for if used. Firing a shot into the air as a frightener can cost you as much as £50 a bullet if you're hiring something exotic like a Luger .35 or a 9mm parabellum Walther. But Steve the Saint couldn't even afford the deposit and was only offered the manky shotgun because of the old-pals act and a promise of £100 after the work was done. He had no choice but to take it.

For the next couple of days Steve and Carol were rarely out of each other's arms, knowing that the worst-case scenario, if they had not even a smidgen of luck in this endeavour, could see Steve going to prison for a very long time. But they convinced themselves to be positive and not even to contemplate the worst out loud. Steve figured that because he couldn't afford a car and he was no good at nicking them, his best bet would be to rob a bank in the West End. The advantage of this was that there was plenty of public transport and black cabs, which he could hail anywhere once he had the money to pay for the ride, plus it would be easier to lose himself in the crowds. He set the date for the robbery and he and Carol spent the night before, talking until the early hours. As dawn broke over the Old Kent Road they swore their undying love, no matter what happened.

Steve had just about enough money for the bus into the West End and, with the ancient shotgun under his coat and his gloves and ski-mask in his pocket, Carol walked him to the stop. She stayed with him until the bus came, her arms round him and her head on his shoulder. Before Steve climbed on they kissed and whispered, 'I love you.' On the platform he called, in a bright and hopeful voice, 'See you later.' Upstairs, he hurried to the back window and waved. As the bus pulled away, he saw Carol standing there on the pavement, a lone figure waving him off with tears running down her face. He blew her a kiss, and then she was out of sight as the bus turned a corner. Deep in his heart Steve knew that this might be the last time he ever saw her. As a free man, in any case. He quickly wiped this thought from his mind and began to psych up for what lay ahead.

It took Steve a good two hours of walking around to spot a bank he was happy with, but he finally found one. Then it took another hour to build up the courage to go and rob it. Steve was well aware of what could happen, and there were three realistic possibilities: 1. he would do the work and get away with the cash; 2. he would lose his bottle and go home with nothing, meaning he would have to go through all this again the following day, or the day after that; and 3. he would be caught and end up in prison for years, losing what little he now had. Steve knew that the money they needed was not just going to drop from heaven, so he girded his loins, sucked in a deep breath, and walked straight into the bank, pulling his mask on as he went.

Once inside, it all came back to him. Just like eating winkles out of the shell, you never forget how to rob a bank once you've done it. Steve pulled out his old gun and took control with a couple of shouted commands. In five hot seconds he had the customers on the floor and a frightened and compliant cashier filling the plastic bag he had brought with banknotes. From what he could judge, there was already more than enough in the bag for his needs, but just to be sure he moved on to the second cashier and got her to add to his tally. Once the bag was heavy with cash, Steve grabbed it, and covering the bank with his shooter, backed his way up to the door. Outside, he ripped the mask from his head and stuffed it and the gun into the money bag. Then he stripped off his coat and hung it casually over his shoulder by one finger and walked swiftly away. With every step his heart seemed to grow lighter as the realization that he had pulled it off hit him. Now he couldn't wait to get back to Carol and see her face – if only he could find a taxi.

Unfortunately for Steve, the manager of the bank he had just robbed was not the usual plump bureaucrat you generally find running a financial establishment but a young white-water-rafting, rock-climbing, paragliding action man. When he saw that his bank was being robbed, he ordered his staff to raise the alarm and then slipped out of the bank to follow the robber. He pursued Steve along crowded streets, never more than ten feet away from him and desperately scanning the crowds for a policeman. Steve had no idea he was being followed, it just never entered his head, but he did want to get out of the West End and searched furiously for a black cab that still had its For Hire sign lit. He wouldn't be completely happy until he was back in south London. Then Steve's worst nightmare jumped back into his head as he saw two uniformed coppers walking towards him in the crowd ahead. He quickly judged their faces and body language and was relieved to see that they both seemed relaxed and were not looking at him. 'It's sweet,' he told himself. 'Just act normal. They don't have a clue.' He was almost level with them when he heard a loud shout from behind: 'Officer! Stop that man! He's just robbed the bank!' And everyone within hearing distance seemed to freeze.

For Steve that split second when the shout had left the mouth of the bank manager and was arriving at the ears of everyone in range, including the two coppers, was when his life was changed for ever. For a second, nobody moved, then the coppers looked in the direction the bank manager was pointing and found their target within arm's reach. One of them went immediately for his retractable steel baton and the other grabbed Steve by the sleeve of his shirt and swung him around. Steve was in the zone now, his animal survival instincts taking over. He had to escape at any cost, so even as he was being swung around by the first copper, his hand was finding the taped wooden stock of the shotgun within the folds of the bag. As he reached the top of the swing, Steve found himself off balance and crashing towards the pavement, but he managed to free the gun. When the crowd of shoppers and tourists saw it in Steve's hand there was a lot of screaming and running. The copper who had swung him to the ground took a step back when he noticed that the gaping barrel of the sawn-off was pointing up at his face. His colleague, who now had his baton in his hand, didn't see the gun and couldn't understand why his oppo was in the way and not steaming in. Steve, with a swiftness and agility born of fear and desperation, almost bounced back up off the pavement, keeping the gun pointed at the first copper. The second shoved his mate to one side and raised his baton before being confronted with the gun. For a split second no one moved, then Steve was clear what he had to do in order to escape. He lowered the gun until it was pointed at the baton-wielding copper's knees and pulled the trigger. Nothing happened.

Steve had forgotten that the gun was a hammer-cock model so, in order to fire it, you first had to cock back the hammer manually. He just had time to mutter, 'Fuck!' before the action-loving bank manager crashed into him from behind and knocked him flying to the hard pavement. The gun flew out of his hand and went clattering across the pavement and into the road, and the two coppers flopped bodily on to him like a tag team of all-in wrestlers. Steve was done and gave up the struggle a good few minutes before the excited trio of law enforcers stopped beating him. At last they cuffed his hands behind his back and, as he lay there bruised and devastated, he saw the money bag about five foot away on the pavement. It had fallen from his hand in the struggle and £20 notes were blowing out and fluttering in the wind. Steve closed his eyes and kept them closed until he was in West End Central police station. He couldn't bear to see his own end.

Nine months later Steve the Saint pleaded guilty at the Old Bailey to armed robbery and using a firearm to resist arrest. He was sentenced to life imprisonment under the Two Strikes Act. The bank manager and the two coppers were commended by the judge for their bravery. While Steve was on remand in HMP Belmarsh, Carol came to visit him just the once. It was a tearful reunion but both knew that their relationship had to end. Steve never saw Carol again, but four years into his sentence he heard that she had married another man and they had a daughter. He has now served eight years in prison and still thinks about her and how it might have been had circumstances been kinder. I still play kaluki and Scrabble with Steve the Saint, and we still argue about politics and royalty. But these days we're both a lot older and, hopefully, a hell of a lot wiser. Whoever said crime doesn't pay must have had Steve and me in mind.

5. Rolex Ronnie

I knew Rolex Ronnie long before he earned his nickname and, as well as being a pretty prolific stick-up man, he was a terrible practical joker. Ronnie's practical jokes had a way of resulting in pain and grief for the targets. Nothing was sacrosanct. Because of this, when the joke was finally turned on him, more than a few people in the underworld laughed long and hard.

Ronnie mostly worked alone as a stick-up artist, walking into banks, building societies, post offices or anywhere that might have a decent payday behind the jump. He never nicked vast amounts of money, and if he pulled over three grand, he'd had a good day, but then he had little to spend his money on: he had no wife or kids and spent most of his days, when not out robbing, nipping between his local pub and the betting shop next door. He still lived with his parents, which in those days was considered a bit under the arm for a man in his thirties. But he was an affable enough drunk and generous to a fault, though he could afford to be when he was getting his wages at the point of a gun. Ronnie had done a bit of bird in his youth – a lagging (three years) for possession of a firearm with intent, and a couple of six-monthers for various drunken indiscretions such as smashing up a kebab shop and assaulting a copper – but he was what is known as a lucky thief, one who has been at it for a long time without getting his collar felt for anything serious. Who knows, maybe Ronnie could have gone through his whole life as a working robber and never got a tug from Old Bill or a long stretch of porridge, but then he met the girl of his dreams and his chakra became naused for ever.

asked to try and pin down the exact moment his life ...ne wrong turning on the road to a happy future, Ronnie ...es one afternoon in the winter of 1985, when he got the idea of playing a particularly cruel joke on a fella named Freaky Fred. That was the afternoon he met Snake-Eyed Sal, the woman he would up his game for, the one who would be instrumental in his downfall. And, by chance, I happened to be there at the time. A few of us were having a rowdy drink in a boozer on Clapham Park Road called the Clockhouse, though local Old Bill called it the Crookhouse because so many of the sawn-off and ski-mask set had adopted it as their favourite watering hole. There was me, Ronnie, Tough Tony, the German and Little Andy the jock, all knocking back the shandies and playing pool for a cockle a game, when Freaky Fred came in looking very pleased with himself. Freaky Fred wasn't a criminal in the strict sense of the word, more what is known as a 'ducker and diver', someone who bought a bit of nicked gear now and then or did straightish jobs but paid no tax. He was a nice fella, if a bit dim, and was well known to all of us. Anyway, it turned out that Freaky Fred had just bought a right bargain. His wife's birthday was coming up and Fred had managed to get hold of a Mini Clubman car for her present. It was a nice little runner and looked the part. His wife had just passed her driving test, so he was going to surprise her on the morning of her birthday, wrap a big ribbon around it and do the whole schtick. He had the car parked outside the pub so we all trooped out to have a butcher's at it. It was definitely a woman's car, small, low to the ground and painted in a sparkly purple colour that looked like nail varnish. All it was missing was furry seat covers, and Fred had them on order. As he wanted it to be a surprise, Fred asked Ronnie if he could park it in the drive of his parents' house until the big day. And Ronnie agreed.

Later on in the afternoon Ronnie got a phone call in the

pub from a mate of his who was selling a couple of revolvers he thought Ronnie might be interested in. He asked me if I wanted to go down to Balham with him to have a look, and I agreed. Fred was still in the pub knocking them back and Ronnie, never one to miss a trick, asked him if we could borrow the Mini to get down to Balham. Freaky Fred, knowing how reckless Ronnie could be, at first refused. But Ronnie cajoled and pulled the old-pals act on Fred until he gave in. He said Ronnie could borrow the motor but on condition that I drove and that we would be back within the hour. I didn't mind driving, even though I'd had a few shants, and I was in better condition than Ronnie, so off we went in the purple Mini Clubman.

Being more used to big fifties Yank motors, I was surprised at the speed and agility of the Mini. I put my foot down and swung it around corners like it was a Dinky toy, and when I reached a long, straight bit of road, I was so heavy-footed that the speedo needle was straining at its zenith. Me and Ronnie were laughing like lunatics as the little car flew across the tarmac like a purple bullet. The road we were travelling on had a slight bend half-way along its length and, as I powered into the turn, I heard a thump at the front of the car and then everything really did seem to happen in slow motion. The wheel jumped in my hand and, as I wrestled with it and pumped the brake pedal, the little car slewed sideways and skidded towards the kerb. I sensed more than felt that I had hit something and that whatever it was had gone underneath the car and was lying in the road behind us. I managed to pump the brakes enough so that when the nearside wheels hit the kerb the impact wasn't too bad and we didn't tip over, though it was enough to burst the back tyre and leave the car trembling in mid air for a long second. When we were completely still I switched the engine off and sat there in shock for a moment. Then I heard several wails of anguish and saw a young woman standing on the pavement with two kids of about seven or eight. The woman was looking at the road behind us with such horror on her face that my worst fears seemed to be confirmed. The kids were screaming and in tears, and one, a little boy, was pointing. I suddenly felt ice-cold, and then sick. 'Fuck!' I said to the now silent Ronnie as I climbed out of the Mini on rubbery legs. 'I think I've hit a kid.' That was the first thought in my mind, knowing how low to the ground the undercarriage of the Mini was and that if it had been an adult we'd have felt more of a thumping. I didn't want to look, I was shit-scared and shaking like a leaf, but I looked over the roof of the car and up the road. I came close to fainting when I saw the smear of bright-red blood and the tiny broken figure, but then I noticed the long black tail and the tufts of gore-covered fur, and my heart rolled back down my throat and into my chest again. 'Oh, thank fuck!' I said. 'It's a fucking cat!'

While I went to examine the splattered carcass of the cat and remove it to the gutter, Ronnie, white-faced and shaken himself, went to comfort the woman and children who had witnessed the whole thing. It turned out that the kids had stopped to stroke the cat, which had been sitting on a wall, when we came screeching around the bend doing 80 mph. Maybe it was the noise from the car that spooked the moggy, but it leapt from the wall and scooted across the road, only making it half-way before we were upon it. Maybe it had already used up eight of its nine lives, but whether it had or not, it was definitely not getting up from this one. I felt bad about the cat, but relieved that it had not been a kid. I vowed then and there never to drink and drive again, the scare had been too much. And that was the last time I ever got behind the wheel after a shant. Meanwhile, Ronnie was doing a pretty good job of calming everyone down. An old woman came out of one of the houses to see what was going on. Luckily, it wasn't her cat that was lying mangled in the gutter, so she offered hot sweet tea all round and lollipops for the kids. I was still very shaken, but I got to work changing the back wheel to keep myself busy. We would have to buy Freaky Fred a new spare wheel before returning the car, but at least it wasn't badly damaged. By the time I had changed the wheel, the kids were sucking happily on lollipops and Ronnie seemed to be getting on great with the young woman, the cat all but forgotten by everyone except me. We said our goodbyes and, with Ronnie now behind the wheel, we headed off for Balham.

The cat incident had sobered us both up but by the time we got to the meeting even I was able to have a little chuckle about it. Ronnie was in top form because, while chatting to the young woman, he had established that she was the children's aunt and he had ended up with her phone number and a date for the following week. Only Ronnie could have turned a horror film into a love story, and I shook my head in wonder. We did our bit of business in Balham and before we drove back we took a look at the damage to the front of the car. The number plate was split in half and hanging down and the grille was dented from the impact of the cat's skull. There was blood, gore and bits of grey brain matter splashed over the bumper and caught up in the metal of the grille, so I suggested we at least run the motor through a car-wash before returning it. But Ronnie held up a hand, a crafty expression on his face, and I knew he was working out a practical joke. 'What if,' he said, slowly, 'we was to go back and tell Freaky Fred that we had run over a kid?'

I shook my head. 'Turn it in, Ronnie,' I said. 'That's not funny.'

But Ronnie was on a roll and he wasn't to be stopped. 'No, hear me out. This will be so fucking funny.' And while he drove us back to the Clockhouse, I listened and found myself warming to his 'joke' despite myself.

When me and Ronnie, grim-faced and pale, walked into the back bar of the pub, Freaky Fred knew that something was wrong. We stopped at the bar and ordered a couple of large brandies, and Fred was stuck to us like shit on a blanket before the drinks arrived. 'You better not have damaged that fucking car . . .' he began, but Ronnie shushed him and pulled him in close.

'Listen, Fred,' he said, gravely, 'I'm not going to lie to you, mate, we had a bit of an accident on the way back and it's pretty serious.'

Fred's face screwed up in anguish. 'You've wrecked the motor, haven't you? I fucking knew it!'

Ronnie shook his head. 'No, the car's parked in the estate across the road, but I wouldn't go driving it for a while.'

Fred looked worried now and bit his lip. 'Why? What have you done?'

Ronnie drained his brandy in one swallow and hung his head. 'We hit a little kid,' he said, and there was a sob in his voice. I didn't know where to look so I took a sip from my glass.

Fred went white and his mouth dropped open in shock. 'Wh– what?' he said. 'What?'

Ronnie made a show of glancing around to make sure no one was earwigging. 'Look, it couldn't be helped. We were doing about eighty down Weir Road and this kid, must have been about five or six, stepped out into the road. We tried to stop but it was too late. He was under the car before we knew it.'

Fred was shaking now and all the colour had drained out of his face. 'H– how is he?' he asked. 'Is he badly hurt?'

Ronnie rubbed one eyebrow and closed his eyes. 'We think he's dead,' he said, and his performance was so good I almost believed him myself.

Fred stared at us. 'What do you mean, "you think"? Didn't you phone an ambulance?'

It was my turn to get involved. 'Fred,' I said, 'we couldn't, neither of us has got a licence. They'd have banged us up straightaway. We had to drive on, mate.'

By now Fred was hanging on to the edge of the bar like it was the only thing holding him up. 'I need a large scotch,' he mumbled, and I ordered one for him.

After Fred had knocked back his scotch Ronnie added a bit more heat to the flames that Fred was now roasting in. He took the keys for the Mini from his pocket and slid them across the bar to Fred. 'Here, mate,' he said. 'It's your motor, not mine. And you might want to give it a bit of a clean-up. We noticed when we were parking it up that there's a bit of blood and that on the front.'

Fred looked at the car keys as though they were covered in blood themselves and wiped a shaky hand across his mouth. 'No, no. I tell you what,' he said, 'you have the motor, eh? Have it. I'll get Angie a bunch of flowers for her birthday instead. She'll be sweet with that. You have the car.'

Ronnie shook his head sadly. 'It's not my motor, Fred. I mean, you can imagine how hot it's going to be if that kid is dead, can't you? And the first place Old Bill will go looking is to you 'cos I'm almost sure we left the front number plate behind. It's your motor, mate.'

Fred was shitting himself, but there was also an edge of outrage in his voice. 'But it was you what run the kid down, not me!'

Ronnie gave him the old fish-eye. 'You wouldn't be thinking of grassing us up, would you, Fred? Because you know what happens to grasses, don't you?'

Fred swallowed hard and began to whine. 'No, course not! Fucking hell, Ronnie! I didn't mean that! No way! I'm just saying, this is really serious and I don't fancy doing porridge for it if it can be helped, know what I mean?'

Ronnie nodded slowly. 'Don't worry about it. With your

lack of previous, you won't get long anyway. What do you reckon, Razor?'

I nodded sagely and looked at Fred. 'Yeah, you'll be OK. Probably won't serve no more than a ten, and you'll do all right in Parkhurst.' This was exactly what Freaky Fred didn't want to hear. He'd never spent more than a night in a police cell.

After a while we convinced Fred to go and have a look at the Mini on the pretext of checking to see if the front number plate was still there. We knew it wasn't, because we had ripped it off and hidden it under the back seat, but we wanted Fred to see the state of the front grille to add to his state of mind. While Fred was gone we filled the other lads in the pub in on the joke, and everyone thought it was hilarious – which goes to show what a bunch of cruel-natured bastards we all were. In the meantime, a fella named Jimmy the Hoister came in for a drink and we brought him in on the joke as well. A few minutes later Freaky Fred, looking decidedly freaked out, came back and ordered another large scotch to calm his nerves. He had vomited all over the pavement when he'd seen the blood and gore on the car and now he was in bits. As Fred poured scotch down his neck and ordered another, Jimmy the Hoister spoke up. 'Here, there must be something going on down in Balham. I've just driven through there and there are police and ambulances everywhere. They've got one of the roads blocked off with that yellow scene-of-crime tape and every-thing.'

To the secret amusement of the watching eyes in the bar, Freaky Fred, in the middle of swallowing his third double since he'd walked back in, spluttered like an old diesel and spilled scotch all down himself.

'What do you think happened, then?' asked Tough Tony in mock interest.

Jimmy the Hoister, enjoying himself immensely, pursed his

lips and frowned. 'Well, I asked one of the coppers, and he reckons it was a hit and run, a little purple motor mowed a kiddie down and drove on. The bastard!'

Fred wiped his face and tried to sidle unobtrusively closer to Jimmy's table. He cleared his throat and tried a nonchalant tone that didn't quite come off. 'The – er – the kid, die, did he?'

Jimmy rubbed his chin thoughtfully. 'Well, with the amount of blood and brains spattered all over the road, I'd fucking think so.' And Fred fainted – to the great amusement and hilarity of everyone else in the bar.

The next couple of days, Fred spent a lot of time in the Clockhouse, afraid to go home in case the police came knocking, and the boys rubbed it in at every opportunity. Whenever Fred looked as though he might have put the car business out of his mind, someone would mention the supposed latest developments about the police investigation they had 'heard'. Eventually someone took pity on him and sat him down and told him it had all been a joke. Fred was like a man who had had his death sentence reprieved at the last minute, but the vinegar in the jam was that the day after me and Ronnie told him about the accident, he had got on the blower to a mate of his who owned a scrap yard and paid him a substantial sum to take the car away in the dead of night and crush it. So for Freaky Fred, the news about it all being a joke was a mixed blessing. His wife had to do with flowers for her birthday, and Freaky Fred never spoke to Ronnie again. Meanwhile, Ronnie was getting on famously with Sal, the bird he'd met the day we ran the cat down, and they became a win double around the manor.

Sal, who quickly became known as Snake-Eyed Sal, due to her snakiness and hunger for money, winkled it out of Ronnie that he was an armed robber. This didn't bother her in the slightest and, in fact, it made her more eager to be his girl because she thought she would be the recipient of his stolen

73

largesse. Sal was after the good life, and she badgered her new man to provide it. Not satisfied with the piddling amounts of cash that Ronnie was robbing, she nagged him constantly to raise his ambitions and horizons by doing a 'big job' so they could buy a house together and drive nice cars. So Ronnie, who had been doing quite well as a lone stick-up artist, took on a partner and started looking for enough dough to rob to keep his sweetheart happy. One day, mooching about in Croydon shopping centre, a favourite target for south London robbers, Ronnie found himself on the second floor of the precinct, staring at the display in a jewellery shop window. The shop specialized in Rolex watches, and Ronnie added up the price tags in the window display and found they came to nearly £200,000. There were watches made of gold and platinum, watches studded with diamonds and rubies, and they were all just sitting there in the window twinkling at him and calling out to be robbed. Ronnie looked inside the shop and saw three members of staff, a woman and two men, and he knew it was a goer.

The plan Ronnie came up with to rob the Rolex jeweller's was simple but very daring. For three weeks he went about arranging everything in a professional manner. He had a meet with a well-known fence, who got in touch with a hot-watch specialist in Coventry who would be willing to come down with cash and buy the lot as soon as they were stolen. Then he got one of the local toe-rags to steal him a 250cc trials bike, one with extended forks and tuned suspension. Luckily, his crime partner, Bimbo, could ride a bike pretty well, so he only had to practise with the bike to familiarize himself with it. He bought a cheapo legal motor with tax on the window for a couple of hundred quid from a car front and got it checked over by a mechanic. And every night he would lie in bed with Snake-Eyed Sal and talk about the great time they were going to have when he pulled this job off. After exes and a split with

Bimbo, Ronnie was hoping to come away with at least forty grand for his whack, which was a tidy piece of change back in '85, as it is now.

Ronnie spent a few days watching the routine of the jeweller's and noted that at noon every day the woman and the older man, who Ronnie assumed was the manager, went out to lunch in a nearby coffee gaff, leaving the younger man on his own to run the shop. It was never that busy between twelve and one, and Ronnie knew this would be the ideal time to strike. In those days mobile phones were not very common and the telecommunications tool favoured by professional robbers was a set of walkie-talkies – simple radio communications only viable over short distances. They could be purchased quite cheaply from most electrical stores or stolen from building sites, where they were used in crane work, which is where Ronnie got his set. The next stage was a dress rehearsal, and Bimbo got into position on the main road outside the precinct and listened for Ronnie's call on his handset. The walkie-talkies worked perfectly over the distance and all that was left to do was for Ronnie and Bimbo to walk the route in and out of the precinct and work out the timings. Ronnie never had any doubt in his mind that he could pull this robbery off. He had always been a lucky thief, and apart from all the off-scene planning, it boiled down to nothing more than a walk-in stick-up, which was his bread and butter. As long as Bimbo performed well on the day, it would be a stone ginger. The day before the robbery Ronnie told Snake-Eyed Sal to book them both a holiday somewhere nice, maybe the Caribbean, so they could relax in the sun and celebrate, and she didn't need telling twice.

On the morning of the robbery everything was in place and at twelve on the dot, Ronnie, dressed in suit, tie, raincoat, trilby and glasses and carrying a briefcase, made his way into the precinct and on to the escalator for the second floor. He walked past the jeweller's to make sure everything was sweet and saw the young fella on his own behind the counter and that there were no customers in the shop. Ronnie put his hand into his pocket and keyed the 'send' button of his walkie-talkie three times. This was the signal to Bimbo to start his run, as Ronnie was going in. There was no going back now, so Ronnie rang the bell on the door of the jewellery shop and smiled pleasantly through the glass at the young assistant, who, seeing nothing untoward, buzzed him in. As soon as he had gained entry, Ronnie went to work. He put the briefcase on the counter and snapped it open. Inside was a white cotton pillow-case and a Navy Colt 6-shot .44 revolver. Taking both from the case, he threw the pillowcase at the assistant and pointed the gun at his face. 'Get those window displays open, load the watches into that bag and keep your mouth shut or I will shoot you in the face. Now, move!' The assistant, looking suitably frightened, grabbed the pillowcase and opened the till. He lifted the till drawer and took out a couple of keys on a ring. As he went to close the till, Ronnie waved the gun impatiently. 'Move it!' he growled, and helped himself to the cash from the open till. The assistant struggled for a moment but managed to get the first window display open. He hesitated. Ronnie, now right behind him, dug the barrel of the Colt into his ribs and said, 'Hurry up!' The man glanced over his shoulder. 'But . . .' he began. Ronnie poked him harder with the gun. 'Shut the fuck up and get those watches in the bag, now!' The assistant seemed to shrug and began sweeping the display into the bag. By the time the second window was cleared, Ronnie could hear the welcome growl of Bimbo's stolen 250 echoing around the precinct. He took the now weighty bag from the assistant's hand and gestured with the gun. 'Lie down on the floor', he snarled. 'And don't come up till I've gone.' The man did as he was told and Ronnie made his exit.

On the three-click signal from Ronnie, Bimbo had started

the engine of the bike and made his way into the massive shopping precinct. He got some annoyed looks from shoppers, but he kept his speed down to around 20 mph so as not to really alarm anyone. At this stage he was more a nuisance than an emergency. He rode through the shopping halls and across a wide, open concourse before reaching the part of the precinct where the jeweller's was situated, and now came the difficult part. His route to the second level was via a moving escalator. Lining up the front wheel of the bike, he gunned the engine and left a bit of tyre rubber on the York stone as he shot up the narrow escalator. Luckily, there was no one on the escalator, as they had fled on seeing what Bimbo intended to do. Coming off the top of the escalator, Bimbo geared down and swung the bike around towards the jeweller's, about fifty yards away. Just as he reached the front of the shop and slowed down, Ronnie came out with the pillowcase in one hand and the gun in the other. He hopped on to the back of the bike and off they went. The game now was to go back the way Bimbo had come as fast as they could. His entry into the precinct had not gone unrecorded by the many CCTV cameras set up on almost every building and the precinct security guards were now on their way to try and stop them. Ronnie tucked the pillowcase full of watches into his coat and hung on to the bike with his free hand while keeping his gun hand free for the security guards. Bimbo negotiated the down escalator perfectly and when they reached the ground level he gave the nippy bike its head, speeding through the precinct at 60 mph and scattering pedestrians all over the gaff.

Ronnie was enjoying himself, perched up on the back of the bike with his six-shooter in his hand, like a cowboy riding double through Injun country. And it wasn't long before the first of the 'Injuns' showed themselves. Everything had happened so fast that the security guards didn't yet know about the robbery and thought they were dealing with a nutter riding a motorbike through the precinct. They didn't know it was two nutters and one of them was armed. Ahead of the speeding bike, three uniformed security guards moved out, crouched and with arms spread, to try and bring the bike to a halt. Bimbo saw them first and gave Ronnie a nudge with his elbow. Ronnie, still with his trilby jammed hard on to his head despite the speed they were travelling, gave a loud '*Yeee-haa!*' and fired a shot in the air. The security guards, suddenly realizing that £3.65 an hour wasn't recompense enough for them to take a bullet in the line of duty, went down like the *Titanic* and covered their heads with their hands as the bike sped through them like a mini localized hurricane. Ronnie, by now almost beside himself with the excitement of it all, looked back over his shoulder at the prostrate guards and shouted, 'See ya, pardners! *Yeee-haa!*' On the way out of the precinct they spotted more guards, but by now they had been alerted by radio and they made no move to hinder the bike. Once out of the precinct, Bimbo shot the bike across a main road and up a one-way street, the wrong way. Getting a ticket was the last thing on their minds. Then, half a mile away, they abandoned the bike and got into the clean change-over car.

As they drove sedately out of Croydon, neither Ronnie nor Bimbo could keep the grins off their faces, and at regular intervals they both burst into laughter. The robbery had been a textbook bit of work and now they were going to exchange the watches for lots of lovely cash. First, they went to the flop, a bedsit in Clapham which Ronnie had originally sorted out as a 'love shack' for him and Snake-Eyed Sal, as she lived with her sister and he still lived with his parents. Snake-Eyed Sal was waiting for them and squealed in delight when she saw the pile of precious metal in the form of wristwatches that Ronnie emptied from the pillowcase and on to the bed. After a celebratory drink and the usual after-job babble fuelled by adrenaline and excitement, Ronnie got on the phone to his fence and told him to get the hot-watch man down from Coventry. The man said he would meet them at the fence's gaff the next morning. And that night Ronnie, Bimbo and Snake-Eyed Sal did the town.

The next morning Ronnie and Bimbo made their way on foot to their fence's flat with the watches in a small sports bag. The man from Coventry was there, with a couple of minders in tow, and after the usual pleasantries they got down to business. Ronnie tipped the sparkling haul out on to the carpet, still with the little white cardboard price tags attached to them, and sat back with a smug grin on his face. The hot-watch man produced a jeweller's loupe from his pocket and picked a watch at random. He used a little tool to swiftly take the backplate off and stared in through the loupe. 'Mmmm,' he said. Then he picked another watch and repeated the process. Then another. At last he removed the loupe from his eye and looked at Ronnie. 'Well,' he said, 'what you have here, my friend, are a pile of Sexton Blakes.'

Ronnie, still grinning, but starting to feel an insistent flutter in his stomach, said, 'You what?'

The man smiled sadly. 'Sexton Blakes, fakes,' he said.

Ronnie shook his head, his grin now gone the way of the dinosaurs. 'No, mate. I don't know what you think you're trying to pull, but I nicked those watches from a reputable jeweller. They can't be fakes!'

The hot-watch man held up a placating hand. 'Oh, I believe you. But what you have there are display watches, copies of the real thing that retailers put in their vulnerable shop windows and not worry too much if someone tries a bit of smash and grab. They look good, but . . .', and here he picked up a men's watch with a price tag of £34,000. 'See, this should be platinum case and strap, and on the real watch it would be, but this one is steel, it's worth about £100. The insurance premium for a jeweller who kept the real ones on display would be astronomical. That's why they keep the real ones in the safe and the likes of this in the window. Sorry, but that's how it is.'

Despite the logic of what he was being told, Ronnie couldn't help but think this was either a very poor practical joke or some sort of scam. He picked up a ladies' watch, price tag £4,500, and handed it to Bimbo. 'Right,' he said. 'We'll see, shall we? Bimbo, take that up to the pawn shop on the high street and see how much they'll pledge you for it. In the meantime, we'll all just wait here. Be quick.' So off Bimbo went while everyone waited. Ronnie wasn't going to be taken for a cunt by anyone, and when Bimbo returned he'd show them that.

Within twenty minutes Bimbo was back, and he still had the watch. 'They wouldn't have it, Ron,' he explained sadly. 'They said it was a moody and threatened to call the law on me.'

Now Ronnie had to accept the fact that he had pulled off the perfect robbery only to leave himself wearing the paper hat. And now that he thought of it, hadn't the fella in the shop been trying to tell him something before he had cleared the window displays? Could it have been that the real watches were in the safe about ten feet from where he had been standing? And that the key to that safe was on the same ring as the keys to the window displays of fakes? The joke, at last, truly was on Ronnie.

In resignation, Ronnie did a deal with the hot-watch man from Coventry and sold him the copies for three grand, out of which he deducted expenses for having had to come all the way to London for nothing. After exes, Ronnie and Bimbo shared £1,600 between them. Ronnie also had a further £1,400 from the till in the jewellery shop, which he shared with Bimbo. When he returned to Snake-Eyed Sal later that day with a pocketful of chump change instead of a fortune, she hit the roof and left for her sister's, but not before giving him a proper mugging. A couple of days later Snake-Eyed Sal read in the local paper that there was a substantial reward being offered to anyone who had information on a dangerous robber who had terrorized Croydon shopping centre, robbing a jeweller's and firing at security guards during his get-away. Two minutes after reading this Sal was on the phone to the police. And in the early hours of the next morning both Ronnie and Bimbo were arrested at gunpoint as they slept in their beds. Soon after their trial, in which they were both found guilty and sentenced – Ronnie to fifteen years, and Bimbo to ten – Snake-Eyed Sal's sister received a postcard from her, postmarked Crete. She was never seen around the manor again.

Since 1985, Ronnie has been known as Rolex Ronnie and has been the subject of much ridicule in criminal circles, though usually behind his back. But he doesn't care. While in prison he worked for and gained a degree in sports and fitness. He now coaches a non-league football team and married a nice girl he met soon after he got out of prison. At the time of writing, they are expecting their first child. Bimbo did his bit of bird and got parole. The last I heard he was selling snide perfume out of a suitcase at Catford market. Freaky Fred still spits at the mention of Rolex Ronnie's name, but he seems to get on OK with me. I saw Rolex Ronnie the last time I was out of prison, in 1998. We bumped into each other on the beach in Sheerness, of all places. He was with his wife and I was with my latest squeeze. He told me he no longer plays practical jokes on people, and I believed him. I noticed he was wearing a particularly nice watch. 'Rolex?' I asked, nutting at the watch. Rolex Ronnie shook his head. 'Timex,' he said, grinning. 'And it's genuine.'

6. The Houdini Kid

Greg, the Houdini Kid, has become a bit of a legend in what you might call the underworld, for want of a better expression, not only for his prison escapes, but also for his rate of not-guilties whenever he goes to trial on charges. The thing with Greg is that he loves a good puzzle, something he can get his teeth into, whether it be working out the logistics of getting out of a top-security prison or combing the details of court depositions for any small mistake that will allow him to bust a case. He became an armed robber in the early eighties when a whole generation of young criminals was hitting the pavement, encouraged in some part by the climate of greed and the me-first atmosphere engendered by the Thatcher government. Up in the City young men of Greg's age who had the advantages of education and contacts, as well as ambition and ruthlessness, were pulling strokes on a daily basis and stepping over the bodies of anyone who fell in their way in their quest for fortunes. And down on the streets their 'underclass' counterparts were doing the same, only in a more overtly criminal fashion. Greg was one of these. Having left school with no qualifications and being faced with the choice of going into a factory for the rest of his working life or taking up a gun and grabbing whatever he could, he chose the latter. I'm not here to make excuses for any criminal – we all have choices in life and we make them how we see fit. All of the men in this book could easily have chosen to work for a living, some of them could even have had great success in the legitimate world due to their natural abilities, and Greg was definitely one of these. But he chose to become a robber, and this is his story.

I first met Greg on D wing at HMP Wandsworth in 1989 when he was serving fifteen years for the robbery of a security van. He was already two years into his sentence and had been at Parkhurst when a big storm blew the roof off one of the wings. As a result, the prison authorities had to ship out sixty prisoners while work was being carried out on the roof. How they went about this evacuation was typical of the prison system. Prisoners at Parkhurst had mixed feelings about the jail. On the one hand it wasn't a bad prison if you had a few years to do – there were no sex cases, the screws took a back seat and didn't strong it with anyone, you could cook your own food, brew as much hooch as you liked, and there was a party almost every night. If you wanted to do a chunk of your sentence in relative comfort, then Parkhurst would certainly fit the bill. But on the down side was the fact that it was on an island and all the prisoners were from the mainland, which meant that getting visits was difficult and very time-consuming and expensive for the friends and families of the cons. The visiting hall at Parkhurst was never full, and to men serving long prison sentences visits are the most important thing in their lives. So when the roof blew off, the authorities decided to sweeten the pot in order to get the cons out without any trouble. What they did was ask for volunteers to be shipped back to Wandsworth jail, nicknamed 'the Hate Factory' and loathed by cons for the restrictive regime and the brutality of the screws, which was the only jail that had the space available to accommodate them. The suits knew that there would be few takers, so they told the cons that if they did volunteer there would be two concessions granted to them: they would be allowed extra visits over and above their two a month for the duration of their stay at Wandsworth, and they would all be relocated in a mainland prison within three months of landing at Wandsworth. This was a pukka deal, and so many Parkhurst cons volunteered they could have emptied the whole jail.

The sixty volunteers were loaded on to prison coaches and bussed off the Island and down to Wandsworth. However, as is standard with the British prison system, it turned out the promises that had been made were not going to be honoured. When the evacuees arrived at the Hate Factory they were informed that they would be getting no extra visiting privileges due, they said, to a lack of staff to supervise them, and in fact they would be staying at Wandsworth for up to six months, and as soon as the roof at Parkhurst was repaired, they would be bussed straight back to the Island. This news came as a bit of a blow to the prisoners, but it was a *fait accompli*, they were stuck in Wandsworth and there was now nothing they could do about it.

Greg was one of the cons shipped out from Parkhurst, as was a mate of mine from the old Borstal days in the seventies, Dave the Gangster, so named because he loved gangster films and could quote reams of dialogue from *The Godfather*. Dave introduced me to Greg and another one of the Parkhurst boys called Squid. I hit it off with Greg immediately but Squid was a fucking string vest and there was something about him I didn't like. He was in for what I class as futile, pointlessly violent mug-crimes. In one he had robbed a corner shop with a crossbow. After pocketing the pittance from the till, he had shot the woman behind the counter. The crossbow bolt had lodged in her chest, but luckily it had missed anything vital and she survived. When I questioned Squid on why he had done this, he shrugged, rolled his eyes a bit and grinned like a loony. 'For a laugh,' he replied. Another one of his charges involved breaking into the flat of a man who owed Squid's brother £20 and holding him prisoner for five hours. Squid, along with three of his muggy pals and armed with a sawn-off shotgun, totally humiliated the man, making him crawl around on his hands and knees barking like a dog and then forcing him to eat his own shit before badly beating him and stealing anything of value from his flat. Squid was a thoroughly nasty individual, capable of serious violence and really quite mad, but he latched on to me, Greg and Dave, and wouldn't take the hint to fuck off. Having to live in close proximity to men like Squid is one of the prices you pay for getting yourself into prison.

At this time I was in the first couple of years of a nineteen-year prison sentence and eager to have a go at an escape of some kind. There was no way I was going to sit still and do my bird. I wanted out, and in Greg and Dave I found like minds. As we walked around the exercise yard we discussed various plans for how we might be able to breach the wall of the jail, looking for any weakness in the security, but nothing seemed viable as we were all classed as high-security prisoners and had no access to the more vulnerable parts of the prison. Then one day, after the Parkhurst boys had been in Wandsworth for nearly four months, word came through that the roof at Parkhurst was finished and the evacuees were to be shipped back on the next National Draft, which was always on a Thursday. With this news, Greg and Dave began putting together a plan to break off the prison bus. I was at Wandsworth waiting to be allocated to another top-security prison, and Greg suggested that I see the allocations officer and try to get on the bus to Parkhurst. I tried, but the trouble was that I couldn't strong my application in case I got the screw suspicious and naused the lads' plan. In the event I was told that I had to stay at Wandsworth for some months yet. I was gutted not to get in on the break-out but I wished the boys luck.

On the Wednesday evening at slop-out, which was the time when cons were allowed out of their cells to get fresh water for the night and empty their piss-pots, Dave, who was on the next landing up to me, asked the landing screw if he could slip down and say goodbye to me as he was leaving the next day. The screw, a right horrible flash bastard, wouldn't allow it and when Dave began to argue the case the screw threatened to ring the alarm bell and get Dave a kicking as a going-away present. 'I run this fucking landing,' he sneered. 'I've got the power here, not you, you mug!' Dave was fuming, but there was nothing to do but go back into his cell. The prison system was always going to win on its own turf, but things would be very different out in the world, and this thought was what sustained us all in the Hate Factory.

Before it became privatized the prison transport system was run by screws on a rota basis. It was considered a plum job to be on escorts because not only did the screws get a chance of overtime and expenses on long journeys but they also got time away from opening and closing cell doors all day. The thing about the rota basis was that you never knew who you were going to get. Sometimes it was lazy, laid-back screws who wouldn't search you properly because it was too much like work for them, so consequently there was quite a spate of bus break-outs in which the cons had managed to smuggle a weapon on board. That morning, when the Parkhurst evacuees were getting ready to be returned to the Island, this kind of laxness worked in their favour and they were able to smuggle not one but two blades on to the bus. Dave had a small razor blade, broken from a prison-issue disposable razor, in his mouth, and Squid had a wicked-looking chiv, made from a snapped-off piece of metal mop-bucket handle filed down to a point, which he placed between the cheeks of his arse before the strip search. There were now six prisoners, on a bus containing twelve, who were in the know about the escape plan, and they were all determined to make it work.

The Parkhurst prisoners were classified as security category B, because it was cheaper to transport category B prisoners than category A, though they were all going to a category A prison. Transporting category A prisoners is very expensive and labour-intensive with usually no more than two cat As to one transport and at least six screws and a police escort, but the system could save money and manpower by classifying dangerous prisoners as 'pot A' (Potential Category A) or category B for the purposes of transportation. These lower-category prisoners could be moved in groups of up to twenty at a time with a minimal escort of six screws. The prisoners were double-cuffed to each other, that is, they had both their own wrists handcuffed and then another set of cuffs linked them to each other. They were then loaded on to a green minibus with steel mesh over the windows and reinforced locked doors. The screws would be in the van with the cons and be instructed to watch for any suspicious moves, while the driver and a senior officer would sit up front behind a mesh screen. Even so, there had already been several escapes from these transports. The gods must have been smiling on the Parkhurst boys that day because, due to the extra numbers to be transferred, they were loaded on to the only vehicle available at short notice – a private coach, with no barrier between passengers and driver and plain windows. The lads took it as a sign.

It was Greg who had come up with the escape plan but Dave was to initiate it. As soon as his cuffs were snapped on in Wandsworth reception Dave started complaining that they were too tight. The screws, never receptive to any complaint by a prisoner, told him to shut his mouth and move on. Dave, a look of pain clearly on his face, got into line to get on the coach. He was cuffed to Greg – they had manoeuvred it this way – and Greg threw in a comment of, 'Come on, guv, you can see the geezer's in pain. Why don't you loosen the cuffs a bit?' Greg got the same short shrift from the senior officer in charge of the escort, but the groundwork had been laid. As they got to the front of the boarding queue Dave noticed that the screw counting them on to the coach, who would be part of their escort, was none other than the one he'd had the argument with on the wing the evening before. For Dave, this day was just getting better every minute.

Once seated on the coach, Dave continued to complain loudly about the tightness of the cuffs and was told several times by the screws to shut his whinging cakehole. Squid had managed to get into the seat behind Dave and Greg, and he gave them a wink as he passed them, handcuffed to a fella doing a ten for GBH who was also in the know about what was going down. When the count had been done for the twentieth time and all the paperwork signed, the coach pulled through the big gates of Wandsworth jail and headed for Hampshire and the Isle of Wight. Because of the openness of the commercial coach, the prison had allocated eight screws to the escort instead of the usual six, and they were positioned four at the front of the coach behind the driver and four at the back where they could watch the prisoners. Every prison transport to one of the prisons on the Isle of Wight (there are three: Parkhurst, Albany and Camp Hill), with the exception of category As, has a scheduled stop-off at HMP Kingston, a lifers-only nick in Portsmouth. The stop is to allow screws and cons to use the toilet before driving on to the ferry for the Island. Once on the ferry, all prisoners are kept chained up in their transport in the hold, despite there being a safety rule about people not staying in their vehicles during the crossing of the Solent. The screws, against prison rules, cut cards for two of them to stay with the cons while the rest shoot up to the bar for a couple of pints. One of the worst things about going to the Island, for me, was having to smell beer on the screws as they came back into the coach when I'd have murdered a pint myself. Anyway, the lads on the coach knew that they had to make their move before reaching HMP Kingston.

Dave continued to complain about the tightness of his cuffs, and as the coach was driving into Hampshire, he surreptitiously slipped the small razor blade out of his mouth and into his hand. He took the blade in his fingers and ran it across the flesh of his wrist just below one of his manacles. He didn't cut too deep, just enough to draw blood, and then smeared it all over the cuff and his wrist so that it looked as though he was bleeding to death. Then he let out a piercing cry that had all the screws instantly on alert. 'Help me!' he wailed, in a good imitation of pain and fear. 'The cuffs have cut into my arm. Please, it feels like my arm is on fire!' Two of the screws at the front of the coach, including the senior officer, who was in charge of the handcuff keys, hurried along the aisle to investigate. Dave was bent over in his seat, hissing and crying in agony, and when he sat up a bit the screws were shocked by the amount of blood that seemed to be coming from his wrist. Without stopping to think, the SO pulled out the hand-cuff keys and opened Dave's cuffs. Quicker than a wink, Dave was out of his seat and had his free arm around the SO's neck in a death grip. Dave liked to work out a lot with weights in the prison gym and he was very strong. 'Anyone moves and I'll snap his fucking neck like a twig!' he roared down the bus. The two screws left at the front of the bus and the one who was standing just behind the SO instantly obeyed this order, but the four at the back stood up and one of them drew his baton and began to quickly advance up the aisle. Squid and his partner stood up in the seats behind Dave, and Squid pointed his deadly little chiv at the advancing screw and leered. 'Come on, fuckface!' he taunted. 'I ain't worried about your stick, but I'll put this tool right in your fucking eye! Come on!' The screw, having read Squid's record and knowing what he was capable of, dropped his arm and stood still. Dave ordered the SO to hand his keys to Greg and in a couple of minutes Greg had unlocked himself and every other con on the bus.

The prisoners then herded all the screws to the back of the vehicle.

While all this drama was unfolding behind him, the driver, a civilian who had come with the hire of the coach, just kept his eyes on the road and carried on driving. Greg came up to the front and assured the man that he was not going to be hurt. He told him to keep driving until they came to somewhere where they could safely pull off the road. Down at the other end, Dave, Squid and the rest of the cons were handcuffing the screws together. First, they told them to empty their pockets and then took all of their cash, which amounted to around £30 between the eight of them. The screws got a few jibes for being cheapskates and not carrying enough money, and they were threatened with all sorts of violence, but apart from Squid, who seriously suggested that they pull the coach on to a bit of secluded ground and torture them, the cons were only really interested in getting away. Once the screws were cuffed together, Dave singled out the screw he'd had the argument with in Wandsworth the night before. He stood in front of him, looking down at the now wilted and shaking man. 'Remember me, mate?' he asked. 'Remember what you told me last night? About how you were in charge?'

The screw was shitting himself now, all bluster and arrogance gone. 'I – I'm sorry,' he spluttered, afraid that Dave was now going to kill him, or worse.

Dave slapped him hard in the face, enough to rock his head back and split his lip. 'Well, today, I'm in fucking charge. Right?' The screw nodded feverishly as blood, snot and tears rolled off his chin. Dave nodded once and then came back up to the front of the coach.

After Dave's slap, the screws weren't touched and sat quietly at the back of the coach, all chained together like a row of sad dummies. Three of the prisoners on the coach didn't want to have anything to do with the escape and asked to be left chained up. One was a black fella who only had eighteen months left to serve out of his sixteen-year sentence and didn't think it was worth escaping and the other two were a pair of brothers from north London who were at the start of twelve and fifteen years for lorry hijacking and possession of firearms. The reason the brothers gave for not joining in the escape was because they had an appeal against sentence coming up and thought they had a good chance of sentence reduction. In the event, they both got nothing off their sentences and, unfairly I thought, became known as the Chicken Brothers in the prison system because it was said they had lost their bottle during the escape. The rest of the cons on the coach were raring to go. Seeing a large pub set back from the road, Greg ordered the driver to pull into the car park and stop.

The cons decided that the best course of action would be to split up and make their own way to wherever it was they were going. Dave and Greg were both going to be heading back to London, so they decided to stick together for a while. Squid was also aiming for the Smoke and tried to suggest he tag along with the other two, but they wouldn't have him at any price. He was just too much of a liability. At that moment a gold-coloured Mercedes sports car drove into the car park and a middle-aged man jumped out, leaving the engine running, and trotted into the pub. This was too good an opportunity to miss. Before the rest of the cons on the bus knew what was happening, Greg and Dave had shouted a hurried 'See ya,' and were legging it over to the Mercedes. In the passenger seat of the idling car was a rather hefty woman, whom Dave wasted no time in pulling out and plonking on the ground and, with Greg driving, they were gone like a cool breeze.

Back on the coach, the black fella who was staying begged one of the remaining escapees to nip into the pub and get him a bottle of lager and some crisps to have while he was waiting. And, surprisingly, the escapee did just that before jogging off up the road in the direction of the Hampshire–Surrey border. The escapees left the coach in ones and twos and spread out into the surrounding countryside. Greg and Dave got quite a way in their newly acquired top-of-the-range Mercedes, and did so in comfort, before spotting a police roadblock, and driving into a forest. They didn't get far into the forest before the car, made for German autobahns, got stuck in the boggy ground and they had to abandon it. The alarm had been raised quite quickly, by the coach driver, who no one had thought to handcuff, and soon dozens of police were combing the countryside for the nine desperate lags.

Meanwhile, back at Wandsworth, the whole prison erupted in cheers and whistles when the escape was the lead item on the radio news at midday. I was glad for the escapees and was pacing my cell smiling when the door was flung open and I was greeted by six grim-faced screws. I was marched to the punishment block, along with several others, pending investigation into the escape. The fact that I had asked to get on that particular bus and had been seen having it with some of the escapees was enough to earn me a month in solitary before being exonerated and allowed back to the wing. I didn't mind, it was worth the month just to see the faces on the screws.

Seven of the escapees were captured within forty-eight hours of the break-out, picked up by the police in various parts of Hampshire and Surrey. Squid was caught trying to cross a railway line and rugby-tackled by a uniformed copper before being dragged, kicking and fighting, to a police van. Dave and Greg managed to make it back to London, where they split up and went their separate ways. Dave was arrested two weeks later in a house in Hackney. Grassed up by one of his so-called mates, he surrendered to the armed police squad who had surrounded the gaff. Greg lasted just over a month before he too was captured by armed police as he was plotting up on a security van, the proceeds of which were to be used to get him to Spain.

The first seven recaptured escapees were brought back to Wandsworth where, deep in the bowels of the notorious punishment block, the screws who had been on the escort, along with many of their colleagues, were waiting for them. Each one of the escapees was brought in, stripped naked, and then beaten like a dog as the screws who had felt unmanned and out of control on the bus tried to reinforce their own masculinity and power. The lads took a terrible hiding, particularly Squid, but it didn't seem to bother him too much, because he could take it as well as dish it out. By the time Dave was recaptured and brought to Wandsworth, the escape was old news and the heat had gone out of some of the screws but not the one who Dave had slapped – never him. Dave was beaten and kicked around the cell and then put into a bodybelt and kicked some more. Still later, Greg's beating was kind of half-arsed, as though the screws were just going through the motions by now. The lads were all charged with everything from prison escape, false imprisonment, assault and theft to aggravated vehicle-taking, and they settled down to await their fate. Greg, as was his way, studied all the statements very carefully and as a result was able to get all his charges dropped except the actual prison escape. At his trial for this he convinced the jury that he hadn't meant to escape but that he had just been caught up in circumstances beyond his control. The prosecution pointed out that he could have said no, as three other prisoners had stayed behind. But Greg, a clean-cut, clear-talking pillar of sincerity when he needed to be, must have made an impression on the judge because he was only sentenced to nine months concurrent. Dave pleaded guilty, as did the rest of them, and received twelve months consecutive. The rest of the escapees received from six to nine months consecutive.

Greg was still serving fifteen years, and this escape had given him a taste of freedom which would only drive him on to escape again. Over the next few years he was to pull off two more spectaculars, one in which he tunnelled out of his cell and scaled the wall of HMP Maidstone using a home-made rope and grapple, and another in which he disguised himself as a visitor and walked out of HMP Swaleside on the Isle of Sheppey. This was how he earned his 'Houdini' tag.

Eventually Greg got a legitimate release, having served his sentence, and got out to pick up where he had left off before being interrupted by prison. Outside, he was a very serious and prolific armed robber. He was quite often mentioned in the tabloids because of his long-standing relationship with the daughter of an established soap-opera star, and this spotlight made it difficult but not impossible for Greg to get on with his main business of robbing security vans. When he wasn't being followed by nosy reporters, he was under close surveillance by the Flying Squad, so he had to be a bit slippery in order to make a living. But that suited Greg. He loved to plan and work out the logistics of a job while pulling the wool over everyone's eyes. During the months he was being watched, the police claimed that he managed to slip away and rob fifteen security vans of substantial amounts of cash, not on his own, of course, but with a notoriously professional crew working out of west London. One morning the police pounced on the gang as they slept soundly in their homes and they were all arrested. Greg was charged with thirty counts – fifteen of armed robbery and fifteen of being in possession of firearms with intent – and remanded in custody to await trial. His girlfriend was also arrested and charged with conspiracy, and though the charge was later dropped, the papers had a right party writing it up.

During his twelve months on remand Greg got stuck into the court depositions, all the statements that would be used in evidence, and managed to winkle out a few important discrepancies that would come in useful in his coming trial. He was being prosecuted for a 'series' of robberies, which meant that the prosecution was saying if he did one, then he did them all. If Greg could throw doubt on one, then they would all fall. Greg was mustard in the witness box and he always chose to give evidence on his own behalf, believing that if he made a connection with the jury he would be half-way home. He always faced the jury members, rather than the judge, and spoke directly to them. He did very well during his three days in the box, two of them spent being cross-examined by a very bullish prosecuting QC. Then came a statement by one of the police officers that was so ridiculous and biased against Greg that it surely pushed the jury that extra inch in his favour. While studying the police surveillance logs, the paperwork kept by undercover officers in covert operations, Greg came across an entry that stated, 'Target 1 Greg – leaving flat and carrying missile-shaped object which he secretes in back of Range Rover.' When reading this in his cell in Belmarsh late one night Greg had been puzzled by what it was referring to. He couldn't remember being in possession of any 'missile-shaped object', and in a case that was littered with references to firearms, this language seemed designed to be emotive to a jury. Greg racked his memory and finally remembered the day it was referring to. He instructed his own QC to call the copper who had made the entry to the stand.

Greg's QC skilfully led the copper down a line that got him to reiterate to the jury just how professional and dangerous this robbery team was, how they had access to all sorts of weaponry and how, in his opinion, they would stop at nothing in order to claim the prize. Then, when the copper was in full flow, he asked him about the entry describing a 'missile-shaped object' and the copper jumped on it. 'That just goes to illustrate the lengths these men will go to,' the copper said, well pleased with himself. The jury were rightly shocked – the statement conjured up a picture of desperate men with rocket launchers, almost terrorists.

Then the QC burst their bubble and brought them back to earth. 'Officer Plod,' he said, 'I have here a statement taken from Greg——'s mother, and it concerns the day in question, when you say you saw Greg leaving an address with this 'missile-shaped object' you have made so much of. I'd like you to read it.' The QC then got the nod from the judge to pass copies of the statement to the copper and the jury. There was silence in court as everyone read the written statement. Then Greg's QC turned back to the copper, who was by now red-faced in the box. 'Officer Plod, perhaps you will have noted from this sworn statement that my client's mother says that on that exact day and at that exact hour when you witnessed him carrying and secreting this 'missile-shaped object' in his car, he was, in fact, collecting an ironing board from his aunt's home for his mother!' With further prodding the copper had to admit that it was an ironing board he saw, and that was the end of the case against Greg. The jury found him not guilty on all thirty counts and he walked out of court a free man once again.

But men like Greg don't just give up and walk away when they've had a result. Getting off only fuels their desire to spit in the face of the system again and again. Less than a year after walking out of the Old Bailey, Greg was under arrest once more, for armed robbery and possession of two firearms. This time the system was taking no chances. The authorities found a car parked on the route his prison transport took to and from the magistrates court for remand every week, and in this car they found ski-masks, a gun and a jacket with Greg's DNA on it. They claimed this as proof that Greg's confederates were planning to break him off the van, so they upgraded his status to double category A. As an AA man, Greg was immediately transferred to the Special Security Unit in the centre of HMP Belmarsh, where he was under constant surveillance and armed police escort, including a helicopter, whenever he went to court. If any jury in this case started to doubt Greg's guilt, then they would only have to look at the armed police positioned about the court to remind them that this man must be dangerous, therefore guilty. But even with all this against him, Greg was still not beaten.

At his subsequent trial at Woolwich Crown Court, Greg put up a plausible alibi for the time he was supposed to be holding up a security van: he claimed he was miles away committing a burglary. By coincidence, one of Greg's pals had been committing a burglary at that time and Greg now claimed it as his own. After much deliberation the jury found Greg not guilty of armed robbery – but his celebrations had to be put on hold when the police immediately arrested him for the burglary he had put up as an alibi. He had no choice but to plead guilty and was sentenced to seven years in prison. The last time I saw Greg, in HMP Whitemoor in 2003, he was looking forward to getting out. Whether he will remain out for long remains to be seen, but one thing's for sure – he'll never stick his hand up to anything.

7. Crazy Dave

I've known Crazy Dave since we were both teenagers, and for some years he was my main crime partner. He was a good thief, always up for anything that came along, but when he got into the armed-robbery game, he found himself a bit out of his depth. The trouble was that once he got on to the roller-coaster of very serious crime he was on until the end of the ride, and, where I enjoyed every twist and turn on the track, it only made him more sick and frightened, but his pride wouldn't allow him to admit it. When we were first starting out on our career of skulduggery, Dave loved the money and the buzz of it all as much as I did, but maybe he matured quicker than me, because by the time we had upped our game and hit the heavy he was already a spent force. With that marvellous twenty-twenty vision of hindsight, I can clearly see that Dave was never cut out for what we were doing, and he was to pay a very heavy price for getting involved. But, when it all began, he was as eager and game as a fighting dog, ready to rock 'n' roll at the drop of a hat or strap on a gun and go for the prize. The world really was our lobster – unfortunately, seafood doesn't always agree with everybody.

By 1986 I had already served a prison sentence for armed robbery but had yet to learn any lessons from it – except, maybe, not to get caught next time. I was a full-time thief, trying my hand at everything from fraud and deception to commercial burglary as well as the occasional walk-in robbery. If it would bring in a few quid and didn't involve too much hard graft, then I was up for it. And my partner in most of these illegal activities was Crazy Dave, a pocket-rocket from

Battersea. Dave looked a bit like the actor Sean Penn but with a bigger nose and blonder hair. He lived in a large bedsit in Streatham and this was often the meeting place where a little crowd of us planned our thieving and brought back the proceeds to be counted. You could knock on Dave's window any time, day or night, and be guaranteed a cup of coffee and a bit of decent music on his stereo. A few of us married lads would also bring our girlfriends and any old slappers we had pulled on a night out and Dave would let us use the gaff as a knocking-shop. The only thing he drew the line at was smoking tobacco in his place, as he was a non-smoker, but only of tobacco. Dave was a serious puff-head and would start every morning with a big spliff and continue the day with the same at regular intervals. Despite his almost constant state of intoxication, Dave was also a fitness freak, preferring to cycle and run everywhere if he could. Smoking copious amounts of cannabis didn't seem to affect this.

One day, me, Dave and a fella named Mark were drinking coffee and lamenting our lack of funds. A few nights before, at the request of a bloke who owned a small building firm, we had burgled a site in the city and stolen a couple of laser levels that were supposed to be worth two grand apiece. It was a custom job – that is, the buyer told us where they were, how much he was prepared to pay and when the security guard would be nipping out for his break. None of us had a clue what these laser levels were really about – apparently they are used in high-rise concrete construction to check surfaces and angles and shit – but the would-be buyer described them sufficiently for us to be able to recognize them, so off we went and did the bit of work. We got the goods no problem and drove them back to Dave's gaff. But then the buyer, who had promised us £1,500 for the pair, started to get cold feet and stopped answering his phone. Perhaps he didn't think we could pull it off, or maybe he was suffering a cash-flow problem –

who knows? But it meant that we were stuck with these fucking things and didn't have 50 pence between us for our labours. Our problems were compounded when Dave noticed the hazard sign on the side of the machines that read, 'DANGER! RADIATION!' Then we started worrying that we might be contaminated with radiation sickness and convincing each other that we'd soon be glowing in the dark and sprouting extra limbs. I suppose a cannabis-induced paranoia started to grip Dave, and he wanted the machines out of his flat immediately. We had to load them back on the van and stash them in a lock-up some miles away. By the time we'd done this it was late in the afternoon and we still had no money, so on the spur of the moment I decided I would do a robbery.

I had an old Navy Colt revolver at Dave's place. I had bought it from a car dealer knowing that it was bound to come in useful at some stage. It had an eight-inch barrel, which made it pretty unwieldy, and I had intended to saw a couple of inches off it for concealment but hadn't yet got around to doing it. I dug the gun out and informed the lads that it was time for action, I was going down to the high street to rob something and they were welcome to join me if they wanted to. They were both up for it, like little kids who had suddenly been offered sweets out of the blue, though neither Dave nor Mark had ever been involved in armed robbery before. From memory, I picked a small building society on Leigham Court Road, facing the *South London Press* building, and threw together a rudimentary plan. We would drive down there in Mark's Mk2 Capri, then Mark would wait in the next street with the car while me and Dave went around to the target. I would go in and do the business and Dave would hang back outside and make sure no one tried to block my escape. The building society was really a one-man job but I wanted them to feel they were doing something for their share.

I disguised myself with the odds and ends that people had

left at Dave's flat – a big suede jacket, a fedora hat, Elton John-type massive glasses – and tucked the Colt into my waistband. Then it was all into the Capri and down to the high street. The plan was for me to do the stick-up and then jog around to an alley behind the parade of shops where I would pass the gun and money to Mark, dump the disguise in a dustbin, and then slip back on to the high street and casually make my way on foot back to Dave's place. After watching my back out of the job Dave would also make his way back on foot. When it came to the actual robbery, everything went as smoothly as planned. I walked into the gaff, waved the gun about, growled a bit, and then walked out with a bundle of cash. It was all over in ninety seconds. I gave Dave a wink as I made my escape and slipped into the alley. But Mark was nowhere to be seen. So I stripped off my disguise and binned it, then, with the gun and money still about my person, I walked back on to the high street. I wanted to get out of the area toot suite and the quickest way was by bus. Streatham High Road is a major bus route into the city and normally you couldn't move for the big red bastards but, typically, when I needed one, there was none to be seen. I plotted up at the nearest bus stop and tried to look casual. As I stood waiting I could hear the sound of many sirens in the distance, coming from the direction of Brixton. I forced myself to look casually interested as about sixteen police vehicles of every description, lights flashing and sirens wailing, flew past me in quick succession as they answered the alarm for armed robbery. I knew their routine. Once they had got a description, they would start combing the immediate area and stop and search anyone who looked even remotely iffy. I was acutely conscious of the big heavy pistol and money bag under my clothes and when a bus finally arrived I almost fell over myself scrambling to get on it.

I stayed on the bus into Brixton then slipped into a Wimpy Bar for a cup of coffee and to get myself straight before heading back to Dave's place. When I got there, the boys were delighted to see me, fearing I had been nicked in the police sweep. Mark explained that a minute after I had left the car to go and do the work the engine had conked out. Realizing he had run out of petrol, he had nipped a couple of streets over and siphoned some from a parked car in the hope that he would be able to get back in time to pick up the kit. He had still been sitting there in the Capri when the first patrol car cruised slowly by, screwing him out, so he had headed back to the flat. Dave in no way fitted the description of the robber and had made it back unmolested. I emptied the money out on to the floor and we began to count. It only came to just under £900, but it was £900 we hadn't had earlier in the day. We all had equal shares and went away happy, with plans to hit the town that evening.

For the next few days Dave and Mark seemed very taken with the idea of doing another robbery, but I tried to explain to them that it wasn't worth the candle to be doing them on a regular basis unless they wanted to take it seriously. They were enamoured and seduced by the lure of what they saw as easy cash, and I told them that they had thought it was easy because I had done the hard part. I wasn't sure that either of them had the bottle for armed raids and told them so. The next day, I turned up at Dave's gaff to find them plotting a robbery, on the same building society that I had already robbed. Like an indulgent parent, I laughed at them but sat back and told them to crack on if they wanted to get nicked. They were determined, so I allowed Dave to borrow my gun and off they went while I sat in Dave's gaff and waited. Dave, dressed in a big zip-up jacket about three sizes too big for him, a flat cap and sunglasses, walked into the building society as Mark waited around the corner in his Capri. At first Dave had trouble getting the huge pistol out of his waistband, and then he couldn't stop his hands from shaking, so the gun was wobbling all over the place as he made his demand in a squeaky voice that finished in a terrified yodel. The counter staff were not impressed and actually shouted at Dave to stop being 'silly' as they phoned the police right in front of him. He was forced to flee empty-handed. When the boys got back to the flat they were crestfallen. I sat them both down and told them that if they really were serious I would teach them to rob properly, and that made them happy again.

Over the next couple of weeks I felt like Mister Miyagi imparting the wisdom of my trade to two novice Karate Kids. I instructed them on the attitude that was needed to convince bank cashiers that you'd just as soon blow their heads off as get the money, how to pick a target and plan your get-away. I taught them a bit of gun-craft, how to point the gun but always make sure the safety-catch was on. And most importantly of all, how to keep your cool and walk away when you got a refusal, as sometimes happened, without resorting to violence born of frustration. When I thought they were ready I picked out a small bank in Balham and got to work. Mark was too nervous and jumpy to be trusted with a firearm so he was designated the wheelman, our get-away driver. We lease-loaned a little .32 Webley revolver from an armourer, and this would be Dave's gun. The small .32 looked just right in his hand, but I only allowed him one bullet in the chamber just in case he got panicky. I figured that, with my experience, I would be able to handle anything that came up and told Dave that if he ever had to fire the Webley he should aim at the sky or the ceiling and make it a warning shot. Nobody would know that he didn't have another four bullets in the gun. Though we were deliberately setting out on a reckless and dangerous course of action, we were not complete lunatics. Actually shooting someone was the last thing any of us wanted to do, so we took whatever small precautions to prevent this that we could. Robbing banks is all about threat in order to get the money and those who really want to shoot people can do so without a banking hall wrapped around them. I'm not making excuses, and there have been people shot by armed robbers, but that was not what we were about. As my old mate Little Andy used to say, 'There are thousands of banks in this country. If I get refused at one I just move on to the next. No drama.'

Over the next six months we gelled perfectly as a robbery team and hit many targets, usually around south London. We were earning a pretty good living, but then the cracks in the team started to appear. Dave and Mark had a falling-out over something and nothing, and their relationship with each other became barely civil. Then one day Mark didn't turn up for a meet, and when I went round to his place he confessed that he didn't want to carry on, his nerves were shot to pieces, he'd never done a day's prison and he was now terrified of being caught and getting banged up for years. I understood this and told him that he was doing the right thing by pulling out. When Dave heard, he dismissed Mark with 'Cunt's lost his bottle.' But I was soon to suspect that Dave was also losing his bottle, and had been hiding the fact for some time. With Mark out of the picture, me and Dave decided to share the driving duties, which made things just a little bit difficult but not overly so. It was nice to have someone waiting at the wheel with the engine running as we came out of a bank but now we would just have to spare the extra minute to do it ourselves.

We planned to hit a security-van delivery in Deptford and had been to look at it a couple of times in preparation. It was a bit of a step up from walk-ins but we only planned to take whatever was going across the pavement when we struck, probably a pony-bag, or two if we got lucky. It was a simple routine: I would pull my gun on the guard and Dave would work crowd control with the Webley, just looking dangerous, waving the gun about threateningly and shouting a few obscenities. Then it would be back to the motor, parked a street away, and into bandit country before the posse arrived.

On the day, we got to Deptford about an hour before the van was due and took a walk around to check for anything suspicious. The last thing we wanted was to walk into someone else's police ready-eye – crossing targets is what Old Bill called it – because Deptford is chock-a-block with armed robbers on some days. We left the guns and robbery paraphernalia in the get-away motor and strolled around the area, eyes peeled for anything sussy. I saw nothing, but Dave reckoned he spotted someone on the roof of a building near where the van would be stopping. When I looked in that direction there was no one there, but Dave swore that the bloke had ducked behind the roof parapet. I asked him if he was sure and he said he was. 'Fuck it,' I said, ever the optimist. 'He's probably fixing the roof. We'll be OK.' But Dave wasn't having it and suggested we were walking into an ambush and we'd better leave it for the day. I was considering his suggestion when he iced the cake and told me that a fella near the bus stop was watching us. 'If he ain't Old Bill I don't know who is!' he said. I nonchalantly checked the bloke out and I had to admit that he did look a bit ploddish. 'OK,' I said, very disappointed but prepared to err on the side of caution. 'We'll leave it for today.' Dave gave a sigh of relief and we headed back to the car.

On the way back to Streatham I asked Dave if he was sure he had seen something, and he started to get very defensive. I told him I was only asking, and he started to argue as though he thought his manhood was being challenged. In order to prove he was no pussy, he said we should go immediately and do one of the other jobs that we had in the pipeline. 'I'll show you who's lost their bottle!' he said angrily, and that was when I realized that he was fucking terrified. I tried reasoning with him, but the more I suggested we just call it a day the more he insisted we do another job. We had another bank in Balham lined up so I drove down there. The idea was to hit the bank just after the security guards had dropped off the cash as the get-away motor had to be parked quite a distance away, and if we hit the prize inside the bank we could get everyone to lie on the floor to give us a head start. If we hit the guard outside, we could hardly order the whole high street to hit the deck and there was the chance, however slim, that we might have to fight our way to the car. On the Deptford job the car would have been right on the plot. We had already cased the Balham job thoroughly, only putting it off because the Deptford job was more lucrative.

We got to Balham with about thirty minutes to spare before the van was scheduled to appear and had a quick look about. This time there was nothing even slightly suspicious, so we sorted the robbery kit out and tooled up. The best place to wait for the van was outside the Underground station, where we wouldn't look out of place. We plotted up under the London Transport awning around the entrance to the station, where we had a good view of the bank. As we stood there in silence, each deep in his own thoughts, it began to rain. I always loved to rob in the rain because it keeps people's heads down and they hurry along, not much interested in what anyone else might be doing. I took it as a good omen.

The van turned up right on time and the guard made several trips into the bank as we watched. As he climbed back into his van, I unzipped my jacket and got my hand on my gun. 'Okay,' I said, out of the side of my mouth. 'As soon as he pulls away, we move. You ready?' There was no reply from Dave, so I turned my head to see what the problem was. I was shocked. Dave was standing there, rigid with fear, all the colour having drained from his face. For a moment I thought he was having a seizure of some kind. 'Dave?' I said. 'Dave, are you all right?'

He swallowed hard and managed to croak, 'I'm not doing it. We'll get nicked.'

I couldn't believe it – he was completely gone and looked unable to move. I heard the sound of the van pulling away and quickly made up my mind. I was here and ready to go, I didn't need Dave, I would leave him here and go and do the job myself. I nodded once at him and then walked quickly up the street towards the bank. I was half fuming at what had happened but determined to have the prize as it was there for the taking.

I was just reaching for the handle of the bank door when I was pushed to one side. Fearing that I was being ambushed by the police, I pulled my revolver half out of my coat and got ready to face whatever was coming. But it was Dave. He had walked quickly up the street behind me, probably driven by a superhuman effort and not wanting to face the shame of bottling out at the last minute. Now he pushed open the door and nipped inside in front of me. I quickly followed. Once inside the bank, Dave completely changed from the bone-white, frightened wreck he had been only minutes before. It was as though he had received an injection of something that turned him into a fucking raving lunatic without an ounce of fear in his body. 'Right!' he shouted, as he stood in the middle of the banking hall. 'This is a raid. If anyone does not co-operate I will shoot them immediately. Play your cards right and you'll all be going home tonight. Fuck me about and I'll turn this place into a slaughterhouse. Understand?' His voice was strong, confident and full of menace, and everyone got the message loud and clear. 'Customers on the floor,' he shouted. 'Bank staff get ready to hand over.' And everyone immediately complied. Usually it was me who handled the verbals and Dave just collected the cash, but I now went up to the counter and swept the money out of the till-wells and into the bag which Dave handed me. When I had it all I hurried towards the door but Dave hadn't moved from his spot centre-bank.

'Come on!' I called from the door, and Dave turned slowly and looked into my eyes. There was not a trace of fear or urgency there, more a calm arrogance.

He turned back to the staff and customers. 'You've done well. We're leaving now, but I ask one more favour. Stay on the floor until we've gone, because if anyone thinks of following us on to the street, I will surely shoot that person dead. OK?' I was almost shitting myself with the need to get away; all this speech-making was playing havoc with my nerves. We were usually in and out in ninety seconds but we'd already been here for over three minutes.

'Come on!' I said again, only louder and more insistently. Dave turned slowly again and strolled over to where I was standing by the door. He was smiling, and there was something a bit scary in it. I pulled the door open and slipped out without looking to see if he was following me.

It was a long jog back to the car and Dave, being fitter than a butcher's dog, left me in his dust. By the time I reached the car he had the engine started and was ready to go. I flopped breathlessly into the passenger seat and he pulled out into the traffic. 'What the fuck was all that about?' I asked when I was finally able.

Dave shrugged and kept his eyes on the road as we put the miles between us and the scene of the crime. 'What?' he asked.

I looked at him. 'What do you mean "What?"' I asked. 'All that "Oooh, I'm not doing it, we'll be nicked" – and then the fucking John Wayne turn-out inside the jug, that's fucking what.'

Dave shrugged again, casually. 'I was just having a laugh,' he said. 'Don't make a big thing of it.' And that was that: he refused to discuss it again.

Thinking about it later, I guess that moment outside the

station had been the start of the complete mental breakdown Dave was later to suffer. We did a few more jobs together but his behaviour became more and more erratic. Then, about nine months after we had started committing robberies together, our pictures appeared in the papers with the headline DO YOU KNOW THESE MEN? and the strapline 'Substantial Reward Offered for Information Leading to Their Arrest and Conviction'. The text was full of clichés about the 'dangerous duo' who had raided banks and building societies all over south London, threatening customers and bank staff with firearms and stealing 'quantities' of money. I was asleep in bed when a mate of mine knocked on the door and pointed it out to me. I immediately phoned Dave, but he'd already seen it. I packed a quick bag and went into hiding about ten minutes before twenty armed coppers kicked my front door in. Dave was equally quick and lucky and also took it on the lam ahead of the gendarmes with arms. During the next couple of weeks, as Dave and I laid low in a 'safe house' in Surrey, the south London papers had a feeding frenzy over us. The police released more security stills from some of the robberies we had committed and some wag at the *South London Press* nicknamed Dave 'the Hooter with the Shooter' because of his prominent proboscis. I got off quite easy as 'the Other One', which suited me fine. But Dave was raging over his new nickname, so much so that he suggested we rob the payroll at the *South London Press* building. But I vetoed that idea pretty sharpish. The last thing we needed was even more coverage.

In due course, and in circumstances I describe in great detail in my autobiography *A Few Kind Words and a Loaded Gun*, both me and Dave were arrested and remanded to HMP Wormwood Scrubs. And this is where Dave's madness really began to surface in a big way. One morning, soon after we were nicked, I came out on exercise and started to talk to him about our forthcoming trial. After I had spoken for a few minutes he suddenly put his finger up to his lips in a shushing gesture. I shut up and waited, then Dave said, in all seriousness, 'I know you ain't going to like this, mate, but do you mind if I check to see if you're wired up?'

I stared at him in disbelief for a moment, and then I had to laugh. 'Are you fucking serious, Dave?' I asked.

He nodded solemnly. 'I think you might be working for the Flying Squad, gathering evidence on me and hoping I'll admit something.'

I knew that by rights I should have been seriously insulted and aggrieved at such a suggestion, but I was more sad about having to witness such a close friend crumbling before my very eyes. So I humoured him and opened my coat and let him frisk me for recording devices. For the rest of the exercise period he talked normally, as though he had not even suspected I was working with the police.

After that incident on the yard, I was worried for Dave but didn't know who to approach to try and get him help. Prison medics are no more than screws who have taken a first-aid course, and the screws themselves would not be interested in the welfare of one more fruitcake in a system where over two-thirds of the inmates have a recognizable mental illness. I mentioned my worries to my brief when he came to visit, but he told me there was little he could do about it. Then I heard that when Dave had been visited by his girlfriend he also accused her of being wired up and working with the police. I guessed that he might be slowly slipping into complete madness, but he had good weeks when he seemed like his old self, and I wondered if the stress of everything that had happened was just causing temporary attacks of confusion.

After twelve months on remand, during which Dave didn't seem to get any worse, I got used to his brief mental episodes and learnt to ignore them. I think that what kept Dave together throughout those months on remand was a bit of false hope.

We had separate legal teams because Dave had admitted to ten armed robberies and related charges almost from the moment he was arrested. Though he didn't say anything in his statements about me or any part I might have played in the jobs, he did detail his own involvement and stuck his hand up. When I found this out by reading the evidence depositions six months after we had been remanded, I wondered again at the depth of Dave's madness – if he had admitted everything, why would he possibly imagine that those close to him were wired up and trying to catch him out? It didn't make any sense. I, on the other hand, had admitted nothing. I kept schtum throughout my police interviews and the only slightly damaging thing was the police 'verbals'. Verballing is an ancient police trick which, I know, is still being used today, though probably not as much as it was in the past, as modern juries are more sophisticated than in days gone by. It involves the police attributing verbal comments and admissions to the suspect, usually at the moment of his arrest, and then reading them out in court as gospel. In my case, I was supposed to have said, just after being ambushed and being chased all over south London in a high-speed car chase, 'I knew it had to come. You can't do as many armed blags as I have done and expect to reign for ever.' It was a little bit more subtle than the classic 'It's a fair cop, guv!', but still pretty unbelievable, given the circumstances. Nowadays, juries and even Crown Court judges are well aware that the police are more than capable of lying under oath and fitting people up but, as late as the eighties, sometimes verbals were enough to get you locked up for many years.

So I had admitted nothing and as a result I was in a position to plead not guilty to everything, but Dave had fucked himself. Now, I don't know where Dave found the solicitor he was using but the geezer was about as much use as an ashtray on a motorbike. Every time he visited the Scrubs he filled Dave's head with a lot of nonsense about how, with his lack of previous convictions and his early-hour admissions of guilt, he could say in mitigation that he had been under my influence, and that because I had the previous convictions for armed robbery and violence this would seem credible, and he would probably be sentenced to no more than eight years – five years if he was really lucky. I didn't mind Dave using my record as mitigation – after all, I was pleading not guilty and would not be sentenced with Dave unless I was found guilty – but I had to tell him that if his brief was saying he would only get between five and eight years after admitting ten armed robberies, then he was talking through his fat arse. But Dave wouldn't buy that at any price, so he certainly wasn't going to have it for free. He became convinced not only that his brief was the voice of reason but, worst of all, that he would definitely be getting the lower tarif of five years. He even worked out how much remission he would get on the five-stretch for good behaviour and told anyone who would listen that he would be out in less than three years. He could handle three years in prison. It would be hard, he knew that, because Dave was one of those people for whom every second in jail is like a week. Every day was a living nightmare for him, and I felt for him, but had to try and disabuse him of the notion that he was going to get a result, or it would hit him even harder when it came. But Dave wouldn't listen.

Because I had kept my mouth shut I was now in a position to have a trade with the prosecution. They only had good evidence on me for two armed robberies, one attempted robbery and possession of the firearms – a revolver and a shotgun – that I was captured with, so, through my brief, a very clever and experienced legal horse-trader, I accepted a deal whereby I would plead guilty to four charges in return for the rest being dropped. The advantage of this deal for the prosecution was that they didn't have to go through a long and expensive trial and they were guaranteed a conviction and custodial sentence. The advantages for me were that I would be entitled to one-third knocked off my potential sentence and would have stuffed them for the other sixteen charges. My brief also got the pros to agree he would press for only twelve years. I could do a twelve not standing on my head by any means – no bit of bird is a walk in the park – but it was manageable. So, though I wasn't what you would call happy, I wasn't too gutted. Dave was still in fairy land with his five-year kick and I agreed to let him still put it on my toes for his mitigation, so he was more than satisfied.

At the last minute, our sentencing was transferred from the Old Bailey to Knightsbridge Crown Court, and we trooped into the dock there one bright September morning to hear our fates made reality by some old duffer in a dusty wig. The charges were read out and we replied with our pre-planned 'Guilty's, then the judge listened to legal arguments and miti-gation. I didn't really have any mitigation, but my brief made that sound like a plus: 'He'll take it like a man, your honour.' The judge ordered us to stand up and said he would deal with Dave first. Dave was excited and eager to get this out of the way and get on with his five. The judge began. 'On count one, you will go to prison for nine years. On counts two and three, you will go to prison for ten years . . .' I winced as I saw Dave slump next to me. He had only reached the third charge and already received double the sentence he was expecting. And it got worse. By the time the judge had reached the last count and made them all concurrent, Dave's total sentence was thirteen years' imprisonment. I had tried to warn him. Dave all but collapsed and had to be helped out of the dock by three screws. Now it was my turn. The judge absolutely coated me for about ten minutes – I was everything from a danger to the public to a habitual and remorseless bandit. He then said that, despite my guilty plea and the prosecutor's suggestion of twelve years, he was sending me to prison for fifteen. It was a bit more than I had been expecting but I took it in good part and told the judge that he was a cunt and that I hoped he got syphilis.

As I was escorted out of the courtroom I was greeted by the sight of Dave being attended by the three screws. One was waving a newspaper over his fevered brow, one was holding a plastic cup of water to his lips and the third was making him a roll-up for his nerves – and he didn't even smoke! When I saw this, I couldn't resist a little joke. 'What did you get?' Dave asked in a wan voice. I rubbed my hands together and beamed. 'A five!' I said, and he nearly fainted again.

Dave never really recovered after the sentencing. He was shipped off to Parkhurst, where one morning he came out of his cell wrapped in nothing but a prison-issue bedsheet, holding a Bible in one hand and a table leg in the other, and proceeded to smash up the wing while screaming out his intention to 'punish the sinners'. At the prison hospital he was sectioned under the Mental Health Act and sent to a secure hospital in Surrey. After a year Dave was judged fit enough to return to prison and, eventually, after serving seven years, he was granted parole. Today Dave lives quietly with his long-standing, long-suffering girlfriend and his children. The life we chose very nearly destroyed him for good and he is glad he has left it all behind. Mark, our nervous get-away driver, never did a day's bird. He was found dead of a heroin overdose in 2003. As for me, I did my time in my own way. But that's another story.

8. Suicide Stan, King of Blades

I first met Stan at HMP Latchmere House back in 1977 when we were both on remand, me for armed robbery and GBH, and Stan for stealing cars. Even back then I knew that if I was going to make criminality my life, then I would probably be seeing a lot of Stan. He was never going to be anything other than a criminal. It was written all over his face and leaking out of his every word and gesture. He was the first kid I knew who was enamoured of the Krays. He had read their life story, *A Profession of Violence*, and Ronnie and Reggie were his heroes. Just this fact alone was a pretty big pointer to where this fifteen-year-old boy wanted his life to go. Stan was from Harrow, which didn't have much of a criminal pedigree in those days, or even today, but he always hinted that he really came from the slums of the East End rather than the sedate and leafy lanes of west London. At this stage in his budding criminal career, Stan was eligible for a Borstal sentence – six months to two years of army-style discipline – and didn't really fancy it. So he came up with a plan so extreme that, when he told me about it, I actually winced in empathy. He was to appear for sentencing at Kingston Crown Court. In those days, you had to be judged 'fit for Borstal' before this sentence could be passed. This usually involved checking that you had both arms and legs and you weren't foaming at the mouth and shouting that the devil told you to do it. The reason for checking on fitness was that Borstal was no tea party and you had to be pretty robust to survive it. Anyway, Stan's plan, which none of the rest of us juveniles who were in the know thought had any chance of working, involved him proving in court that he was not 'fit' at all.

On the day of his sentencing Stan smuggled a razor blade into the court under his tongue. Then, as the judge was just about to pronounce sentence, Stan took the blade from his mouth and, holding his arms up where everyone could get a good view, he slashed his wrist. Stan wasn't fucking about, he knew that any half-hearted moody little scratch was not going to impress anyone, so he dug deep and opened an artery. The blood shot out of him, splashing the court reporter and half the prosecution team, and caused a lot of screaming and panic in the courtroom. The judge almost fell over himself in his rush to vacate the bench, and the escort screws who were in the dock with Stan, getting their priorities right as usual, drew their batons and beat him to make him drop the razor blade, which he had dropped as soon as he had opened himself up anyway. Stan was dragged from the court by several shouting and panicky screws, leaving a trail of bright red blood in his wake. He was rushed to hospital and had to have six stitches in his wound. When the court reconvened the next day there wasn't one person who could, hand on heart, stand up and say that they thought Stan was fit for Borstal. After much discussion, the judge told Stan that he would have been going to Borstal but, due to his obviously unstable emotional state, he was to have two years' probation instead. Stan walked from the court to freedom and went straight back to crime.

Nobody was really surprised when Stan turned up back at Latchmere House less than two weeks later with even more charges against him. But he wasn't worried, as he reasoned that the old wrist-cutting coup had worked before and there was no reason why it shouldn't work again. For Stan, every razor blade in the nick was a get-out-of-jail-free card. Eventually he went up for sentencing again, and this time the screws at Latchmere gave him a proper good search before he left, but they found nothing, as Stan had the blade wrapped in a wad of toilet paper tucked between the cheeks of his arse. He was searched again before being put into his cell under the courthouse, but again they found nothing, so the screws relaxed. Once in his cell, Stan extracted the blade from its hiding place and then popped it into his mouth. He was given a last rub-down search before climbing into the dock, but again nothing was found. Stan listened carefully to the reports and arguments from defence and prosecution and could see that there was no legal result imminent so, as soon as the judge started his sentencing remarks, Stan whipped out his blade and did his other wrist. The result was almost exactly the same as the first time, and he was dragged from the court in a trail of his own arterial juice. This time his wound required nine stitches, and the next afternoon he found himself back in the dock again. As he stood there, both arms heavily bandaged, he could barely suppress a smile, knowing that he would be back on the street within the hour. But this judge was made of sterner stuff than the first. He told Stan that it was obvious he had a few emotional problems but they were nothing that a good dose of Borstal discipline wouldn't iron out in time. He then sentenced him and recommended he be held in a closed Borstal where he could be properly supervised. Stan was gutted. When I saw him seven months later he commented, 'I went in too soft, see, I should have done me neck, that would have got me another whack of probation for sure.'

Eventually, I got weighed off with three years' detention for my own criminal indiscretions and, after a sojourn in a special unit for violent juveniles, I too was dropped into the Borstal system to do my bit of bird. My first stop was Dover, or Her Majesty's Borstal Institution Western Heights, to give it the full title. One of the first familiar faces I met was Stan, and he had a plan. Not happy with being deprived of his liberty in such unfair circumstances, Stan wanted out. His idea, as you might already have surmised, involved cutting himself to bits. We were being held in a six-man dormitory and at night the door was locked, but there was a toughened glass panel through which the night watchman could check on us every hour on the hour. Stan's plan was to cut his wrist and spray blood on the glass panel so that the night watchman would panic and open the door. Then the rest of us would jump him, take his keys and tie him up before making our way to the works shed and breaking out a ladder that we could use to cross the deep, empty moat that surrounded the Borstal.

It sounded simple enough, and the simple plans are usually the best, so I agreed. We had to find something sharp for Stan's wrist, and we settled on a light bulb from the ceiling fixtures. Stan broke the bulb so that there was a length of jagged edge and the metal cup to hold on to. We knew the night watchman was on his way because we could hear his keys rattling on the landing below. Next, Stan got me to tie a prison-issue sock very tightly around his bicep – he had really thought this through. But when it came to the actual cutting, I think Stan lost his bottle because he asked me to do it. I didn't really want to, but I had a bit of a reputation as a cold bastard, which helped me to survive the gladiator school of juvenile prison, so I couldn't back down. I took the light bulb in a good grip and got ready. 'Deep now, don't fuck about and have to do it twice,' Stan told me. I took a breath and ran the jagged glass over Stan's wrist just below the bright pink scar tissue of his previous cutting. I felt the glass ripping through his flesh and watched as it parted, leaving a gaping wound. There was very little blood, but Stan was just about to remedy that. As the screw reached the door Stan loosened the sock around the top of his arm and blood fountained from his wrist, splashing over the glass panel. Through the blood-drenched window, I saw the screw's mouth form a shocked 'O'. 'Get ready,' Stan cried, holding his wrist and spraying his blood on the door. But the screw, instead of opening up, shouted, 'Hang on, I'll get some help!' And off he went down the stairs to raise the alarm.

The escape was a failure. Within a short time the screw was back with a medic and several reinforcements. By then we had managed to get the sock back on Stan's arm and slow the bleeding. We had to be philosophical about it, we had no choice. Stan was removed to the prison hospital, where he was kept for some weeks on suicide watch, and the rest of us got on with our lives. I didn't last too long at Dover and after a series of violent incidents I was shipped to Rochester, another closed Borstal with a reputation for toughness, also in Kent. When I eventually got on to the wing – via the hospital where I had been kept in a padded cell under 'mental observation' and forcibly injected with tranquillizers, and the block where I had been put in a straitjacket for assaulting a screw and attempted escape – I was unsurprised to see Stan already there. And he had another plan. But this one, I was pleased to hear, involved cutting the bars rather than himself.

This time Stan had managed to get hold of a couple of hacksaw blades, worth their weight in snout behind the walls of HMP, and had put together a team to saw out the bars on the shower room. As a former trusted confederate of Stan's, I was immediately given an invite to the break-out party. As well as the blades, Stan had miraculously managed to get hold of several items of civilian clothing, an FS car key that would fit any Ford, a chisel and about £10. The idea was that we would cut the bars, which were made of thick, reinforced steel, and then go out the window during evening association and scale the wall using a couple of kitchen barrows which were kept chained to a post at the back of the wing. The chisel would be used to smash the padlocks and free the barrows, and then we would change out of our Borstal uniforms into the civvy clobber, nick a motor from the screws' car park and head to London before they even knew we were gone. It sounded good to me and I was happy to get on the firm. There were six of us involved and we worked in shifts, in teams of two. While one team was in the shower room cutting, another team would keep watch on the screws, and the third would deter other cons who might be thinking of having a shower. The bars were so tough that it took us five evenings to make a hole big enough to get through. But for some reason known only to himself, Stan decided to take another kid into the coup. Maybe he felt sorry for him, but the bloke he brought in was a right fucking melt. His name was Nobby, and he lived in the cell next door to Stan. He was in for criminal damage, having got drunk on cider one night and kicked in most of the shop windows in whatever hick town he came from, and he was an oddity. He never showered and smelled like a goat, and he was also a 'swooper', which was the Borstal term for kids who would pick up dog-ends from the floor and smoke them. None of us was happy with Stan bringing Nobby in, but it was Stan's operation, so there was little we could do.

With Nobby on board, Stan decided he should take part in the bar-cutting. But when the screws started noticing a noto-rious soap-dodger like Nobby spending time in the shower room and coming out smelling exactly the same as when he went in, they smelled a rat. The day before we were due to make our break a couple of screws went nosing about in the shower room. We had the loose bars stuck in place with some putty that one of the lads had nicked from the works department, and when the screws casually gave them a whack with a truncheon the bars fell out like soldiers on parade. The alarm was raised and the whole wing was locked down for a count and a search. Stan had entrusted the escape kit to Nobby to hide and, being a fuckwit, he had stashed it all under his bed. The screws found the kit in double-quick time and Nobby was marched down to the block. When we heard him going I know we all hoped that he would have the bollocks to keep his mouth shut and not grass the rest of us up. But that was a forlorn hope, and within half an hour of his going the screws were back for the rest of us. We were held in the punishment block pending investigation but we all, except Nobby, denied everything. The screws only had Nobby's word that we had been involved, though they knew the score, and he was too frightened to confront any of us with his accusations, so after a month held in solitary we were not charged. Stan was shipped out to the Borstal wing of the Scrubs and Nobby was put on protection in the block, where he became the cleaner, but the rest of us were allowed back on the wing.

Years went by and I occasionally heard news of Stan whenever I was back in jail. True to his youthful ambitions, he had gone on to bigger things and had got into armed robbery in a big way. He was having it off and enjoying the easy life that comes with bundles of money and plenty of free time. Stan had teamed up with a fella from his manor named Buster, and they specialized in robbing security vans picking up takings from commercial premises, such as supermarkets. With all due respect to Buster, who was a very nice bloke, he wasn't exactly the smartest geezer in Harrow. Probably not even in his own house. And he lived alone. But he was a willing and fearless disciple, and Stan had him doing all the dangerous work. Armed with a pump-action Magnum shotgun, Buster would do the actual robbing of the guard while Stan, who did all the planning, would be waiting in the get-away car as far away from the robbery as he could get without Buster realizing he was actually doing the work on his own. Buster would threaten the guard, grab the cash box and then run half a mile to the get-away motor, but he was very fit and it all worked out quite well.

This went on for two years or so, with a robbery every couple of months, before some citizen dobbed them in and the Flying Squad put them under surveillance. The police pounced during the robbery of a security van that was picking up from a DIY superstore. They arrested Stan where he sat in the car, with no trouble at all, but Buster wasn't giving up that easily. With the gun in one hand and the cash box in the other, he didn't hesitate at the shout of 'Armed police!' Instead, he took off at great speed and vaulted a wall behind the shop, landing in a garden and not stopping there. He jumped a series of fences like he was thinking of entering himself in the Grand National and needed the practice before landing in a garden that offered an open back door into a house. He legged it in the back door, through the length of the house and out of the front door. Duckwalking his way across the street, he had to throw himself under a parked car on the other side as several armed coppers came running around the corner. He waited there until Old Bill moved on, and then he jumped another wall and did the whole garden-hopping thing again. It was then that he suddenly realized he had left his gun on the ground under the parked car and it was now too late to go back for it. He was still clutching the cash box, so at least he had his priorities right.

By now the police had saturated the area and Buster had about as much chance of getting away as he did of getting a blow-job from the queen, but he wasn't bright enough to know this. He spotted another open back door and went through it. This time he could see the police through the glass front door and ran upstairs. Finding his way to a bedroom, he flung himself on the floor and crawled under the bed. The owner of the house, a woman in her fifties, had been watering her garden when she saw the desperate figure of Buster run into her house. She hurried through just after he legged it upstairs and opened her front door, to see several dozen coppers, most in flak-jackets and carrying sub-machine guns. At her urgent request, the police flew up the stairs and found

Buster resting under the bed with the cash box still clutched in his sweaty little mitts. He was arrested, of course.

Twelve months later, both Stan and Buster pleaded guilty at Harrow Crown Court to attempted robbery and possession of a firearm. Stan got seven years and Buster got nine. And off they went to prison to serve their sentences. Stan got a bit of a cushty job working in the laundry at HMP Wandsworth, but Buster, true to his luck, got sent to HMP Albany on the Isle of Wight, then the most violent dispersal prison in the country. I was at Albany at the time and got the whole story about the work from him. Since he had been in prison, a lot of people had opened his eyes to how Stan had been treating him like a mug and using him. He told me that one time he had robbed a pony-bag and handed it over to Stan, who said he was going to hide it until the heat went down, and when they went back later the bag was gone. Stan told him that Old Bill had probably got it, but now, with his newly acquired enlightenment, Buster believed that Stan had taken the money. Buster now hated Stan and admitted to me that the only thing that kept him from going crazy was knowing that his one-time crime partner was doing his time in a shithouse like Wandsworth. He couldn't believe that Stan had actually requested that he stay there. I also found it very suspicious as no con in their right mind would want to do their bird in the Hate Factory. I was soon to find out that there was plenty of method in Stan's madness.

Wandsworth was one of those nicks that was locked down so tight that no one had escaped from there since the Great Train Robber Ronnie Biggs had gone over the wall in 1965. Many had tried (including me, by attempting to hijack a JCB that was doing work inside the jail and crash it through the wall in the summer of 1990 – and, of course, Big Bad Bob's try, which I mentioned in an earlier chapter) but no one had made it from inside the jail. But Stan had spotted a weakness and was determined to exploit it and make his escape. While working in the prison laundry he had noticed that the loading bay for deliveries into the building was right next to the lowest part of the wall, and the way out to the bay was not by a locked door and barred gate, as in every other part of the prison, but via a set of steel shutters. He figured that if he could knock up some kind of pry-bar, then he could lift the shutters enough to crawl under and then, with the use of a rope and grapple, he could easily scale the wall and escape. Stan planned to be home by Christmas.

The reason Stan was desperate to escape, apart from the natural desire to be free and get one over on the prison system, was that he had heard that his long-time girlfriend was having an affair, and Stan couldn't have that. He was told that the man who was cuckolding him was a nightclub bouncer and would usually visit Stan's gaff, where Stan's girl was living, in the early hours of the morning when he had finished his shift on the door. Apparently he would turn up very quietly and then leave that evening when it was dark. Like most men in prison, Stan was burnt by this news. It's not only the betrayal by a loved one that hurts but the fact that you can't do anything about it. It's like you are being mugged off and are unable to fight your corner. A lot of men in jail crack up when this happens, but not Stan. He was determined to get out and show this geezer exactly what he was risking. So Stan made his plan.

First, he found himself an escape partner, as it was always better to have two brains on the firm, plus, you never knew when you might need another bod to help out with something. Stan recruited a young kid who was doing a seven as well and wanted out almost as much as Stan did. They managed to break about five feet off a disused iron pipe in the laundry toilet and spent about a week flattening the end into a wedge shape by putting pressure on it in a door jamb whenever the screws weren't looking. At the back of the laundry, over several days, behind piles of dirty sheets and pillowcases, they plaited a thirty-foot rope. Made from tough prison-issue bedsheets, the rope would support their weight no problem. Then they used the broken frame of a swivel chair that had been put out for rubbish to fashion a grapple. Then they were ready to go.

Stan and his pal chose a time in the mid-afternoon shift when everyone was busy at the front of the laundry. They gathered up their escape kit and went to the back shutters. The pry-bar worked like a dream. It slipped in under the shutters, and with both of them using their weight on it, they managed to force the shutter up about eighteen inches, high enough for them both to roll underneath it. The noise of the washing machines covered the slight screeching of metal and nobody noticed they were gone. Outside, they quickly attached their grapple to the rope and flung it up at the top of the wall. It took four throws before the hook took, but once it did, they were both up the rope like rats in a drainpipe. They hung by their fingertips and then dropped the length of the wall on the outside. Stan landed OK but his pal twisted his ankle. Stan helped the other fella to hobble away from the jail, and they were soon moving through the residential streets that surround it. They made it to a cab office, and using money Stan had smuggled in on a visit, they were soon on the other side of London and out of the reach of the prison authorities. The first I heard of the escape was when Buster turned up at my cell that evening with an incredulous half-smile on his face. 'You'll never guess,' he said, with a mixture of admiration and exasperation. 'Stan's only had it away from Wandsworth! It's just been on the radio news. The fucking jammy bastard!'

Stan and his escape partner soon split up and went their separate ways. Top of the agenda for Stan was nicking a few quid. Being on the trot is a very expensive business and he would have to pay out for places to stay. To start with, he crashed with a pal, but as soon as he could get his hands on a shotgun he was back on the rob and set up in a gaff of his own. He kept contact with his girlfriend to a minimum, saying that Old Bill would be watching her, which they would, and he didn't let on that he knew about her affair with the bouncer. After a couple of months, when things weren't so warm on his manor, Stan set out to take his revenge. One night he pulled up across the road from the girlfriend's place on a powerful motorbike, and with all that he needed in a duffel bag over his shoulder, slipped into the front garden of the house opposite where he could see everything and lay down under a hedge. It was two in the morning when he got there, so there was no one about. Inside the duffel bag was a sawn-off twelve-bore shotgun, fully loaded with magnum rounds. His plan was to wait quietly for the bouncer to appear on Stan's own driveway and then jump out, jog across the road, and give him a little message about fucking around with a jailbird's missus, courtesy of the Remington Arms Company.

But Stan had been having a few late nights, enjoying his freedom – which is always that little bit sweeter when you have nicked it back from the prison system – and the area was very quiet and peaceful, so he dozed off. He wasn't sure how long he'd been asleep, but when he was awakened by a sound dawn was just breaking. He looked over in the direction of his house and saw his target walking up the drive. Still half-asleep but knowing he had to be quick, Stan grabbed the shotgun and jumped out of the bushes. He was wearing full motorbike leathers and a crash helmet and dew had settled on the dark-tinted visor while he slept. He wiped it with a gloved hand as he jogged across the road, but that only smeared the water and made it harder to see. There was no time to clean it properly because he was now only five steps from his target and he needed both hands for the gun. His target heard Stan coming up behind him and half-turned, to be confronted by a figure all in black leather pointing a shotgun at him. Stan pointed the gun at the man's legs and took a deep breath. 'This is for you,' he said simply – though he had planned to deliver a speech at this point – then he pulled the trigger.

There was a loud *whumpth!* and flames shot out of the shortened barrel of the gun as sixty lead pellets of magnum shot, tightly grouped together, hit the target just below the knee and blew his leg clean off. Stan had no time to stop and admire his handiwork as the sound of the shot was loud enough to wake up the neighbourhood. And if that wasn't, then the piercing screams of the now one-legged man were. Stan jogged across the road, stuffed the gun into the duffel bag slung over his shoulder and kick-started the big bike. Less than a minute after he had fired the shot he was revving out into the street. Then he noticed a milk float double-parked in the road in front of him, and as he powered the bike around it and up the open road wondered if the milkman had witnessed it all. Stan decided it didn't really matter because the crash helmet was a perfect disguise, and even if he had noticed the number plate it was no drama, because the bike was going into a canal in about ten minutes.

Later on that day, after he had got rid of all incriminating evidence, Stan was having a celebration drink in his new flat. He decided to turn on the midday news to see if he'd got a mention. That's one fucking musclehead who's certainly learnt not to fuck with Stan the man, he thought. There was nothing on *Thames News* about a nightclub doorman being shot but, to Stan's horror, there was an item about the mystery shooting of a milkman in the same area. Stan cursed his luck without a thought for the poor milkman, but that was Stan all over. The milkman was in hospital in a stable condition and doctors thought there was a good chance they could sew his leg back on, but Stan was gutted that he would now have to come up with another plan to get the bouncer. In the event, he never did, because when the man, who had been in bed with Stan's girlfriend as Stan was shooting the milkman on his driveway, saw the scene he guessed exactly what had been meant to happen and he disappeared up north at a rate of knots.

Some months after the shooting, Stan was nabbed in the commission of a robbery. There was no evidence against him for the shooting, though he was interrogated extensively about it, and for the other crimes he had committed while on the run. Stan was sentenced to thirteen years consecutive (i.e. in addition to the seven he had been serving when he escaped) making a total sentence of twenty years. This time they only kept him in HMP Wandsworth for a couple of days before sending him to a top-security dispersal prison in Cambridge-shire, HMP Whitemoor. At Whitemoor Stan once again did the near-impossible and managed to get hold of some tungsten-tipped hacksaw blades. There was no way he was going to spend the next twenty years in jail, and as long as there was breath in his body he would be planning an escape. But during a security search, Stan was caught in possession of the blades and charged, under the new, more draconian approach to prison discipline pioneered by then Home Secre-tary Michael Howard, with conspiracy to escape from prison. He was taken to an outside court, instead of appearing in front of the prison governor for adjudication, and pleaded guilty, thinking he would only get a slap on the wrist. Instead he was sentenced to eighteen months' imprisonment on top of his twenty years. This only made him more determined to escape.

The next time I bumped into Stan was in 1992 in the punishment block at HMP Swaleside on the Isle of Sheppey and, as usual, he had a plan. Finding out through a bent screw that both he and I were due to be transferred to the Isle of Wight on the same escort, he suggested that we break off the van. He had a syringe and needle that he had bought from one of the junkies up on the wing, and his plan was to break open a red pen and pour the ink into the syringe. Then he would smuggle it on to the van and, at some stage during the long journey, pull it out and use it to threaten the screws and get them to undo the cuffs. The idea was to tell them that it was filled with HIV-infected blood. I still had years to do so I was up for it, but when the escort screws looked at my and Stan's combined prison records, there was no way they were going to take the slightest chance with either of us. Stan did manage to get the syringe through the strip-search but we were double-cuffed and chained, with eight screws on the escort, and even scratching my nose had them fingering their truncheons. So we reached the Island without incident.

When I was granted unexpected parole in the summer of 1997, Stan was still on the wing and still plotting to make one. I had a chat with him the night before I was released and asked him what his plans were. 'Dartmoor,' he said. I couldn't believe that anyone would choose to go to Dartmoor, as it was another brutal khazi, on a par with Wandsworth. 'Ah,' Stan replied to my comments, 'but plenty of people have escaped from there. I mean, how hard can it be? Yeah, it's the Moor for me, and the quicker the better.'

Stan did manage to get himself to Dartmoor, but he didn't manage to escape again. In 2002 he was granted parole. Two weeks after being let out on licence he was breached and brought back to prison for being caught in a stolen car. For breaching his licence, he'll have to serve more years. Stan is one of those fellas who has been at it for over three decades now, but I sincerely hope that when he next gets out he will stay out and not go back to crime and prison. I hope so. But I wouldn't take any bets on it.

9. Naughty Nick – Goodfella, Badfella

My old pal Nick is a straight shooter, one of those blokes who, if he wasn't a criminal, could probably have succeeded in most walks of life. He's got it all – good looks, charm, charisma and style. After speaking to him for just a couple of minutes, you cannot help but like and trust him, he's just that sort of fella. Unfortunately, Nick also has a wild streak, and like a lot of serious criminals, he's an adrenaline junkie who gets his fix from crime. He's not a violent criminal as such – that is, he doesn't go around coshing or shooting people – but he has been involved in armed robbery, and we all know that this crime entails the threat of violence and a large degree of psychological trauma for the victims, which cannot be dismissed lightly. Apart from crime, Nick is a fighter. He was a pretty good amateur boxer in his youth and went on to become a cage-fighter, so he does have the capacity for serious physical violence. He just chose never to use it in his crimes. Like all criminals, Nick was forever chasing the Big One, and though he came close a few times, he never actually managed to get his hands on it.

When I met Nick in HMP Highdown in Surrey in the early nineties, we were both in 'patches', which is the uniform that prison escapees have to wear, a bib-and-brace overall with a bright yellow stripe down its length. While in patches you are on what is known as the E List and have to be escorted everywhere by two screws and a dog. The prison authorities take all your clothing every night at bang-up and hand it back the next morning. Being an E man is bad enough, but I also had the added restriction of being category A, which meant that, instead of two screws, I had to be escorted by at least four. In order to get on the E List a prisoner has to have made a successful or serious attempt to escape from prison or court custody. Nick had tried jumping the dock in his local magistrates' court when he was up for a routine remand. He had made it out of the courtroom but not the court building, having been steamed by a dozen screws and coppers when he was about twenty yards from freedom. Nick ended up a couple of cells away from me and we immediately hit it off.

At this time Nick was on remand for car theft, half a million pounds' worth. He specialized in top-of-the-range sports cars, particularly Porsches. He was also charged with blackmail and demanding money with menaces. Nick and his crime partner, Shorty, had been going about their business and keyed a brand-new 928 Turbo from a car park in the West End. As Nick drove the motor to their lock-up in Surrey, Shorty was rooting through the glove box and under the seats. Under the passenger seat he came across a crocodile-skin Louis Vuitton briefcase. Obviously, it was locked, but that was no problem to a tea-leaf of Shorty's calibre, and he had it open in a hot second. Inside, he was shocked to find a set of full-colour glossy eight-by-ten photographs of several men engaged in homosexual acts. He pushed a particularly naughty picture in front of Nick's face and shouted, 'Take a look at that!' Nick almost ran the Porsche off the road.

When they got the Porsche safely under wraps and ready for an ID change in the lock-up, they made a closer examination of the dirty pictures. Nick noticed that the same man appeared in every photo, though his sexual partners were different, and surmised that he must be the owner of the photos. It was only a small step then to assuming that the man in the pictures was the owner of the Porsche. From the odds and ends of paper-work they found in the glove box they had the man's name, address and phone number, and also his business address. It turned out he was a barrister. It didn't take much pondering for Nick to realize that they could have stumbled into a nice little earner. He wondered exactly how much a respected barrister might be prepared to pay in order to stop his mucky photos going public. It might be quite a sum.

That evening Nick went to a public phone box, with Shorty in tow, and phoned the number. When the target answered, Nick didn't bother going round the houses. 'I'm the geezer who nicked your Porsche,' he said. 'I've also got your photographs, and I want £10,000 in cash, small bills, or I send a copy to the *News of the World*.'

The barrister, as you might expect from a man who made a living from putting people under pressure, was cool as an iceberg lettuce. 'OK,' he replied. 'Let me know when and where.'

Nick couldn't believe his luck. This was working out just like one of those old blackmailing films with the respectable bod prepared to pay for silence. Nick had already thought it all through, on the off chance that the man would be willing to wear the demand. 'Twelve o'clock tomorrow at Victoria train station. Put the money in a blue sports bag and leave it in the first cubicle as you go in the door of the station toilets. No police.'

The man sighed. 'And what about my photos?' he asked.

Nick assured him that if he paid up, he would send the pictures back to him. 'You can forget the car though,' he ended, 'that's not part of the deal, it remains stolen.'

The man agreed, and that was that. Nick and Shorty were well happy – this was the easiest ten grand they had ever earned.

The next day Nick and Shorty, suitably disguised in dark glasses and baseball caps, were hanging around the station pretending to read newspapers. The station was very crowded, but they easily spotted the target walk into the toilets with the blue holdall as ordered. He was in there for less than five minutes, and they let him leave the station before jogging into the toilets to collect their prize. The money was there, and it was a couple of happy bunnies who walked out of the toilets and straight into ten plain-clothes coppers. They were arrested on suspicion of blackmail and taken into custody. They found out in the police station that, far from being worried about the photos being made public, the target didn't give a fuck. He was openly homosexual and had a reputation for hardcore sexual shenanigans anyway. In fact, he said, having his photos splashed across the pages of a Sunday tabloid might be a bit of a turn-on. As soon as Nick had phoned him, the man had called the police and informed them of what was going down. The Old Bill had set up the operation at the train station and moved in to mop up when the lads had shown themselves.

So Nick had tried to make his own way out of custody and ended up in patches with me in Highdown. He was a good fella to do a bit of bird with because he had a great sense of humour and was able to laugh at himself as well. He also loved a good scam, and when he was moved on to another wing after about five months, I inadvertently became the victim of one of his flim-flams. At this time I had taken up a bit of drug-dealing in order to keep the wolf from the door. It wasn't something that I had planned to do but I just kind of fell into it. It happened because of my own use of cannabis. I liked a couple of spliffs in the evening after bang-up. I found they took the edge off the cell and ensured me a good night's kip. And in a prison full of lunatics, some of whom like nothing better than to hang off their window bars shouting and scream-ing into the early hours, getting a decent sleep was like winning the lottery. So my pal, Big Al, used to come up on a visit every couple of weeks and bring me a parcel of hash, which I would then smuggle back to the wing. One week he turned up on the visit but said that there was a bit of a puff drought in south London, due to some large police and customs seizures. I was gutted, but he said he had brought me some heroin instead and I could use this to buy a bit of hash inside the jail. I wasn't too pleased with this as I didn't really want anything to do with heroin – I had seen too many good people fucked up on it. But, being a mercenary and selfish bastard, by the end of the visit I had decided I would take the heroin and try to deal it for a bit of hash.

As soon as it was whispered that there was skag up for trade I had every junkie in the prison bringing me lumps of hash they had been holding on to for just such an opportunity as this. I ended up with plenty of hash and had skag left over for cash trades, and there seemed to be no shortage of these. Money in prison is usually not that common, despite being easy to smuggle in, because it's not really the currency of jail – drugs are – but there were a couple of serious skagheads who kept turning up at my cell with £20 notes clutched in their sweaty mitts looking to buy a bit of tackle. I did wonder where this pair of melts were getting all their cash from as they were the sort of geezers who had probably never had more than £50 in one place before, even on the out, but as long as the cash kept coming, I kept serving. Heroin in jail is sold in wraps called £10 bags, though, in reality, there is probably no more than £2 worth of genuine narcotic in each wrap, but it seems to do the job. There is an unwritten but accepted rule that if you buy two bags for hard cash then the dealer will throw in a third bag free. The three-for-the-price-of-two deal is traditional and encourages people to pay up-front. So when I was being approached with cash, I was giving three for the price of two. Over a period of three months I cleared over £400 in cash and had become a regular skag-dealer, with Big Al supplying me from the out. I decided that the cash was becoming a nuisance to hide, so I would smuggle it out on my next visit and start over again.

By chance, when I went on my next visit, Nick was also

having a visit from one of his pals, and after the visits were over, we had a chance for a bit of a chat as we were waiting for the screws to take us back to our wings. We had barely seen each other in months and we were soon laughing and joking. Then Nick told me that he was living like a king on the proceeds of a get-up he was working and went on to tell me the details. A mate of his outside had bought £100,000 in counterfeit £20 notes and was having it off passing them up and down the country. At Nick's instigation he had brought up a couple of parcels of the notes and Nick smuggled them in on a visit, and now he had a team of junkies working them into all the skag-dealers for him. They would get three bags for £20, out of which the junkies would get one free bag and Nick would get the two remaining, which he would trade up for phone cards, groceries from the prison canteen and whatever else he might need to make life in a top-security jail a bit more comfortable. Nick didn't take drugs, not even tobacco, so he was delighted that not only was he earning out of it but was also sticking it to the skag-dealers. I was gutted and told him that I had just handed out £400 worth of his hooky money. But we had to laugh over it since there was no way Nick could have known that I was dealing skag as we were both so anti. He offered me, by way of a refund, a chance of getting my money back and stuffing one into the prison system at the same time. All I had to do was get the money sent back in, officially, in medium amounts, and it would be credited to my prison account. There was a lot of cash coming into a jail that size and no one would know which note was which or who had sent it in when the fakes were discovered. The money coming in was placed in the prison safe and banked once a month, and I managed to get the majority in before the shout went up. Because of this scam, the prison changed the rules on money being sent in and every note had to have its serial number recorded on arrival.

Nick eventually went up to court and got six years on reduced charges. He used this time in jail to plan his future and do a bit of research on anything that might help him in his ambition to become very rich. He soaked up knowledge like a sponge and sought out anyone who might be able to impart a bit of inside info about anything interesting and possibly lucrative. One fella who Nick sought out and nurtured was a straight-goer turned attempted murderer who we called Biggles. Biggles had been recruited by a tasty firm of drug smugglers because he had a pilot's licence, which is a very attractive prospect to anyone who's in the business of shifting large loads of cocaine from one country to another. He also had a gambling problem, which is how they hooked him in the first place. He had no police record and was just a nondescript middle-aged man, which was perfect cover. Unfortunately for Biggles, his new-found wealth and an introduction into the champagne and charlie lifestyle, along with the free-loving, beautiful young women who inhabit this world, were too much for him, and he went a bit mad. He decided that he would be much better off without his wife, from whom he was keeping everything a secret, and plotted to murder her. At the height of his madness, he figured that the perfect crime would be to make an explosive device, at which he was somewhat expert as his hobby was pyrotechnics, and then fly low over his house in his two-seater Cessna and drop it on her. How he thought he was ever going to get away with that one is beyond me. But his wife had become suspicious about his frequent disappearances and wondered what he might be building in his shed. What she saw when she broke in was enough to get her on to Old Bill double quick and have him arrested. Biggles, by the time of his arrest, hated his wife so much that he coughed the lot about his plan and ended up with five years for conspiracy to murder and possession of explosives. This was a particularly lenient sentence given the charges, and it raised a few suspicions among the real criminals, but he was given the benefit of the doubt and most of us figured that his lack of criminal record and previous good character had done the trick for him. As far as any of us cons knew, he hadn't mentioned a word about the drug smuggling, but some years later it was to emerge that he had, in fact, spilled his guts about that as well, and after he was given early parole on his sentence, he went on to work under cover for Customs & Excise and caused a lot of damage to the drug operation.

Nick had dreams of getting a pilot's licence of his own and pumped Biggles for hours about how he could go about it, how much it would cost, how many lessons he would have to take. Nick also spent a lot of time talking to some of the big-time drug barons about the ins and outs of their game, as well as to the top armed robbers. Nick was such a pleasant guy and he had such charisma that people would tell him things they wouldn't normally even tell their lawyers. He picked up a lot of information during his sentence. He also got every book on antiques, precious metals and gemstones from the prison library and studied up on what stuff would be worth nicking. He didn't really have any specific plan in mind; he just knew he wanted to be ready for anything that caught his fancy. Nick wanted the Big One, and he wanted it before he was too old to enjoy the benefits. And for him, prison really was a university of further criminal education.

Nick served his time and got released around 1996. The first thing he got into was a couple of walk-in robberies. From these he garnered enough money to buy the equipment he would need for his next criminal enterprise. His plan was to burgle museums and break his way into the display cases with a Hilti-gun, a nail-firing tool used in the building trade, to steal valuable relics. He had a few in mind, but when he started looking into the possibility of unloading such pieces for the right price, he was disappointed to find no one was interested. No doubt, somewhere out there is an international fence, with money and contacts, who is absolutely gagging to get his hands on Edward VII's gold- and diamond-encrusted snuffbox, but Nick couldn't find him. So he teamed up with his old gang, Shorty and Billy the Bullshitter, for a bit of work they had on the agenda. They were planning to rob a safe, and there was supposed to be a nice few quid in it. They would break into the warehouse under cover of darkness and have a good few hours to crack the safe with the tools they were bringing along. Billy the Bullshitter had put the work up and said he would have no trouble popping the box as he had done it before on a previous bit of work before joining the team. Nick had his doubts, but he needed the money so he agreed to come along.

Now anyone who has seen an old black-and-white film about safe-crackers will have the idea that it's an easy business – you just pack the door with 'gelly', stand well back and *boom!* there's the money. But, in reality, safe-crackers are an all-but-dead breed. For one thing, hardly anyone keeps anything of value in safes these days: it's always a short walk to the bank, and for another, you can no longer just snap the padlock on a shed in a stone quarry with your trusty 'jemmy bar' and walk away with a couple of bundles of dynamite. This kind of stuff is now guarded more closely than money. Most safe-breakers now have to use a more primitive method. The weakest part of most safes is the back panel, so the trick is to tip your safe over and expose the back. You then use an electric drill or an angle grinder to make a hole in the outer skin, which is usually half-inch-thick steel, before using a lump hammer and cold chisel to smash the inch-and-a-half-thick steel-reinforced concrete inner lining. Then it's back to the power tools to breach the inner skin. Then, if you're lucky, there'll be some money in it. Breaking into a safe is hard graft and it's a long and noisy job, not to be undertaken by amateurs.

The best way of doing it is to load the safe on to a vehicle and transport it somewhere you won't be disturbed, and then crack it at your leisure.

Nick and the boys broke into the warehouse with no trouble, but when it came to actually breaking into the safe, Billy had to admit he was lost. 'I thought you said you could fucking well do it?' Nick accused. Billy shrugged his shoulders. 'Well, I've seen it done on the telly and I thought once we were here it might just come to me.' Nick was not amused, and neither was Shorty, but there wasn't a lot they could do about it. Then Nick suggested that they cart the safe away so that at least the night wouldn't be a total loss. They could ask about for a bit of advice on how to break it the next day. The lads agreed and so began the long, painful process of dragging the two-ton hunk of metal out of the warehouse to their van. Even with the three of them working together, the safe was a bastard to move, and after a couple of hours of pushing and pulling they still only had it half-way to the door. It would have been easier to drive the van into the gaff, but it was too big to fit through the doorway and negotiate the narrow corridor to the safe. Nick then had an idea. He had a Porsche Carrera parked in a lock-up about four miles away – old habits die hard for the performance car thief – and after quickly measuring the gaps he realized he could drive the little car straight in. So, leaving Billy to guard the prize, Nick got Shorty to drive him to pick up the Porsche.

Nick's idea worked a treat and the Porsche slid through the gaps with inches to spare right up to the safe. It took the boys a further twenty minutes of sweating and straining to lift the dead weight off the ground and tip it into the Porsche. They had to take the convertible roof down, and once the safe was in, there was barely room for the driver, but they had it. It was still only three in the morning and the roads were fairly empty as they drove back to the lock-up in convoy, Shorty and Billy bringing up the rear in the van as Nick handled the safe-filled Porsche. Once in the lock-up, they decided to leave the safe in the car for the night and come back the next day armed with the information they would need for an opening ceremony. But the lock-up was on a residential street, and the noise they had made getting the Porsche back in had alerted their nearest neighbour, who, being very pissed off at the disturbance of his beauty sleep, came down in his dressing-gown to remonstrate with the noise-makers. He got there just as the door was wide open and his mouth dropped open when he saw the little sports car kitted out with what was obviously not an optional extra – a fucking big safe. The lads tried to laugh it off, telling him they were very sorry for the noise and that they were just leaving, but they could tell by the crease of his brow that he had clocked the safe and wasn't happy. They told him that they were scrap-metal merchants and that the safe was scrap they had picked up earlier in the day. The neighbour seemed to accept this explanation, though in his mind he was probably wondering what sort of scrap-metal merchants used a brand-new Porsche for their pick-ups. But he headed back into his house, asking them to keep the noise down in future.

Nick was a bit dubious, but the other two thought they might have got away with it. They decided to pretend to leave, drive around the block, and then park the van up and watch the lock-up for a little while to make sure. In the meantime the rudely awakened man went into his house and immediately phoned the police to report what he had seen. By the time the lads had traversed the block and arrived back at the top of the street, there were blue flashing lights all over the pavement and a couple of burly uniforms were breaking open the lock-up. The lads made a swift but quiet exit from the scene, cursing their luck and all light-sleeping nosy parkers. Back at Shorty's gaff, they lamented the loss of the safe, the Porsche, the lock-up and their tools, and speculated on the fortune inside the safe they had missed out on. Nick felt particularly cheated. 'That's our fucking safe,' he declared angrily. 'We put a lot of graft in on that, and I'll be fucked if I let Old Bill walk away with the fruits of our labours!'

Then he got to thinking. Nick knew that Old Bill would load the Porsche, complete with safe, on to a low-loader and take it to the police-evidence compound at the local station to await forensic examination for fingerprints. He suggested, to the complete horror of Shorty and Billy, that they wait until just before dawn and then go and steal their prize back from the police. Nick had broken into the police compound several times when he was a kid and nicked stereos from the stolen cars so he knew his way around. He also knew that there was only one guard there, an old boy who spent most of the night asleep in his hut. Shorty and Billy told him that what he was suggesting was utter madness. You can't steal from the police, it had just never been done. Nick told them that if they weren't going to help him, then he would do it on his own. The boys refused point blank to risk it and tried hard to talk Nick out of what they saw as a suicide mission. But Nick was adamant. He was having the safe back, and if he did it alone, he would be keeping whatever was in the safe for himself.

So Nick, armed with a small pair of bolt-croppers and his Porsche keys, made his way through the quiet, pre-dawn streets to the police compound. He made his way around the chain-linked fence and spotted the Porsche, still with the safe on board, parked up near the front. There was a signboard in front of it with the words EVIDENCE AWAITING FORENSICS DO NOT TOUCH. There was no sign of the old guard so Nick slipped up to the entrance of the pound and used the bolt-croppers to cut through the chain that kept the gate locked. Being as quiet as he could, knowing that there were plenty of coppers awake in the adjacent well-lit police station, he slid the double gates open wide. Then he crept into the pound and up to the Porsche. He climbed inside and keyed the ignition before loosening the handbrake and putting the stick in gear. The engine purred like a big cat as Nick gently toed the accelerator and set the little car rolling out of the open compound. There was no movement from the police station or the guard's shed, and the car was out in the road and away before Nick put his foot right down and began to sing. He drove the car to another lock-up he had about five miles away and didn't see another soul on the roads. As dawn broke, Nick was just climbing into his bed, happy that the night had not been a complete loss and looking forward to spending all that lovely money in the safe.

The next day, after getting some advice on safe-breaking from one of the local faces, Nick spent six hours cutting and hammering his way through the back of his safe. Inside, he found £17,000 in cash, which he considered a very good wage for all the hard graft he had put in. As a gesture of goodwill he gave Shorty and Billy a grand apiece, and when the tale of his daring act started getting whispered around the underworld, Nick's already pristine reputation went up a notch. You would think that stealing the safe back from the police compound would be enough to satisfy Nick's ego, but he couldn't resist taking it a bit further. He phoned one of the daily tabloids, the *Star*, and asked how much they would be willing to pay for a funny story. The *Star* sent one of their reporters to meet with Nick and, for £1,800, he told them the story of how his 'mate' had left the police looking like complete mugs. The newspaper published the story as an exclusive on page five the next day and Nick chuckled all the way to the bank. Embarrassed police officials had to confirm the story and said they had plans to upgrade their security.

Now Nick was still on the look-out for the Big One when he was approached by a kid who, impressed by Nick's reputation, had an earner in mind. The kid, who was nineteen, had worked for NCP car parks and been sacked for nicking a few choice items from customers' vehicles. He brought news of large amounts of cash being deposited daily in the ticket machines at the car parks. He wanted Nick to help him hold up the security guards who did the collections. Nick, never one to pass up a financial opportunity without full examination, listened carefully to what the kid had to say and then asked a few questions of his own. The kid estimated that each ticket machine, of which there were thousands in the hundreds of NCP car parks up and down the country, took an average of £700 per week. And they were emptied every week. The parking fees were very expensive and Nick was surprised to learn that they took banknotes as well as coins. He decided to go and have a look at one of these machines, and an idea began to form in his head. Why go to all the trouble and danger of doing an armed robbery on the guards when you could break into the ticket machines themselves? After closely examining one of the machines, he abandoned his original idea of cracking the money boxes with a hammer and chisel and realized that he was already in possession of a tool that would probably do the job more quickly and easily – the Hilti-gun he had bought for his museum-breaking idea.

Late one evening, he and the kid decided to give it a try. They drove into one of the multi-storey car parks and up to a deserted level. Nick hopped out of the car with the Hilti-gun and pressed the muzzle up against the lock of the cash box. He pulled the trigger and there was a sharp crack. When Nick looked he saw that the entire lock had been bent out of place and was badly damaged. He went to the boot of his car and got a lump hammer from his toolbox. With two hard whacks the lock on the cash box dropped into the interior and the box was free. But the freeing of the lock had activated a high-pitched screamer alarm inside the machine, and an ear-splitting noise filled the concrete interior of the building. Nick slid the box out and found that it was almost full. Without panicking, he passed the box to the kid and made his way to the next machine. This too was popped in seconds and Nick got back into the car and drove away with just over £1,100 for three minutes' work.

For the next six months Nick and the kid travelled the length and breadth of the country hitting ticket machines. They honed their MO so that they would drive in one end of a car park, hit the first machine with the Hilti-gun and then move on to another machine in the centre of the car park before doing the last one on their way out. They could take three cash boxes in less than five minutes, and by the time the police responded to the alarms they were miles away. Then one night, just outside Rugby, in Warwickshire, they were unlucky enough to run into a police patrol as they were leaving a job. When the cops searched the car they found the Hilti-gun, the lump hammer and fifteen cash boxes containing a total of £4,500. The gig was up for Nicky and the kid. They were charged with stealing £94,000 in cash and criminal damage to the machines to the sum of £735,000. The kid got five years and Nick got ten because of his previous.

By the time Nick got out he was approaching thirty-five, though still fit and still hungry for the Big One. The only lessons he had learnt in prison were the kind taught by other criminals, and Nick had been a willing student and a quick study. But he now understood the value of patience and intricate planning when it came to business. This time he would take it slow. The first thing he did when he got out was get back into the fighting game. He had always been a good boxer, and one of the things he had apprenticed at in jail was kick-boxing. He had been taught by an ex-champion and trained every day in the prison gym until he surpassed the skills of even his teacher. So he put himself up as a cage-fighter, fighting for cash prizes against other lunatics inside a cage and for the delectation of blood-hungry fight fans. He did pretty well for his age and used his winnings to take the flying lessons he had long been dreaming about. It wasn't long before Nick had his pilot's licence and, with his reputation and contacts in the criminal world, he was now much sought after by the big drug teams as a smuggler. Nick earned a bundle flying parcels of illegal drugs to various countries, and soon he had bought his own plane, a two-seater Piper Comanche, and a house in Spain, and had shares in a cage-fighters' gym in London. He met a girl and settled down in Spain, where they had a son. When his boy was born Nick gave up drug smuggling and moved his family to Costa Rica. Life was good, and as he lay by his pool sipping cold beer and watching his young son playing in the garden of his villa, he must have thought he had come a long way from his days in the grim cells of British prisons. And he was right.

If Nick hadn't been such a genuinely nice guy he might still be living *la dolce vita* in his tropical paradise, but one of his old contacts in the drug business approached him and asked for help. The man said he needed someone to captain a yacht for him, from Morocco to England, and he was desperate as his captain had been nicked at the last moment for an unrelated incident. While living in Spain, Nick had owned his own yacht and often sailed to England and back for business and pleasure, so he was more than capable. He knew there were illegal drugs on the yacht and there was always a slight risk of getting caught, but his mate almost begged him to help out and Nick agreed. Just off the coast of southern France, the yacht was boarded by French customs officials, the French navy and Interpol. A search uncovered sixty-two kilos of pure cocaine.

I recently received a letter from Nick. He's being held in the top-security *maison d'arrêt* in Aix-en-Provence, France. He doesn't know when he will be up for trial – it could be a couple of years yet – but his brief has told him to expect twenty-five years. Now close to forty and having had a taste of paradise, those years are going to be long and hard for Nick, which is a shame, because for a badfella, Nick was always one of the goodfellas.

10. Shotgun Johnny

Shotgun Johnny is an East Ender, not one of the ones off the popular BBC soap opera but a real one – born and bred in the East End of London. At about five foot eight and ten stone wringing wet, he is one of the most dangerous men I have ever met. It's not that Johnny goes around growling all the time or picking fights with everyone, because he doesn't, and if you met him in any circumstances other than when he's on a mission, you would find him a totally normal and decent human being. But stand between Johnny and something he wants, or try taking what he might consider 'a liberty' with him, and you had better be prepared for all hell to break loose. Johnny was an old-fashioned post-office blagger, and he took his job seriously. Personally, when I was robbing, I couldn't be doing with post offices, particularly sub-post offices. Yes, there is money in them, and yes, some people do make a good living out of relieving them of said money but – and I don't mean this to come across as in any way racist – most of them are owned and run by Asians. It is common knowledge among the armed-robbery fraternity that Asian sub-postmasters are notoriously hard work around a pound note. Maybe it's because they are proud and stubborn, and being used to grafting for a living themselves, they don't see why they should hand over to some lazy bastard with a gun and a loud voice. If I seem guilty of stereotyping here, then I can only say that I am speaking from experience, and you can take it or leave it. But Shotgun Johnny did love a post office and the reason I think he was always able to claim the prize was because his victims recognized that he really did not give a shit whether they lived or died. Most armed robbers are actors, able to convince their audience of their deadly intent, but Johnny was as serious as cancer.

Johnny's MO was to enter a post office wearing a ski-mask and carrying his trademark sawn-off sixteen-gauge shotgun and immediately fire a shot into the ceiling to get everyone's attention. The firing of the ceiling shot was pioneered by a little firm known as the Wembley Mob in the sixties and early seventies. The Wembley Mob, who came by their name after robbing Barclay's Bank on Wembley High Street of £138,000 in just under four minutes in 1969, used to fire a doctored shotgun cartridge. Before each robbery they would saw the end from a plastic shotgun cartridge, empty out the lead shot and replace it with either rock salt or dry rice. Then, when they fired their warning shot, it would look and sound like a real shot but cause little injury or damage. Nearly thirty years later Shotgun Johnny was doing something similar, only he was firing real lead shot. The Flying Squad came to recognize Johnny's jobs by the fact that half the ceiling would be hanging down or on the floor at the premises he had robbed. He left a trail that the most stupid copper could have followed and provided much-needed jobs for local builders.

Johnny was doing OK as a post-office robber. He liked to work alone so he didn't have to share the prize with anyone other than his many beautiful girlfriends. Johnny was a big hit with the women. Perhaps it was the air of danger he exuded or the way in which he splashed his money around, but the general consensus in the underworld was that it was down to his eleven-inch dick, which he wasn't shy of flashing about when the mood took him. It was said that if Johnny ever lost his shotgun, he could go on a bit of work with his dick in his hand and people would only think he'd bought a bigger gun. Women loved him and Johnny loved women, so there was a nice bit of symmetry working in his life. He had done the odd short prison sentence, mainly for theft, when he was a kid, but with his MO at the old blagging game it was a foregone conclusion that he wasn't going to reign for very long. To the Flying Squad, any robber who fires a shot on a bit of work becomes top priority. They know that blasting out a ceiling with a sawn-off is only a short step away from blasting out someone's head. And Shotgun Johnny was about to prove the truth of that.

As well as post offices, Johnny was also up for robbing drug-dealers. In fact, he preferred robbing the latter because they were unable to go to the police when he relieved them of their cash and valuable merchandise. He would keep his ear to the ground and pick up any hot whispers about who was having it off in the drug game, then rob them. Here, too, Johnny was a bit more reckless than your usual blagger. He didn't care what sort of dangerous reputation these men might have. To Johnny, they were just targets who had better hand over double lively or suffer the consequences. He would rob Turkish heroin-dealers, Jamaican crack-dealers or Colombian charlie men – to Johnny they were all the same: he truly was an equal-opportunities blagger. One day he picked up a bit of info on a Turkish mini-cab driver who was supposed to be transporting the take from a large heroin deal and knew the whereabouts of the cash and a large shipment of brown powder, so Johnny decided it was as good as his.

Sticking his trusty sawn-off under his coat, Johnny waited for the Turk to come out of his premises one evening and got the drop on him. He made the man drive him to Wanstead Flats, a quiet bit of ground a few miles from the East End, and asked him nicely where the money and gear was. When the man had no reply, Johnny then asked not so nicely, putting a few dents in the butt of his shotgun for emphasis. I have spoken at length to Johnny about this incident, and I'm still not sure whether the Turk was just one tough cookie who would rather die than reveal his secret, or whether, as it was said in court, that Johnny had got the wrong man. Anyway, after asking the same question several times without getting the right answer, Johnny started thinking the man might be trying to take liberties with him. He ordered him out of the car and, standing less than three feet away, ordered him to reveal all or get his head blown off. The Turk just shrugged silently, and Johnny shot him in the head.

When speaking about this moment Johnny is colder than Eskimo shit and calmer than the Dead Sea. He says that he felt the gun jump in his hand as he pulled the trigger and saw the flame shoot from the barrel to where the man was standing, but by then the Turk was no longer there; instead he was flying through the air, propelled by the force of the sixty lead pellets that had slammed into his skull at about fifteen hundred feet per second. The man came to rest about eight feet from Johnny. You would think that having just blasted someone in the head at almost point-blank range would add a bit of urgency to your next movements, but Johnny told me that he walked over to where the man was lying. He had never shot anyone before and he was interested in seeing exactly how much damage he had caused. He naturally assumed the man was dead but was surprised when he approached to hear him moaning. Johnny got down on his haunches and stared intently at the bloody mess he had made of the man's head for a couple of minutes. The man was breathing strongly and Johnny patted his hand consolingly. 'Sorry about that, mate,' he told the bleeding, moaning Turk. 'You should have told me what I wanted to know. Hope you pull through, but it's your own fault, remember that.' Then Johnny climbed into the victim's car and drove off.

It was something of a miracle that the man didn't die, and the surgeons who were later to operate on him attributed this to the thickness of the human skull bone and the fact that

Johnny had been packing birdshot in his no. 6 cartridges. Nonetheless, had Johnny used a bigger bore of shotgun, a twelve-bore, say, the man's head would probably have been blown clean off, birdshot or no. As it was, the victim made a pretty full and rapid recovery, though he did have some damage to part of his brain and a horrible patch of scar tissue. The shooting was in the local newspapers and, with a reward offered for the arrest and conviction of the gunman, it wasn't long before Shotgun Johnny's name was being bandied about in police briefing rooms all over the East End.

Shotgun Johnny was arrested in a dawn raid by enough armed coppers to start a war on crime – and the causes of crime. He was questioned at length about the shooting of the Turk and then about several outstanding post-office blags. Johnny refused to say anything and claimed a brief as soon as he was able. Old Bill then put Johnny on an identity parade and the Turk, sitting in a wheelchair and with a massive bandage around his noggin, picked Johnny out of the line-up in a hot second. That, and the fact that they had recovered a sawn-off sixteen-gauge shotgun loaded with no. 6 birdshot cartridges at the side of Johnny's bed, was enough to get him remanded in custody as a category A prisoner. For Shotgun Johnny the future was now bleak and barren, something he would just have to get used to. If you shoot someone in the head, you can't expect to get a probation order, no matter how hard the tabloids try to convince people otherwise.

Johnny was held in HMP Belmarsh, as a category A prisoner, and in order to fill the long days in this very restricted atmosphere, he read a lot. Law was one of the subjects he became interested in and he managed to pick up a rudimentary knowledge of it. He was particularly interested in civil law and how to sue for damages in the small-claims court. Johnny had noticed that a lot of his fellow prisoners had gripes and complaints about their treatment at the hands of the police and the prison service, and he thought it might be amusing to help a few of them write up writs and cause a bit of agg for the authorities. Johnny was typically anti-authority and would go out of his way to poke and annoy the system. It turned out that he was very quick, and the role of advocate came quite easily to this East End lunatic. In fact, he was more ruthless than any regular lawyer in pursuing his clients' claims and won the first few cases he took on. Suing the police and the prison system through the small-claims court is a pretty simple (but tedious) business but Johnny had the patience and the will to succeed. A typical case would involve the loss of prisoners' property, and Johnny became an expert at getting monetary compensation for those whose goods had been 'lost' by the system.

Whenever someone is arrested for a serious crime, the police have a habit of seizing every piece of moveable property in the vicinity of the suspect. They take vehicles, raid his home or business address, take any cash or jewellery, clothing and tools – in fact, anything that the suspect might have had contact with and may be considered as 'evidence' at a later trial. They even take the clothes he is standing up in and give him a white paper suit to wear instead. The seizing of this property serves two purposes: one, for any possible evidential or forensic value; and two, to throw the suspect completely off balance and put him at a financial disadvantage – in an uncomfortable zone, if you will. It can be very demoralizing and disconcerting to have to appear in the magistrates' court dressed in nothing but a paper suit and government-issue plimsolls. Then, when the suspect is remanded in custody, he will struggle to get someone to purchase the essentials for him because the police are holding all of his goods and money. Every item seized by the police is listed on the Property Seizure Sheet, a copy of which is given to the suspect. Then the property is searched for items which might be evidence, usually sent to a forensics laboratory for examination. The rest is bagged up and sent to a central property store.

If the suspect is found not guilty at his subsequent trial his property will be returned to him, but if he is convicted and sent to prison, then his property remains in the store. With so much property being taken, the store soon reaches capacity, and if no one has claimed it, it is either destroyed or sold off. Though they do this on a regular basis, the police have no right to destroy or sell property without a court order. A suspect is entitled to have his property returned on request up to four years after it has been seized.

A lot of prisoners lose their property in this way, and this is where Johnny stepped in. He would ask around the wing for prisoners who were sentenced and had had property seized by the police, then he would draft a letter to the arresting officer in the case demanding the return of said property. Usually, the police will not reply to these letters, but the important thing is to register them and keep a copy for evidence. The next step is to calculate the value of the seized property. You do this on a cost-of-replacement basis, so if the police have seized all your old favourites – every pair of footwear that you own, for example – it doesn't matter that half of them have holes in the soles, they now have to be replaced as new. If the claim is under £5,000, it is classed as a small claim and can be dealt with by way of issuing a summons, on the Commissioner of the Metropolitan Police in the case of a London nicking. Issuing the actual claim does not cost anything for the unemployed and serving prisoners. So now the court and the police have your claim and the legal dance begins.

The police have their own top-notch legal retainers whose job it is to fight any claims laid against them, and fight they certainly do. It has always amazed me, having also been a jailhouse lawyer myself, how much time and money these legal eagles put into fighting unwinnable cases. I have made claims of less than £1,000 for prisoners and then watched as the police lawyers have run up bills of twice that in man-hours and unnecessary letters at £50 a pop only to settle out of court months later. The thing with these property cases is that the police, and the prison system to a certain extent, have absolute liability and must pay up if they sell or destroy someone's property without a court order or permission from the owner. The legal-dance steps in such a case are as follows: you ask for £2,000 in compensation, about £500 over what the property is actually worth; the police lawyers offer £50; you write back and laugh; the police lawyers wait a while and then offer £600; you write back again and say you might be willing to accept £1,500; the police lawyers offer £900; you refuse; then, the day before the case is due in court, the police lawyers offer £1,200 in full and final settlement – and if you've got any sense you accept it. All parties involved know that actually going into court with a small claim is a very risky business, as each case is judged not 'beyond reasonable doubt' as in criminal cases but on 'the balance of probabilities', and this is open to a particular judge's interpretation of the case. For the claimant, even winning can be a Pyrrhic victory. If, say, you have been offered £1,200 in an out-of-court settlement and you go to court, win the case, and the judge awards you £1,199, then you get nothing, as you are liable for court costs. It's safer to settle.

Shotgun Johnny, from his top-security cell in Belmarsh prison, took to the law like a pig to truffles and started carving out a name for himself. He did the first few cases pro bono, but then became inundated with eager cons looking for a bit of compo and decided to charge a 10 per cent legal fee for juggling the paperwork. This is how he passed the months awaiting his trial for the shooting of the Turk. Johnny may have been ruthless, but he was far from stupid, and when he received the court depositions, he realized that the weight of evidence against him was overwhelming. So he worked out a deal, through his lawyer, whereby he would plead guilty to attempted murder and possession of a firearm, with several counts of armed robbery being left on file, in return for a bit of leniency in the sentencing. Johnny was under no illusion that he was looking at any mere slap on the wrist and knew his sentence would run into double figures. He just wanted a '1' at the front of the amount rather than a '2'. He appeared at the Old Bailey one cold morning and was sentenced to fifteen years' imprisonment on his guilty pleas. He took it with a shrug and went off to do his bit of sparrow in the same way he had done his remand time – by being a thorn in the side of the authorities.

As a category A prisoner, Johnny could only be housed in a handful of top-security prisons in the country, and he was such a handful that he had soon spent time at every one of them and was coming around for a second go. Figuring that he had little to lose and that prison was now his world, Johnny decided he would live in it however he pleased. As well as being both verbally and physically confrontational when he felt the need arose, Johnny also increased his legal load and set up in business as a jailhouse lawyer willing to take on any case. He didn't exactly hang a shingle outside his cell but he did get plenty of business and earned a regular few quid from winning cases. Johnny also became well known for his propensity to 'hang one up', and this upset the system much more than any of his legal writs.

'Hanging one up' is prison slang for going on a dirty protest, and Johnny developed it into an art. The dirty protest, as far as I can ascertain, was originated by IRA prisoners in the Maze prison in the seventies. It involves covering your cell and, in many cases, yourself in your own shit and then adding a fresh coat to it over a period of time. Its purpose is to shock and disgust your captors, stop them from laying hands on you in any way and to cause as much aggravation for them as is humanly possible. When a prisoner is on a dirty protest his cell has to be sealed, with him in it, and only opened to pass in meals and offer medical treatment. The screws who handle this have to get suited up in bio-hazard gear at least three or four times a day and are paid an extra allowance. No matter how much yellow hazard tape you put over the cracks in a cell door, the smell will always find its way out. The cells on either side of a prisoner on a dirty protest have to be kept empty for health reasons, which costs the prison two spaces for as long as it lasts, and the whole block in which the protest is taking place becomes a stench-filled hell to work in. The screws hate it, the prison service hates the expense of it, and this made Johnny love it. He would hang one up at the slightest excuse and stay with it for as long as it took for the system to meet his demands. Though Johnny doesn't hold the record for the longest dirty protest in the English prison system – that dubious honour belongs to another London robber, Ronnie Easterbrooke, who did it for eighteen months in 1993–4 in HMP Whitemoor – he does come a strong second with over six months at HMP Full Sutton. That's a long time to be covered in shit. Even if it is your own.

As well as handling claims for other prisoners, Johnny was also not shy about making his own and was always on the look-out for breaches of safety by HMP to exploit. One evening in HMP Long Lartin, in Worcestershire, he noticed that one of the strip-lights in one of the narrow corridors on the wing had blown and not been replaced. This put a part of the windowless hall in shadow, and this gave Johnny an idea. He got someone to go and report the lack of lighting but made sure to point him in the direction of the laziest screw on the wing, who Johnny knew would simply mark it up in the works repair book but not actually get on the phone and report it as of any urgency. Then he walked down the darkened space with his water jug and managed to 'accidentally' spill some water in the shadows. Not long after that Johnny happened to be passing that exact spot when he slipped on the wet floor and fell, injuring his back and causing the medics to be called to stretcher him down to the hospital wing. Johnny's 'bad back' kept him in bed for two weeks and, as he mentioned on his claim form, he was still getting painful twinges months after the accident.

He claimed £4,900 in damages, citing the prison's failure in its duty of care by not replacing a light bulb that had been reported as out. He claimed that the lack of light in the corridor meant that he could not see that the floor was wet and this had resulted in his injury. The case dragged on for over a year and, as part of their defence, the Home Office issued Johnny with a floor plan of the part of the prison where he said the accident had occurred, their aim being to show that there were more than enough light fittings around the spot and that replacing one light would not have made much difference. In the meantime, Johnny was on the move again, to HMP Whitemoor, in Cambridgeshire.

HMP Whitemoor is now probably one of the most secure prisons in the system, but back in 1994, soon after it opened, the lax attitude by staff there led to a spectacular escape from the Special Secure Unit, a prison within the prison that houses the most dangerous double and triple category A men. Five IRA prisoners and a London robber managed to smuggle in handguns, ammunition and enough Semtex to blow up the entire jail. They cut their way through four security fences before being picked up on CCTV scaling the perimeter wall. As the screws rushed to stop them, they were shot at by the escapees, two screws being hit and requiring hospitalization for gunshot wounds. The escapees were eventually over-powered just outside the prison. This escape had far-reaching consequences for the prison system as a whole and for Whitemoor in particular. The result was that Whitemoor staff became the most security-conscious in the entire prison system, and it has never suffered an escape since. This was where Johnny landed in the middle of his case against Long Lartin.

A couple of days after reaching Whitemoor Johnny's cell was spun, given a routine security search. This was at a time when screws had just been given the right to search through prisoners' personal paperwork, so they had a good old mooch through Johnny's legal papers. When they found the floor plan for the wing at Long Lartin, it was like they had been goosed with an electric cattle-prod. This was obviously some sort of plan to escape from a top-security dispersal prison, the floor plan the starting point. Already paranoid to the point of dementia, the Whitemoor security department flew into action. Instead of asking Johnny where he had got the document – he could have explained that it was issued by the Home Office – they immediately upgraded his security category to double A and ordered up an emergency police escort, including helicopter. The first Johnny knew of this was when the door of the holding cell, where prisoners were put as their cells were searched, was flung open and he was faced with ten jump-suited security screws and a governor. The governor quickly read from a form. 'During a routine security search of your cell, certain items were discovered that give rise to security concerns. As a result you have been upgraded from category A to High Risk category A. You are now being transferred.' Before he had a chance to protest, Johnny was being frog-marched down to reception and double-cuffed. He was then loaded on to an armoured prison transport, and when the vehicle exited the prison gates, it was picked up by two similar vehicles, one in front and one behind, two Range Rovers filled with machine-gun-toting police officers, and a police helicopter, which followed the journey from the air. Johnny had no idea what it was all about but he suddenly knew where Franz Kafka had been coming from.

The transport hit the outskirts of south London and then HMP Belmarsh, where the escort was waved through the gates without delay and sped to the centre of the prison and the Special Security Unit. Here Johnny was unloaded and taken through the airlocks into the most secure unit in Europe, usually used to house international terrorists and the most influential and dangerous prisoners in captivity. It was two weeks before he was actually told why he had been brought to the Belmarsh SSU, and then he could scarcely believe what he was hearing. He tried explaining that it was actually the prison authorities themselves who had given him the floor plan but his explanation fell on deaf ears. When the prison system makes up its collective mind on something it will not be persuaded against it by anyone as inconsequential as a prisoner. There had to be a full investigation, and that was just the way of it. So Johnny settled into the SSU and stayed there for the next five months until the investigation had tracked down where the paperwork had come from.

It has been medically proven that the ultra-high security inside HMPs' SSUs causes mental and physical deterioration in its denizens. The psychological trauma that results from being watched twenty-four hours a day, seven days a week, sometimes for years, is deep, and even after only five months of it, Johnny was starting to feel the strain. Visits from friends and family are made very difficult, with anyone who wishes to visit having to be security vetted and interviewed by police intelligence operatives who often refuse to pass the would-be visitor, without explanation. So when he was eventually cleared by the prison-service investigation, Johnny wasn't even bothered that they offered him no apology for their over-reaction. He was just glad to get back to the normal restrictions of a single category A.

Though he was completely exonerated, Johnny was informed that he could never again go back to Long Lartin due to the 'unique knowledge' he had gained during his possession of the floor plan. But we have an old truism in prison: how can you tell when the prison system is lying? You can see their lips move. And less than a year after leaving Belmarsh SSU, Johnny was back at Long Lartin. While he had been in the SSU, he had lost his claim against Long Lartin for the back 'injury' he sustained there. Johnny put it down to the fact that he couldn't appear in person to explain his case, and he was now gunning for a claim on the governor of Long Lartin once again.

The handful of dispersal prisons in this country are very violent places, which should be obvious given the fact that they are used to house dangerous and violent offenders in close proximity to each other. Long Lartin in the early 2000s was a particularly violent jail, mainly due to the influx of young black 'gangsters' from cities like Manchester, Birmingham and London. These youngsters are even more brutal and violent than the traditional dangerous prisoners of the past and most of them are serving massive sentences for casual and senseless murders committed outside. Usually their crimes involve spraying thousands of rounds from automatic weapons because somebody trod on their toe in a disco or looked at them funny in a fried-chicken outlet. Once in prison, these kids re-form their gangs and carry on the wars they began outside, only with makeshift knives and coshes instead of guns – so Long Lartin started being called Stab City.

The vast amount of stabbings within the dispersal system began to worry the prison authorities. They didn't really give a shit about cons stabbing each other, but when the screws' union started demanding stab-proof vests for their members before they would work in these war zones, things were getting out of hand. The governor of Long Lartin, the worst-hit jail, decided that he would close down all areas in which prisoners had previously been allowed to congregate in large numbers, and this included the sportsfield exercise area, where the majority of stabbings took place. In order to gauge the mood of the cons before taking such a step, the governor issued each prisoner with a copy of a memo stating his intentions and citing thirty-odd stabbing incidents and the seizure of over sixty bladed implements in the three months leading up to the decision. Reading this memo gave Johnny an idea for a claim, and it was one that could eventually take him all the way to the House of Lords.

The governor's memo and the issuing of Long Lartin screws with stab-proof vests was all the proof that Johnny needed that, contrary to the Human Rights Act, the system was putting his life in danger by holding him in such an environment. He demanded the right to be able to purchase his own stab-proof vest from the prison canteen, and when this was refused he got working on the writ. His case got a mention in the local papers, and then in the nationals, and pretty soon Johnny had the backing of expert prison-law specialists who agreed with his very cogent argument and offered to help. Soon Shotgun Johnny, East End gunman and pain in the arse to the British prison system, was something of a *cause célèbre*, with those at the very top of the legal profession rushing to offer opinions on his case. When the case came to court, it was argued long and hard by the Treasury solicitors, appearing for the Crown, that to issue violent prisoners with stab-proof vests was tantamount to inviting anarchy into our prisons. Johnny's argument was that anarchy was already well ensconced in prison and he just wanted the right to protect himself from it. It was very close, but the judge ruled in favour of the Crown and refused the prisoners the right to stab-proof vests despite the vast amount of evidence that prisoners' lives were in danger. Johnny and his now large legal team appealed to the High Court. He expects to win his case at the High Court, but if he doesn't he's fully prepared to go to the highest court in the land and appeal to the House of Lords. One way or another, Johnny is determined to get a result, and if he doesn't, then it won't be for want of trying.

I'm happy to say that in some respects the years have mellowed Shotgun Johnny, and he is no longer the ruthless, cold-blooded gunman he once was. It is education that has been responsible for whatever small steps Johnny has made towards rehabilitation. When we were at Whitemoor together Johnny showed me a couple of short stories he had written and I encouraged him to stop fucking about and brought him to work on the prison magazine with me. He learnt to love writing and took to it with the same zeal he had put into suing the system. He purchased a typewriter, and in the last couple of years he has taken and passed a feature-writing course with the London School of Journalism and regularly contributes articles and features to many publications. In 2004 he was assessed for and accepted by the experimental Dangerous and Severe Personality Disorder unit at HMP Whitemoor, where he is receiving treatment and therapeutic intervention for his problems. He is still a category A prisoner and has another three years left to serve. How his life will pan out is anyone's guess, but one thing is certain – when he gets out this time, he will not be the same man who came to prison all those years ago. None of us is.

11. The Little Firm – Have Guns Will Travel

The Little Firm was a gang of south London robbers who operated in the eighties, so called because of the stature of the four main members of the gang, none of whom was over five foot eight. Working in a gang can have its advantages, the main ones being you can go for the bigger targets and nobody wants to fuck with you. There's definitely safety in numbers, especially when you all have guns in your hands. The disadvantages, though, are the short shares when you nick a mediocre prize and the fact that the more criminal egos you put together, the more personality clashes. There is no doubt whatsoever that the Little Firm was a danger to the public, but when the members started to fall out with each other, they were more of a danger to themselves. To say this gang were prolific at the robbery game is like saying that Boris Yeltsin liked the odd vodka: they were almost non-stop, and that's what led to their downfall. That, and their quick addiction to class A drugs and adrenaline.

The acknowledged leader of the Little Firm was a fella from Glasgow called, appropriately enough, Little Andy. Andy was a good pal of mine and I knew him years before he formed the firm and went to war on financial institutions everywhere. Before coming to settle in south London in 1981, Andy had already served a three-year sentence for armed robbery in his native Glasgow and had left the city to try and make a new start. Unfortunately for Andy, he landed in an area where there were more thieves and robbers per square mile than anywhere else in the world apart from Rio. In his book *Crime in London* the author Gilbert Kelland says that in the eighties almost

92 per cent of armed robberies committed in the whole of England were carried out by men from one small part of south London. That's a pretty amazing statistic – nothing to be proud of, but pretty amazing nonetheless. Some areas produce great sportsmen, politicians or shopkeepers, but south London is bandit country.

Little Andy started hanging around one of the pubs where a lot of the local criminal fraternity congregated and was soon accepted by almost everyone. He was a typical Glasgow hard man despite, or maybe because of, his height and would fight anyone at the drop of a hat with no hard feelings afterwards. In those days it was all about drink. Everyone wanted to get smashed off their face every night, and drugs were not acceptable, except maybe the odd spliff and line of speed. And speed was only tolerated because it helped you drink more. Coke was still a rich man's drug at £60 a gram (compared to £8 for a gram of speed) and though we had vaguely heard of heroin, none of us knew anyone who had taken it. Andy fitted right in and started to get involved in a lot of the criminality that was going on. He became a pretty good 'kiter', able to work the stolen chequebook and card turn with a lot of panache. He was always well dressed, usually in a nice suit, expensive shoes and a cashmere overcoat, and he loved a bit of tom, particularly thin, understated gold watches and diamond rings. The word 'dapper' immediately springs to mind when I think of Little Andy back then.

Once he was established on the south London criminal scene, Little Andy was a regular in the various clubs and pubs where the leering law-breakers would spend their ill-gotten, and he picked up a lot of work. He would buy clean chequebooks and cards that were stolen either on burglaries, dips or direct from hooky postmen who were supposed to be delivering them, and would pay the standard £5 per page. The average chequebook had thirty-two pages, each with a cash limit of around £50 with the card that accompanied them, so Andy would pay £160 for a brand-new book and card. Then, over a couple of days, he would go through the large shopping centres using the cheques to buy goods to the value of £1,600. He would then sell the goods at half-price for a quick sale and end up with around £800, a profit of £640 on each book. Of course it didn't always turn out like that. Sometimes you could lose the book to a suspicious shopkeeper after the first hit, and in those cases you just had to swallow and take it, which is why Andy, like most kiters, would often get the books on bail and pay the supplier out of the proceeds. But Little Andy looked the part and rarely lost a sheet. He would also take advance orders for goods that he was going to kite. If you wanted a new kettle, say, or some clothes for your nippers, then you would just tell Andy what you needed and where he might find them and he would be back, usually the same day, with your goods for half the price you would have paid in the shops. It was a lucrative business, and Andy was coining it.

Andy was mustard at working the restaurants, and he would often take a crowd of us out for a meal after the pub. We'd order wine, beer and spirits and as much food as we wanted and then Andy would pay for the lot with one of his bent cards, always making sure to tell the waiter to take a £10 tip and just put it on the card. The waiters in all the late-night gaffs loved him for it and were always very welcoming whenever he turned up. They knew the cards were bent but they didn't give a shit because their money was guaranteed by the insurance company. He would sometimes do night runs on dodgy credit cards he didn't think would pass in the daytime. He would be driven around London and the suburbs in a car with false number plates, stopping at the all-night petrol garages and buying cigarettes and tobacco for resale the next day. At night there was no number that the cashiers could ring to check if the card was kosher, so they would normally swallow and hand over the cartons. Andy couldn't drive and didn't want to learn, so his driver always earned a nice few quid for very little work. Andy was well loved by almost everyone, except the insurance companies.

But Little Andy wasn't all sweetness and light. He had a terrible temper on him and loved to fight. One night, outside a pub in Clapham, he got into an argument with one of his best pals, the German, who was also my cousin. The fight that ensued can only be described as epic. The two little men fought up and down Clapham High Street for almost an hour. They were evenly matched in height, weight and determination to win. At one stage a passing police patrol car pulled up. At the cry of 'Old Bill!', both Andy and the German immediately ceased hostilities and wrapped their arms around each other's shoulders as though they were best mates having a mess-about, which deep down they really were. The coppers, seeing nothing that they could get a nicking out of, had to move on. And the two boys broke their temporary truce and steamed into each other again. In the end the German, after a particularly damaging butt to the face from Little Andy's head, decided to end it by resorting to the use of a weapon. He slipped off one of his shoes, a sturdy lace-up Oxford with cleats on the heel and smashed it over Andy's head several times until the latter lost consciousness and slid to the pavement in a pool of blood. The German's use of a non-sanctioned weapon was considered bad form by the watching fight fans, but Little Andy, when discussing the evening's festivities with the German over a pint the next day, had no problem with it. As far as he was concerned, a good fight was a good fight, and that was that.

Andy had a younger brother named Chick, who was still in Glasgow, and as the money was flowing in, he decided to invite Chick down to the Smoke for a little holiday. Chick was a nice fella, and we took him out and showed him the sights and a general good time. One of the pubs we frequented at this time was the Swan, in Stockwell and, though it is probably perfectly respectable these days, it was then a kip. A lot of pimps and prostitutes from nearby Brixton used to get in there in the evenings, though they mostly kept to their own corner and didn't bother the mainly Irish and Scottish crowd. One night we were in the Swan with Chick when, in his naivety, he thought he was getting the eye from one of the scantily dressed women in the corner. He started chatting her up while we watched, greatly amused that he hadn't twigged that she was a prostitute and he could dispense with the chit-chat and just wave a tenner under her nose. Chick thought he was doing great and wasn't amused when her pimp, a very large black man with a shiny bald head and a mouthful of gold, offered to sort things out for them if Chick had the dollars. Chick, seeing this as an insult to himself and a slur on the character of the young lady in question, replied by punching the pimp right in the snoot. The pimp got off the floor and thought about retaliating then and there, but he heard the scraping of many chairs as several villainous faces close by stood up and got ready for action, and this changed his mind. So we sat back down again. The pimp, his pride in tatters and his nose all bent, shouted a bit of patois about us all being 'blood clots' or some such, and then marched out of the pub.

We all had a good laugh at what had occurred and were still chuckling fifteen minutes later when the pimp strode back into the bar with an axe in his hand and a mission in his stride. Before anyone could react, he had buried the blade of his axe in Chick's neck, pulled it free in a shower of blood, and was lining up his next blow. But he never got a chance to complete his second swing, as he was hit by the weight of many bodies and dropped his axe. Little Andy rushed to his fallen brother and, seeing the amount of blood coming from his neck, thought he was dead. Spotting the dropped axe on the carpet, he grabbed it and went after the pimp. The now panicking pimp managed to fight his way out of the side door of the pub and ran around to the busy Clapham Road. By now he was being pursued by a crowd led by Little Andy, who was waving the bloody axe in the air intent on decapitation. Nothing else would do. The pimp, in desperation to be away, ran straight out into the busy four-lane road. He might have made it to the other side if the traffic hadn't been so heavy, but I have no doubt he wouldn't have made it much further than the opposite pavement before Andy caught him. The pimp was destined to die that night, one way or another. Death came in the form of a Range Rover travelling at nearly 70 mph. He was thrown into the air and flew about thirty feet before crashing into the road head first. He was stone dead. Little Andy, not to be denied his vengeance, reached the broken body of the pimp and raised his arm to give him a whack with the axe, but he was pulled away and held by the now satisfied mob.

Chick, thanks to the quick reactions of the bar staff, who staunched the blood with bar towels and quickly phoned an ambulance, survived with nothing more than a nasty scar, though it was touch and go for a while. Little Andy was arrested for murder, but with so many witnesses willing to testify for him the charge was duly reduced to manslaughter and he was released on bail. Over the next two years Little Andy had two trials on the manslaughter charge, and each time the jury could not agree on a verdict. He remained on bail for the whole of this time and kept working at the kiting game.

No matter how skilful and careful you are when committing crime, if you make it your living, then it's inevitable you are going to have to suffer a nicking sooner or later. The best you can really hope for is a decently long run and to make enough money to see you through the lean times. But Little Andy wasn't prepared when it came to his turn to have his collar felt. The trouble was that, though he was a big earner, he was also a big spender and never more than £50 in front of his last score. So when he was stopped in a car outside Catford shopping centre in possession of six chequebooks and cards all in different names and a boot and backseat full of fraudulently purchased goods, it wasn't good news for the little Scotsman. Typically for Andy, he gave his driver the out, telling police that he had merely hired him for the day and that he knew nothing about any illegal acts. Charged with fraud and deception, Little Andy had no option but to stick his hand up. While he was on remand in Brixton prison the prosecution in the manslaughter case offered him a deal whereby if he pleaded guilty to the manslaughter charge, they would press for a maximum sentence of three years' imprisonment. Andy weighed it up. On the one hand, he had been lucky with the juries on his first two trials and he could take the chance that he would get lucky on the third trial. If they couldn't agree on a verdict again, then the Crown would have to drop the case. On the other hand, if he was found guilty by the next jury, he could quite easily get a life sentence. He agreed to accept the three years. Soon after, he appeared at Inner London Crown Court, where he was sentenced to two years for the fraud charges, concurrent, and sent to HMP Wandsworth to serve his sentence.

In prison Little Andy got involved in the drug scene and spent what little money he had left on hash, pills and then heroin. At this time he didn't get hooked on heroin because he could never afford enough of it to get a habit, but pills were very cheap and he left jail with a Valium and Mogodon craving that he didn't have when he went in. The world had moved on by the time Andy got out and the people he used to buy his chequebooks from were either nicked themselves, doing other things or working with new buyers, so he was out in the cold and facing the prospect of starting again. Like a lot of career criminals who have spent a bit of time parked up in prison, Little Andy felt as though he had time to make up, and he became willing to cut corners. One of the drug contacts he had made in Wandsworth came from the sprawling council estates of Tulse Hill and said there might be a bit of work available if Andy was willing to up his game. So Andy went to the area and met up with a fella named Mark whose family is well known in south London crime circles. Mark had a contact who was selling a couple of guns, and his plan was to buy them and put together a crew for a bit of armed robbery. After about two minutes thinking about this offer to get in on the ground floor, Andy accepted. And the Little Firm was formed.

Along with Andy and Mark in the new robbery crew were Burt, another south London boy with big ambitions, and Tony, a good wheelman who could heft a shooter and double as a frightener if the need arose. These four were the nucleus of the gang, but there were also several other characters who were in and out for various bits of work over the next couple of years. The Firm's first hit was on a bank in Clapham High Street and, with Andy and Mark wielding sawn-off shotguns, Burt collecting the money and Tony driving the get-away car, they cleared around twenty grand. From then on, it was happy days, and the gang was out working most weeks. They were not that choosy and would rob anything that looked as though it might provide a few quid – banks, post offices, building societies, jewellers' and supermarkets all made it on to their list of targets, and they didn't stick to London either, often travelling out in all directions looking for places to rob. One week they would be blagging a jeweller's in Devon, the next hitting a bank in Coventry. They were modern motorized bandits.

You would think that, with the amount of blags they were doing, they would be flush with money and be able to give it a rest now and then, but the more money the Little Firm nicked, the more they spent. They loved to party, and champagne and cocaine were big on their menu for a typical evening out. Money was easy to get for these boys, so they considered it their duty to spend it in the same way. At the height of Thatcher's culture of greed and consumerism, the Little Firm truly was living the dream.

As they became more proficient at their trade and started building a rep in the underworld as serious pavement merchants, they began to be approached by people touting work. For robbers, the tout is a good source of information. They are usually straight-goers or people on the fringes of crime who maybe drink in the same pubs as the serious criminals and know they can earn themselves a nice chunk of change by offering up information on possible targets. It is usual for robbery firms to pay a 10 per cent 'finder's fee' to touts who come up with the goods, which can be a decent reward for very little work and practically no risk. One such tout who came to the Little Firm was a kid who did his YTS in an insurance and loan firm and informed the boys that there was a stack of money in the counting room of the business every Friday afternoon awaiting collection by a security firm. The boys took a look at the kid's job and it seemed easy, but they weren't able to establish exactly how much the take would be. All the kid could say was that there was 'loads of money', more than he had ever seen before except in films. The boys had a free Friday afternoon coming up and decided to spend it nicking 'loads of money' from the loans company.

On the following Friday afternoon they burst into the office, sawn-offs at the ready, and got the startled security manager to open the counting room. On a table there they found the money laid out in little piles ready for tallying and bagging. Burt swept it into the bag they had brought along specifically for the purpose while Andy kept Mark covered as he handcuffed the five staff together and then secured them to a radiator before the gang made its get-away. Later, at the flop, when they counted the take, it came to just over £7,000, which, to the kid who'd put the work up, must have seemed like a fortune, but it was peanuts to the Little Firm. They had to go out again that afternoon and hit a bank in order to bump their take up. They gave the kid a grand for his whack and he was over the fucking moon. The Milky Bars were definitely on him that night.

The Little Firm was hitting the odd security van but only robbing the guards of pony-bags, which didn't go far among four of them, and they were anxious to get into the really big money that came from taking a whole van over and cleaning it out. To this end, they were in the market for a .22 long-case rifle, which was one of the few things that could pierce the toughened security glass on the vans' windows and allow them an opening to get inside. They managed to hire a .22 Remington at great expense, although the owner wouldn't sell it at any price as he was in the same game and doing quite well thank you. They plotted up on a security van that was picking up from many major supermarkets around north London and was carrying nearly £2 million by the end of its route. The job was planned meticulously, and a lot of money had been laid out for expenses, such as several get-away cars and vans to cart the money away in, the .22 hire and the rental of a derelict bit of land with a large outbuilding where they could take the security van for clearing. This was going to be the Little Firm's Big One, and they were well up for it.

They brought the security van to a halt in a quiet sidestreet by sandwiching it between two old Transit vans. Then Burt scrambled up the back of the security vehicle and on to its roof with a pair of bolt-croppers and cut the communications aerial so that the guards couldn't radio a distress signal. Andy wielded the .22 and put a hole in the windscreen, then stepped back and picked up his sawn-off as another member of the firm widened the bullet hole with a couple of swings with the pointed end of a pick-axe. Once the hole was wide enough, Mark stuck the barrels of his shotgun into it and threatened to give the two guards inside both barrels unless they opened the passenger door. The guards, realizing that if the triggers were pulled they would both be cut to ribbons by the hot lead shot ricocheting around the small cab, immediately complied and opened the door. All of this took less than two minutes and, to all intents and purposes, the ruthless robbery gang now had a security van containing £2 million. And this was where they lost it.

In the rush to get inside the van, Andy had wrenched the passenger door back with some force, buckling the hinges. He and Mark jumped up into the cab, sticking their shotguns in the faces of the terrified guards and shouting threats. Once they saw that the guards were completely cowed, they ordered the driver to start the engine and follow the vehicle in front, which was to be driven by Tony and would lead them to the unloading point. Unfortunately, one of the fail-safes in the security van's system was that the engine would not start until all doors were securely shut. The driver quickly explained this and told the robbers to shut the passenger door through which they had entered the cab or the van couldn't move. Andy reached over and tried to close the door, but it was so badly bent it wouldn't close all the way. A moment of panic ensued, but Andy, leaving Mark covering the guards, jumped out of the vehicle and tried to force the door. He shouldered it, pushed it and gave it several hefty kicks, but it was going nowhere. By now a crowd of onlookers was starting to gather on the pavement and Tony was honking the horn of the lead van and revving his engine impatiently. Andy put his shotgun down on the road and gave it one last superhuman effort to close the door, but it just wouldn't latch.

The Little Firm knew it was beaten – they couldn't push or

tow the van away, and there was no way it was moving with the door open. But determined not to leave empty-handed, Andy climbed back into the cab and ordered the guards to open the security door behind them which led into the back, where the money was. If they couldn't take the whole van, they could at least take as much as they could carry. The driver, already shit-scared and fearing for his life, now had to inform these two masked and armed men that another security feature of the van was that the door into the back would not open. This too depended on the cab doors being firmly locked. When they heard this, Andy and Mark turned the air in the crowded cab blue with curses. But they knew there was nothing to be done. The best they could hope to salvage now was an escape without being nicked. Without bothering to make their excuses, they left.

The failure to get the prize from the security van was a bit disheartening after all the planning they had put into it, but at least the gang now knew that the MO was a good one. And next time they wouldn't be careless enough to damage the door. They renewed their efforts to purchase a rifle of their own, and pretty soon they had two. One was a Remington six-shot semi-automatic .22, which was perfect, and they bought it from a couple of tea-leafs who had a habit of breaking into the homes of the hunting and fishing set and stealing antiques and any firearms that happened to be lying around. They were also approached by a junkie who sold them a proper sniper's rifle he had lifted from the boot of a Bentley in a hotel car park in the West End. It was a professional piece of kit and can only have belonged to a serious hunter or an assassin. It was just like the ones you see on the films – broken down into several components and all slotted into a foam-lined aluminium briefcase. The telescopic sight could be adjusted for night shooting and the ammunition was 7.62 full metal jackets. This was a gun that was made for no purpose other than to kill things, of that there was no doubt. The junkie wanted a monkey for it, and the ammunition was probably worth more than that, but the boys knew he was clucking and beat him down to £250. This was a bargain that would lead to their downfall.

By now, drug-taking was coming second only to robbing on the Little Firm's daily agenda. First LSD, then heroin and crack cocaine, or 'freebase', as it was known in those days, became the drug of choice for these thrill-seeking desperados. The more drugs they took, the more erratic they became and the more arguments they had. Little Andy had taken to slipping off and doing robberies on his own – small building societies and television rental shops being his favourites for quick cash – and the rest of the crew formed loose associations with other freelance robbers for one-off jobs. The drugs were also making Little Andy paranoid and reckless. One night, in a pub in Brixton, he got into an argument with a barman and went back with his shotgun, and stood on the pavement outside and blew out every window in the building, reloading several times before he was satisfied. Towards the end, he wouldn't go anywhere without a black leather sports bag loaded with two sawn-off twelve-bores and enough ammunition to blow out all the lights on Oxford Street. But he was still working, and when not acting as an 'enforcer' in internecine criminal disputes, he was robbing regularly.

One night he turned up at my place and offered me five grand to come with him to a police station on the London– Essex border where his brother-in-law was being held, having been nicked at an airport with eighteen kilos of heroin in his luggage. I needed the money so agreed to go and help Andy break the fella out. Armed to the teeth and dressed in black, I drove us over to the place and we plotted up in a park across from the police station, drinking beer from the can and preparing the guns for what was to be a full-frontal assault.

Back in south London he had said that it was a little country police station with about four coppers on duty at night. We would just mask up, walk in the front door and take over, locking the coppers in their own cells and walking out with the brother-in-law. But when we got to the gaff it was busier than West End Central, with vanloads of cozzers in and out all the time. I expressed some misgivings about Andy's planned assault on Precinct Thirteen, but he was so full of class A drugs that he was touting it as 'a good laugh' and one up on the filth. The more I looked at this job, the more I didn't like it – I mean, five grand's OK for putting a scare into Dixon of Dock Green, but it's peanuts when you are going up against a station full of SPG. It was almost dawn before I managed to convince Andy that it was a suicide mission, but he finally saw sense, thank fuck. On the drive home he fell asleep and looked very peaceful slumped there in the passenger seat, apart from the loaded shotgun still clutched in his hand.

The Little Firm, despite their differences, was planning another Big One and already had a security van in mind, but they were also doing their bread-and-butter jobs as well. One late afternoon in October 1987 they were driving back from a job in Surrey when they were ambushed by the Flying Squad at the entrance to the estate in Tulse Hill where they lived. They had just robbed a supermarket, and in the get-away car the cops found three loaded guns, masks and a large bag of cash. The boys didn't put up a fight, which was just as well, as they were surrounded by thirty armed coppers. It turned out that the police had had them under surveillance for a couple of months and knew a lot about them. The junkie who had sold them the sniper's rifle and been jibbed out of his full price had been nicked for something unconnected and put the Little Firm up as bargaining chips. And now their reign had come to an end.

Andy, Mark and Burt and their new driver, who had only

driven on the last robbery, were charged with several counts of armed robbery and possession of firearms. They were all remanded in custody in different London prisons in order to make it difficult for them to concoct any cohesive defence between them. This is standard procedure when the police nick criminal gangs. Andy ended up in HMP Pentonville, in north London, but he didn't plan on sticking around for his trial.

Pretending to settle in and accept his lot, Little Andy managed to get hold of a digging implement, and over Easter weekend he dug a hole through the wall of his cell. Pentonville is a Victorian prison and, back in the eighties, before it was thoroughly renovated, the brickwork of its walls was old and crumbled easily. In the middle of the night, Andy, using a rope made of plaited sheets, crawled through the hole and climbed down three storeys to the ground. He then scaled the perimeter wall using another rope and rudimentary grapple and found himself above the Governor's garden. Deciding to work his way around to a better dropping spot, Andy balanced along the top of the wall but was spotted by one of the guard patrols inside the prison. When the cry of alarm went up, Andy was startled and fell from the wall. The good news was that he fell outside the prison, but the bad news was that he shattered his right leg in the fall and became almost unconscious with shock and pain. The screws found Andy trying to crawl away from the jail, leaving a trail of blood behind him from his ruined leg. He spent the next six weeks in traction in Whittington hospital and then three months in the hospital wing in HMP Wandsworth. For the rest of his life he walked with a bad limp.

Faced with the overwhelming evidence of their misdoings, the Little Firm decided to plead guilty and hope for a bit of a result on the sentencing. They knew they were looking at double figures and were prepared. In Court Two at the Old

Bailey the boys received a total of forty-three and a half years between the four of them. Andy and Mark got thirteen years each, Burt got ten, and Chrissy, the unlucky get-away driver who hadn't earned a penny from his crime, got seven and a half. The newspapers made a meal of the Firm, and the financial institutions and cashiers breathed a sigh of relief. The boys themselves went off to Parkhurst to serve their bit of sparrow.

In 1996, in Parkhurst hospital, months away from the end of his sentence, Little Andy was diagnosed with cancer. He died a few days after being granted compassionate parole. Mark never managed to kick his drug habit and has been in and out of prison a few times since completing his thirteen years, but always for petty crime. I recently had a letter from him saying he was in rehab, but it didn't last long and he's now back on his toes again. As far as I know, both Burt and Chrissy have settled down and no longer have anything to do with crime. Good for them.

The Little Firm, like all armed robbers, were ruthless and dangerous men who caused a lot of grief and terror to innocent people. But they got their comeuppance in the end. We all do.

12. The Laughing Bank Robbers

Andy was originally from Tooting Broadway, south-west London, and was one of those geezers who grew up cheering for the baddies at Saturday-morning pictures. Even as a kid he knew what he wanted to be – a criminal – and he was to achieve his ambition. Andy had a fiery temper and it was said that he could start a fight in an empty house, and that he often did, just to keep himself amused. He was the kind of fella who never did things by halves, and one of my memories of working with him is him suggesting, in all seriousness, that we should purchase a box of British Army hand-grenades that had come on to the market because 'they will be handy for launching at police cars if we get a chase!' I've never had any great love for Old Bill, but even I drew the line at fragging the bastards with high explosives. To Andy it was simple: no police car behind you equals no jail. Despite this, he wasn't a totally ruthless man, just a bit of a lunatic.

In the mid-eighties Andy teamed up with a north London bandit called Curley, and they pulled off a series of heists around Central London. Hitting targets in places like Park Lane, Regent Street and Shaftesbury Avenue is a very high-risk business for any robber as Old Bill absolutely smothers those areas with its presence. If you live on a high-crime estate outside Central London, you'll be lucky to see a copper from one week to the next, but stick a few rich businesses and a bunch of tourists on your manor and the police will be crawling all over you in no time at all. So robbing on a patch like Central London is not for the nervous type. Another disadvantage is that there is nowhere to park the get-away car without attracting the attention of wardens in about two minutes flat. Getting a £60 penalty notice on some old ringer that you are only going to burn out anyway as soon as the job is done is no drama, but having it lifted on to a low-loader and carried off to the pound while you are in robbing the jug can be a bit of a fucking nuisance. A lot of robbers avoid Central London for bread-and-butter robberies and only hit there if it's absolutely necessary – or to snaffle the odd pony-bag using a motorbike as transport.

The one advantage in targeting Central London is the fact that the banks do massive amounts of business and therefore the prize can be bigger than a similar bank outside the hub. And this is what attracted Andy and Curley. They were traditional walk-in robbers who worked on spec and usually got away with till money rather than robbing the vault. Still, a good four minutes' work could earn them up to ten grand, which wasn't to be sneezed at back in the eighties. The boys did a few nice bits of work, never having to fire a shot and earning enough to keep them in the manner to which they had quickly become accustomed, but Old Bill was not happy that a couple of upstarts were playing on their hallowed patch and put an extra bit of effort into their manhunt. Rewards were offered for the capture of Andy and Curley, and pretty soon someone decided to collect. The boys were arrested by armed police as they were plotting up outside their next job and they were captured in situ with masks and guns.

At their trial at the Old Bailey they were found guilty of armed robbery and possession of firearms. Both boys had a long list of previous convictions, but whereas Andy's were for the normal kind of stuff – TDA, GBH, burglary and theft – Curley, it turned out, had a bit of a darker past that his crime partner had known nothing about. While still a juvenile, Curley had been involved in a robbery in which a security guard had been killed. Curley had been given three years' detention for manslaughter. He'd been done on what the law calls 'joint enterprise', which is where all criminals in a team can be held guilty for whatever crime is committed by one of their number while the others are present. The law does not have to show any intent by the others, but if one member kills someone, they are all held accountable. As a result of his previous conviction, Curley was sentenced to eleven years' imprisonment, while Andy received ten. A small disparity, but a disparity nonetheless, which shows how even after you have served a sentence for a past crime, the British justice system will keep punishing you for it in little ways.

Andy, due to his aggressive nature and willingness to duke it out with anyone who even looked at him sideways, was assessed as suitable for HMP Albany, a top-security dispersal prison on the Isle of Wight which at that time held the reputation of being the most violent prison in the system. Albany was the dumping ground for the mainly young and cocky serious criminals of that era, and as a result there was an average of three stabbings a week. Andy settled right in. This was where I met him. As fellow south Londoners and armed robbers, we naturally gravitated towards each other in a jail where it was important to have someone to watch your back for you. Andy first helped me out by tipping me the nod that there was a 'hitman' waiting for me on the landing one day. At the time I was involved in a black-market snout-buying business whereby I would, for a small fee, change up cash for tobacco. The going rate in the tobacco–cash exchange was two and a half ounces of tobacco for £10. If anyone smuggled in cash on their visits, I would get them two and a half ounces of snout from my contacts. I would get half an ounce on each deal, and everyone was happy. Then a lifer named Tufty, who was serving a twenty-five-year minimum for shooting a man dead on an aggravated burglary and thought he was the 'daddy' of the wing, decided that the rate should now be two ounces of tobacco for £10. He gathered all the money-dealers and got them to form a cartel so that the two-ounce limit was prison-wide. This was bad news for the money-smugglers and middlemen like me, but most just accepted the new exchange rate with a bit of moaning. I had never got on with Tufty – he was a bit too friendly with the screws for my liking and I classed him as a mug – so I decided to challenge his rule. I went to see a pal of mine, an East End face with plenty of tobacco, and borrowed twelve ounces of snout on bail. I agreed to pay my pal in cash as soon as the money started rolling in. Then I set myself up as a snout-dealer, offering the old rate of two and a half ounces a tenner. As the only one offering the higher rate, naturally everyone came to me to do business.

I did a roaring trade in cash and snout, and it wasn't long before I got a summons from Tufty and his pals. A runner named Gilbert, a right melt from out of Kent who thought he was a gangster because he ran errands for Tufty, turned up at my cell one afternoon and informed me that Tufty wanted to see me down in the laundry room on the ground floor of the wing. It wasn't a request but a demand, and this got my dander up straight away. I smiled coldly at Gilbert. 'Tell Tufty that if he wants to see me, he knows where I live.' And I closed my cell door in Gilbert's sour mooey. I can only imagine Tufty's rage when Gilbert passed on my message. He was the fucking daddy, and I was mugging him off!

Tufty, while brave enough when shooting unarmed home-owners, didn't have the bottle to confront me full on. Instead he waited till the next day and then sent Gilbert up with a request: would I, if I had the time, drop down to the laundry room for a cup of coffee and a chat? I agreed to the meeting and strolled down to Tufty's 'office' for a business meeting. Tufty, like a big fat spider in the centre of his web, greeted me in a friendly manner, and as Gilbert busied himself making the coffee he asked me if I knew how much damage I was doing by offering two and a half ounces for a tenner. I shrugged. 'I don't give a fuck,' I said. 'I'm doing good business. And you know what the score is in a jail like this – survival of the fittest.' Tufty spent twenty minutes trying to convince me of the advantages of joining his two-ounce cartel, and there *were* obvious advantages, but the truth was that I didn't like Tufty and my main motive for undercutting him was pure malice. As I left he started to get a bit lemon and said that my refusal to negotiate would have 'consequences'. I gave him my hard look. 'Mind how you go, Tufty,' was my parting shot.

In top-security jails there is no shortage of lunatics who are willing to do 'hits' for payment. Calling on a hit is as easy as putting the word out that there are drugs or money to be earned; the fruitcakes, desperados and knuckle-draggers will fall over each other in their rush to take the contract. It is relatively cheap, £20 worth of heroin in some jails, to get someone tea-bagged (left with plenty of perforations), but Tufty, being a tight-fisted bastard, decided to use Gilbert for the job on me. Gilbert was only doing five years, for GBH, a relatively short sentence at Albany, and though he looked the part – a big bodybuilder with a good line in war-faces – he can't have been much cop if he was working for a fake like Tufty. I heard about the hit through the grapevine and kept my eyes open for the next few days. Then, one morning, I came in from exercise and was pulled to one side by Andy. He informed me that Gilbert was mooching around up on my landing and he was dressed for action – prison overcoat, gloves, and with several thick magazines strapped around his body. Andy told me he thought he saw a chiv in his hand before he slipped it into his pocket. The prison-hitman kit is easily recognizable to any con with a bit of experience. The overcoat is to stop the hitman's clothes from being splashed with blood: after the hit the coat is bundled up and thrown into a bin, leaving the hitman in a pristine forensic condition when the alarm goes up. The gloves are so that no fingerprints will be left on the chiv, which is usually thrown out of a window after the deed is done. The magazines strapped around the body are in case the victim is armed himself, not unusual in a jail like Albany, and fights back with a blade. Along with his warning, Andy slipped me his own chiv, a sharpened six-inch nail set in a wooden handle, and offered to come upstairs and back me up if I needed it. I was touched by Andy's offer but had to refuse as it would be seen as a weakness if I accepted.

I walked up the stairs and on to the landing and, sure enough, there was Gilbert skulking around as though it was midwinter in the Arctic instead of July on the Isle of Wight. He must have been sweltering in his big greatcoat, with an extra thirty pounds in magazines strapped around him. With Andy's chiv in full view, I walked straight up to him and stared into his eyes. 'You looking for me?' I asked. This wasn't in Gilbert's script – I was supposed to come up the stairs and go to my cell, where he would catch up with me and stick his chiv into my back several times before making his get-away. Now he was fucked. He would either have to pull his weapon and fight it out with me or wipe his mouth and walk away. His bottle now shattered, he chose the latter. 'Yeah, go on, fuck off!' I shouted down the stairs after his scurrying form. 'And tell that other fat cunt he's just declared war!' Andy came up the stairs then and we had a good laugh at the unmanning of Gilbert. From that moment on, Andy and I became an inseparable win-double. He was a good geezer to go two-of-toast with, as not only was he intensely loyal to his mates, he was also a good laugh. After a couple of days shitting himself Tufty decided to change the exchange rate back to two and a half ounces a tenner as it 'wasn't really working out'. But, due to his massive loss of face, hardly anyone would do business with him. The last I heard, he'd had a reduction in his minimum recommendation and got his sentence cut to fifteen years, so he must have been sucking up to the right people somewhere.

Me and Andy went through the next six years and several prisons together before I left him behind when I escaped from an escort on my own. The next time we met was when we were both outside, in 1997. Andy got out a couple of years before me, and he had teamed up with a cannabis-grower turned robber named Tommy. The two were earning a living robbing cannabis-dealers, but times were starting to get a bit lean for them as they began to run out of targets. The dealers they robbed couldn't report them to the police, but they could hire a few heavies to guard their premises so the duo couldn't strike a second time and also to hunt down and punish the perpetrators. Andy and Tommy weren't worried as they had covered their tracks pretty well and were both more than capable of putting up a fight if it came down to it. When I got out I was trying to go straight, just to see what a 'normal' life was all about, though I have to admit my attempt was pretty half-hearted and I was looking for any excuse to get back into the armed-robbery game. I met up with a few of my old mates for a drink and a trip down felony lane, all telling war stories and generally having a laugh. Andy could see that I was struggling to keep interested in my £90-a-week road-sweeping job so he offered to set me up with a lucrative low-risk sideline in selling some of his stolen cannabis. I accepted.

Being a street-level puff-dealer requires a lot of patience, and I soon realized that this was something I was very short of. I would go to work in the morning, sweeping roads on a few south London sink estates, up to my ankles in crack vials and used needles, and then come home in the evening and have to answer the phone up until two in the morning to people looking for £15 or £30 worth of puff. I would tell them to come around and then cut and weigh up their draw before taking the next call. I grew tired of this very quickly, and instead of going through the rigmarole of weighing up, I began biting off chunks of hash that looked about right and taking the money at the door. The puff-heads loved it as they always got over the weight for their money, but I was left short of cash at the end of every week. After four months of trying to go straight (ish), I'd had enough. There was an incident on the job – I assaulted a member of the public – and I decided that the straight life was not for me. I quit and ended up getting in touch with Andy and Tommy and suggesting that we form a crew and get back into the blagging game. The boys were up for it, and pretty soon we had a fourth member in Curley, Andy's old crime partner. We purchased the requisite kit of firearms, masks and cars, using the last of the drug money, and were ready to rock 'n' roll.

Though we all took robbing banks very seriously – after all, it was our job and only source of income – we all had a sense of humour, an essential for surviving years in prison without going mad, and couldn't resist having the odd laugh while going about our business. On the team, I was the gunman, or 'frightener', who would announce our intentions and make sure nobody got ideas about tackling us. It pains me to admit it now, but I was very good at this job and I could absolutely terrify a bank full of customers with just a few words and gestures. Andy was the bagman, collecting and bagging the cash. Curley was the doorman and made sure that anyone who came in during a robbery would be staying in for the duration, and Tommy was our wheelman.

We were all experienced robbers and fell into our roles very easily. Our first job was a bank on Balham High Street, and it went like a dream, except we forgot to bring a bag for the money and about £7,000 ended up on the carpet with me and Andy on our hands and knees scooping it up. We were using a Ford Sierra that I had bought off the side of the street for £350, and after legging it out of the bank and across a busy road Tommy drove us less than a mile through the backstreets to where the second, straight, car was waiting. It was November, and just beginning to snow as we changed cars. We left the Sierra with all of its windows wound down, so as to fuck up any DNA that might have accidentally been left behind, parked badly and made our get-away in the next car.

About a week later, when we were planning our next job, Tommy mentioned that he had come through Balham that morning and had seen our get-away Sierra still parked up with the windows wide open. Andy, who wasn't one for wasting money if it could be helped, suggested that we go down and have the car back to use on our next robbery. He argued that it can't have been sussed as the get-away car or the Old Bill would have had it on a low-loader and into a pound for forensic examination. Therefore, the car must be sweet and we could use it again. I wasn't so sure – maybe it was my paranoia, or the fact that I knew how devious the cops could be in setting traps. But in the end I was swayed by Andy's argument and agreed that we should at least go and have a look at the car. It seemed to be OK, and sitting in Tommy's own motor further up the street, we agreed to toss a coin to see who would go over and drive the Sierra away. Typically, I lost, and it was down to me to get it and drive it back to Croydon. Tommy handed me the keys, which he had taken with him on the day of the robbery. As I approached the abandoned Ford I kept expecting a cry of 'Armed police! Halt!' and for flak-jacketed coppers to start jumping out of gardens all around me. Nothing happened.

The interior of the car was wet and cold and some enterprising tea-leaf, probably one of the local kids, had nicked the radio, leaving a bunch of bare wires hanging in its place, but when I turned the key in the ignition the engine started up first time. The boys pulled out in Tommy's car and tailed me up as I headed for Croydon. I still wasn't 100 per cent convinced that the police hadn't got to the car and I began to imagine they might have planted a tracking device on it, standard operating procedure for C11 (the surveillance squad), and that they were now following and waiting to pounce. Then, at the top of Streatham Hill, the Sierra's engine suddenly cut out. I was sure that it had been cut by a remote device and that now, caught in rush-hour traffic, I would be nicked. But again nothing happened. Andy and Curley jumped out of Tommy's motor and helped me to push the Sierra up on to the pavement, and it was Andy who noticed that it was out of petrol. I took a can from the boot and Tommy dropped me at a nearby garage. Once the Sierra was juiced up, it started and ran perfectly. But, even so, when we got it back to Croydon I went over it with a fine toothcomb looking for bugs or devices. It was clean.

We used the Sierra on a bank job we did on the morning of Christmas Eve and, just for the crack, we bought some of those Santa hats that street traders sell at that time of year and wore them over our ski-masks, wishing everyone in the jug a merry Christmas and ho-ho-ho-ing it all the way to the getaway car. It was this incident that earned us the sobriquet 'the Laughing Bank Robbers' from the Flying Squad. The Sierra was parked up right outside the job, and once again we drove it to the change-over car and then dumped it, this time with the windows secured. We didn't expect the car to last too long as we had left the doors unlocked and the keys in the ignition in an area well-known for its car-thieving, joy-riding youngsters. But two weeks later the Sierra was still sitting there. Maybe it just wasn't up to the usual standards of the local twockers, or maybe they thought it had to be a police set-up, but nobody took it. Criminals are, on the whole, a superstitious bunch, and we were beginning to see the Sierra as our 'lucky' get-away motor. We had used it on two very lucrative robberies and no one had even so much as jotted down the number plate. We knew that it could be tempting fate but we decided to use the car on a third robbery.

The target was a bank in Rosehill, Sutton, and it was on a one-way traffic system, so the best escape was to drive the wrong way up the road and then spin a left into an alley that led to a fence. Beyond the fence lay the car park for St Helier Hospital, where we would have a van parked up and waiting. The idea behind the get-away route was to make it difficult for any following squad cars, just in case they happened upon the blag in progress. The robbery itself went without a hitch, and we came running out of the jug and jumped into the by now familiar Sierra – but it stalled right outside the jug. Tommy turned the key but the engine wouldn't catch. We were sitting there, masked and gunned up, as a crowd of onlookers started to gather on the pavement. Then I heard a police siren in the distance. We would have to abandon the car and make our way to the van on foot, a prospect unattractive to all of us. I had my hand on the door handle when Tommy tried the engine one more time and it burst into a roar. We flew down the one-way street, scattering oncoming traffic, spun left into the alley and traversed it at high speed until we reached the fence. We left the Sierra, engine running, all lights on and all doors swinging wide, and scrambled over the fence. Three minutes later we were lying in the back of a Fiat van on our way back to London as police cars, sirens wailing and blue lights illuminating the gathering twilight, passed us going the other way. This time we would not be going back for our lucky Sierra.

Our quirky sense of humour could sometimes land us in tight spots. On the get-away from the robbery at Rosehill I had thrown myself over the fence into the hospital car park and landed face-down in a mud-filled puddle. Much to the amusement of my compatriots, I had to climb into the van looking and feeling like a Victorian mudlark. I was the source of much ribald jocularity for the next couple of days. When I went around the car fronts to purchase our next get-away motor I noticed a Rover 3500 CDi with a number plate with letters that made up the word 'MUD' and took this as a sign that this was to be our next lucky motor. I purchased it, paying over the odds for what was, to us, a throwaway commodity. But I felt the number plate had some sort of mystical connection to me. When I showed up in the Rover, Tommy had a look under the bonnet and pointed out that what I'd actually bought was an ex-police car. This only added to my good feeling about it, as the notion of robbing banks in an ex-cop car appealed to my sense of humour. I decided to use the Rover as my personal car until the day of our next job, and this was how I managed to blow the engine. I took it down the length of Kings Avenue, a long, straight road between Streatham and Brixton, and when I got it up to 125 mph there was a loud bang and smoke began to issue from under the bonnet. So, despite my mystical connection to the MUD car, the rest of the firm wouldn't spring for a new engine before our next job. This setback left us without a get-away motor and with a job in Hendon, north London, just around the corner. I nipped down to a little car front in Clapham North and bought a four-door Ford Orion with a month's tax on the windscreen for £200. Maybe it was because I was in such a hurry, but when the seller asked me for my name and address for his records, I gave a false name but my parents' address, only changing the door number. I realized this when I was driving the Orion away and glanced at the receipt lying on the dashboard. I didn't worry too much about it at the time as I thought, with our record up until then, it wasn't likely the police would get the car, and even if they did, it was proof of nothing.

The Hendon Central bank job was one of our pranks in keeping with our nickname. We had chosen the bank because it was less than two hundred yards from the police training college and we thought it would be a nice touch to hit them right on their own doorstep, so to speak. It would be one in the eye for the coppers and one up for the Laughing Bank Robbers. We drove over to Hendon in convoy, me driving the Orion, with Andy in the passenger seat, and Tommy driving a four-door Vauxhall Astra which was to be the change-over car. We parked up on a council estate close to the job, got changed into our robbery kit and tooled up. The Hendon robbery turned into a bit of a disaster. Robbing a bank next door to the main police training college was always going to be risky and, with hindsight, we shouldn't have been taking those kinds of risks. The job was already difficult without the police neighbours: there was nowhere to park except on the red-lined and busy roundabout of Hendon Central itself; the double doors into the bank were electronic and could be locked from behind the bullet-proof jump; and police response time to the silent alarm was bound to be negligible. But we thought it would be 'a laugh' so we did it anyway.

Tommy parked the Orion on the roundabout with his hazard lights flashing while me, Andy and Curley masked up and went into the bank. Curley dropped an already prepared obstacle, a holdall with a breezeblock inside, on to the sensors of the electronic doors. This kept them open, but he stayed next to them just in case. I got the customers on the carpet with a few choice expletives and a pointed gun, and Andy hit the jump with his bag looking for the cash. The manager of the bank, hearing the commotion, came out and told the cashiers not to hand over any money. 'The police are on their way,' he assured them, as Andy and I banged the screen and screamed at them to start putting the cash up. I knew early on it was going to be a no-go. The manager was too calm and confident and his cashiers drew their strength from him. He padded up and down behind the screen tapping each petrified cashier on the shoulder and telling them to keep calm and hold their ground, and they did. Time was ticking by, and I knew that it didn't matter how much shouting we did – the cashiers were not going to hand over. The choice I faced was whether to fire a shot, which might galvanize them into action, or to beat a retreat. Remembering the words of my old pal Tough Tony, I decided to retreat and ordered the pull-out. Andy and Curley, being professionals, obeyed immediately and began backing up to the door. I noticed a blue money bag sitting on my side of the counter and grabbed it on my way out. The bag weighed a fucking ton and we later found it contained over £400 in two-pence pieces, which one of the customers, a shopkeeper, had been paying in.

We got to the Orion, but Hendon was already turning into robbers' hell and the sound of sirens seemed to be coming from every direction. It was now that I began to contemplate the value of Andy's hand-grenade suggestion. Tommy took us off the roundabout and down a sidestreet within sight of forty or so coppers, most hatless and in shirtsleeves, running like cheetahs towards the bank. They spotted us masked up in the car and ran after the speeding Orion, but we left them in our dust. At the bottom of this road was a path through some common land that led to Brent Cross shopping centre, in whose car park our change-over Astra was parked. We left the Orion parked in a bay and legged it up the path to the shopping centre, changing our clothing as we went and stuffing the robbery kit into bags. We were into our get-away car and well away before the police were able to follow our trail.

The Hendon job had been a bit of a wash-out, but at least none of us had been nicked and we were able to go again on the next bit of work. Unfortunately, this was when I started to worry about having given those details when buying the Orion. I told the lads my fears that Old Bill, who obviously now had the car, would trace it to the Clapham car front and then to me. Everyone thought I was worrying unnecessarily but I knew it was the small details that get you nicked, so I suggested that we drop down to the car front and take the paperwork back, by force if necessary. This sounded like a bit of an adventure and the boys were up for it.

We plotted up across from the little car front, which was run by two ropey-looking black fellas, one of whom had long dreadlocks tucked up into a multicoloured hat, and watched. There was a third fella, who seemed to be a mechanic, as he was working under the bonnet of an old Austin van, and the first two kept mainly to the large portacabin they were using as an office. Andy said they looked like a bunch of criminals and not the sort of bods who would willingly give information to Old Bill. I agreed, but looks can be deceiving and we couldn't take the chance. We decided to wait until it was getting dark and then go and pay them a visit. There was an argument about whether we should go pretending to be coppers or tax inspectors or whether to just go in masked and have a demand up. In the end we flipped a coin and it was in favour of going in masked. Around five thirty it was fully dark, and the mechanic packed up his tools and left in an old Mk4 Cortina. We decided that me and Andy would handle the job and Curley and Tommy would wait in the car, only being used as back-up if we called for them.

The car front was in a yard just off a main road, but no one noticed me and Andy as we slipped on our ski-masks and walked briskly into the yard, our guns ready. When I walked into the portacabin with Andy close behind me, the two men were startled. 'We ain't got no money here, mate,' one of them pleaded as we quickly tied them up. I rooted through the drawers of a desk and found their registration book and their receipt book. I stuffed them inside my coat and grabbed a bag of weed and about £200 that was also in the drawer to make it look like a genuine robbery. In minutes we were back in the car and driving away from the gaff. A couple of hours later we were at Andy's place, drinking beer, smoking weed and burning the two books. There was now no way the Orion could be traced back to me.

I was eventually arrested for the Laughing Bank Robbers jobs, and after being convicted on a retrial I was sentenced to the eight life sentences plus eighty years concurrent that I am now serving. So I guess the joke was on me in the end. But two funny things came out in the evidence depositions at my trials. The first was that the 'lucky' Ford Sierra we used on our first three jobs was never recovered by the police. When they searched the alley we had left it in after the Rosehill bank job, it was gone. No trace of that car has ever been found. And the other thing was that when they got the Ford Orion used on the Hendon Central job and checked the registration, they could only trace it to a woman who lived in Plumstead who had had it stolen from outside her house three years before I bought it. The car was a ringer, and we had robbed the car front for nothing, as the police would never have made it that far.

As I write this, I am in my ninth year of imprisonment for the Laughing Bank Robbers jobs, with no end in sight. Nobody else was ever convicted of those robberies, but the years have not been kind to the rest of the gang. We gave new meaning to the phrase 'laughing all the way to the bank', but today none of us is laughing any more. Armed robbery has many victims, and sometimes they include its perpetrators.

13. Deadly Dave

Deadly Dave was unusual for an armed robber in that he didn't enjoy the actual act of robbery. Most robbers get a buzz from it but Dave was happiest at either end – planning the job and counting the money afterwards. He must have been doing something right because he didn't take his first conviction for the heavy until he was in his mid-forties. He had a bit of form for handling stolen goods when he was a kid, but throughout the late seventies to the mid-eighties Deadly Dave was one of the most successful armed robbers in the country and Old Bill never even got a sniff of him. If he had not taken on a new partner of dubious repute, then Deadly Dave might have retired a very rich man; his downfall came when he went to work with a notorious supergrass. Dave was under the impression that the man had learnt his lesson and would never betray anyone again. Nobody in the history of British crime had ever become a supergrass twice; it was unheard of. But it turned out that Deadly Dave was very wrong and his poor judgement of character was to cost him plenty.

Dave was really a planner, a man more at home with logistical problems and blueprints than with a gun in his hand, but he also had that wild streak that most career criminals seem to have in their nature. To all intents and purposes, Dave was a respectable pillar of the community. He owned his own house – a bungalow on the outskirts of north London – and ran a small business which kept him, if not exactly wealthy beyond his wildest dreams, financially secure. But Dave wasn't happy being a straight-goer. He had grown up with a lot of the criminal faces in the fifties and sixties and had the kind of contacts that could get him anything from a hooky television set to a semi-automatic pistol. He watched some of his schoolmates setting out on their lives of crime, and it jarred him because he had an idea that he could do what they were doing, only better. They made too many silly mistakes because they didn't have the patience to plan things properly.

Then, when Dave was in his thirties and thought he had achieved about all he could in the straight world, he took up crime full time. And for Deadly Dave it was a case of starting at the very top. He had noticed a spate of security-van robberies in which the robbers only got away with a couple of cash bags or nothing at all and wondered why these stupid men didn't go for the whole prize, as some of these vans were carrying absolute fortunes. Dave decided he could do better and spent the next year researching his first job. The amount of time and patience that Dave was prepared to put into the planning of a robbery was phenomenal. He would spend months in different disguises and using various hire cars just following one security van. By the time he was ready to do the actual robbery, he would know every stop on the van's route, the timing of every journey, how much the guards were loading and delivering, the lot. Deadly Dave would leave nothing to chance.

Yet the first time that Dave robbed a van, despite all his careful planning, it was a bit of a disaster. Along with a partner, Dave was waiting for the van at its first drop, a supermarket. He knew from his research that there would be in excess of £200,000 on the van and thought it would now be a pretty simple task to get it off. He figured that the only way to get the money was through the crude but sometimes effective full-frontal method. He grabbed the guard who was delivering the bags and took him, at gunpoint, to the front of the van. There he warned the van driver that if the money bags did not start dropping out of the chute in the side of the van immediately, then he would execute the guard. This was the only weakness in Dave's plan. He knew from others that sometimes this worked and sometimes it didn't. It depended entirely on the personalities of the guards who were locked inside the van. If they were strong-willed or uncaring about their workmates, then they would not budge, no matter what the level of threat. As Dave's partner waited in vain for the cash chute to open Dave realized that they were on to a loser. Never one to chase a lost cause, Dave made do with the bags the guard had been carrying and he and his partner made their get-away before the police arrived.

It was back to the planning table for Dave. He had to find a way that would guarantee the guards' co-operation, and it was obvious that fear of their colleague being shot was not going to cut it. It was too hit-and-miss for the amount of planning that Dave was putting into the jobs. He realized that a direct threat to the safety of the guards inside the van was what he needed, but what? And how could he get it in there with them? Then, one day, as he was changing channels on his television with his remote control, he had an idea. Dave already had another security van researched and ready to rob, so after making the equipment he would need in his small workshop, he decided to test his idea. From scrap metal he constructed a box, around the size of a cigarette packet, with a tiny bulb on the outside that shone bright red when he switched on the pencil battery inside with a remote-control handset. It was a completely harmless piece of fakery, but he was hoping that the guards would never know this. He attached his box to a leather belt and he was ready to give it its first outing.

This time, the delivery guard was held up at gunpoint by Dave and his partner inside the vestibule of the premises he was delivering to, well out of sight of the other guards in the van. As Dave's partner held his gun on the guard, Dave put the leather belt around his waist, locking it into place with a small padlock. He explained to the guard, 'This box contains enough Semtex to blow up a tank. I am now going to arm it.' And here he pressed the right button on his moody remote and the red light came on. 'You will now go and get back into your van. Once inside, you will tell your mates to start throwing the cash bags out or I will detonate the bomb and you'll all be a smear on the road. If you try to tamper with it, or if you raise any alarm or if those bags don't start coming out within a minute of you getting into the van – then *Boom!*' Dave then let the terrified guard walk away and get into the van. Dave held his breath for a moment, and then the chute on the side of the security van opened and cash bags began to tumble out on to the pavement. Dave was buzzing. He and his partner grabbed as many bags as they could and launched them into the back of a Transit van that had been backed up by their wheelman. When the pavement was empty Dave and his partner jumped into the van and were gone. The whole thing had taken only six minutes, no alarms had been raised and they had cleared over £100,000.

It was while they were counting the take that Dave realized the guards had jibbed them out of another £150,000 by throwing out several 'dummy' bags, which are filled with plain paper and designed to fool robbers. His good humour over the plan being a success and their getting away with a substantial amount of cash was coloured by knowing that they had missed out on over half the take. Dave was a meticulous man and knew exactly how much the van would have been carrying, so it rankled with him that they hadn't got the whole whack. It wasn't the money so much that bothered him, but the loose end of his plan. He thought about it for a couple of months and came up with another innovation which would help him to clear the next van. For Dave, robbing security vans was a learning curve, and he relished each new setback as it gave him a chance to use his thinking skills.

Dave spent nine months researching his next job, following the van to every stop on its route again and again until he had the routine down pat. He knew that he would have to use a different security company to the first as they would surely be on to the fake-bomb coup. He had read in the local papers that on his last job the bomb squad had been called to make his device 'safe'. But it had been a long time ago and with a different firm he knew his chances were better than good. He got the fake bomb on to the guard, impressing on him that this was no joke and he would be mince if he fucked about, and sent him back to the van, this time with a typewritten list of details of each bag, the address of the premises it was destined for, the amount in it. This was to show that he knew how much was on the van and that if the right amount didn't pop out of the chute there would be trouble. This time Dave and his partner cleared the van.

It would be another eighteen months before Dave struck again with his fake-bomb ploy, this time on yet another security firm. In the intervening months Dave's original partner, now happy with his financial solvency, had decided to call it a day. The split was amicable and the man went off to live in Malta, where Dave and his wife would take their holidays for the next few years and be treated with great hospitality. Now Dave had to find another professional to work with. As he was going after so much cash, his crew needed a minimum of three members – one to drive, and Dave and another to do the business and load the cash. So he asked around the underworld and was pointed in the direction of a big old heavy who had let it be known he was in the market for a nice bit of work. The man, who went by the name of Tony, was about the same age as Dave and looked vaguely familiar to him. They chatted over a few drinks and Tony seemed to know his stuff. Dave liked him instantly, and after a few more meetings, just to make sure, he took him on board as a partner and laid out his coup. Tony was all for it and they began to put the next job together.

Dave had been following a particularly lucrative security van for over a year and had spotted that its last cash pick-up of the day was from a crematorium in north London. Dave, in disguise, visited the crematorium posing as a prospective customer and got a good gander at the staff and premises. He asked a lot of questions, but nobody would suspect that anyone could contemplate robbing a crematorium, so the director answered everything. Then, one afternoon, Dave and Tony entered the crematorium in business suits and ski-masks, and armed with revolvers, and proceeded to kidnap the five members of staff on duty and handcuff them. They made the staff lie down on the office floor and put tape over their mouths so they couldn't raise the alarm. Dave then removed his ski-mask and manned the front desk, his gun now out of sight.

When the security van arrived and the guard came into the premises for the pick-up, Dave greeted him and escorted him to the office. The guard later said in his witness statement that when he entered the office and saw all the staff lying on the floor in a line he thought they were dead bodies awaiting cremation. He was shocked that the dead were being treated in such a way but when he turned to Dave to protest he found himself looking down the barrels of two Smith & Wesson .38 revolvers. Tony covered the guard as Dave strapped the fake bomb to his waist. The guard was given his instructions and went back to the van. Three minutes later Dave, Tony and their wheelman were scooting out of the crematorium with £190,000 in cash.

Dave was smart enough to know that he had torn the arse out of the fake-bomb coup and that all the security firms would now be on to it, but his next plan was so audacious that it would take almost three years in the planning, and by then the box could be used again. Not happy with just clearing out the security vans. Dave now planned to clear a whole security depot. This was to be his Big One, the job on whose proceeds he would be able to retire and live out the rest of his life lying on sun-kissed golden beaches sipping exotic drinks. The fact that Deadly Dave was too intense to relax for even ten minutes and so lying on a beach doing nothing would drive him mad never even entered his head. He had the dream and that was enough until the next one came along.

Any robber worth his salt has, at one time or another, taken a look at the possibility of robbing an actual security depot where all the cash is kept before being loaded on to the vans. All that lovely cash in one place is a big temptation, but usually the amount of risk and the work and organization you have to put in deters your average blagger. Often, so-called criminal masterminds come up with a theoretical plan to do a depot and tout their ideas around the underworld – sometimes for several years – without getting a serious nibble. Depots are just so secure that it's not worth the candle, but every now and again an enterprising crew will take a punt, with varying success. The four biggest depot robberies have been the Security Express depot in 1983, where the robbers escaped with £6 million in cash; the Brinks-Mat gold-bullion job in 1983 (£26 million in gold); the Northern Bank robbery in 2005 (£26.5 million in cash); and the Tonbridge Security Depot robbery in 2006, where the robbers got away with £25 million in cash and left a further £50 million behind. But for every successful depot robbery there are another ten that fail or never even get off the starting blocks. Now Deadly Dave had his eyes set on a depot robbery of his own, and if anyone was going to pull it off, then it would be him.

Dave chose his target depot and set to work finding out everything he possibly could about it. Time meant nothing to Deadly Dave and he immersed himself in his research. He was able to find an ex-employee of the depot and spent months getting close to the man, even joining the same golf club and drinking with him in the clubhouse. Eventually Dave managed to inveigle himself so far into the man's life that they became friends. Carefully, Dave introduced the subject of the security depot into the conversation, and the man, classing Dave as a straight, upstanding member of the community, coughed the lot. The information Dave was able to gather about his target from the ex-employee was invaluable and helped him to formulate his plan.

By the time Dave was ready to do the job he knew everything he would need to know about the running of the depot. He knew every personal detail of all the staff who worked there, including the names, addresses, telephone numbers, dates of birth and extended family details of the two men who held the keys and codes for entry to the main vault where the cash was kept. Along with Tony and the wheelman, Dave recruited a fourth member to his crew, a reputable robber who came highly recommended in criminal circles. This was to be another bomb job, and Dave set to work making up another box in his workshop, only this time there was one small refinement – the box was no fake. What Dave rigged was a small and crude but very effective explosive device. It was a metal box of the usual size, but now, as well as the battery, it contained a twelve-bore-shotgun cartridge and a firing pin. Dave could arm and detonate it with the remote control, and when strapped to the small of a target's back, it was powerful enough to blow out someone's spine. This time Dave couldn't afford to be bluffing and he had to make his target fully aware of this for the plan to have a chance of working. This job would be all about instilling absolute terror into the victims so they had no time to think about anyone else.

At ten o'clock in the evening on a dark November night there was a knock on the door of the Ketcher family home in

Potters Bar. Jack Ketcher was a key-holder at the Guardian Security Depot and enjoying an evening in front of the telly with his wife and twenty-year-old daughter when the knock came. On the way to answer the door Jack Ketcher did wonder who could be calling so late, but he wasn't suspicious in any way. He had worked for Guardian Security for over twenty years and never so much as heard a voice raised in anger. But when he opened his front door on this particular night all that was to change. He only had time to register the 'old man' masks made of latex rubber and the bristling guns before being bundled through the hallway and into his front room. The family, faced with three armed and masked men, could do little but comply, and the wife and daughter were quickly tied up and placed together in an upstairs bedroom. Dave showed the bomb box to Jack Ketcher and carefully explained how it worked before strapping it to his body. He was told that he and his family would remain safe and unharmed as long as Jack followed the robbers' instructions to the letter. The next morning he was going to drive to work as if everything was normal, though he would have the bomb strapped under his coat. He would be followed by Dave and Tony, who would keep him in sight at all times, and if he deviated one jot from his normal routine – which, Dave explained, they knew almost as well as Jack himself did – then Dave would get on the blower to the third man, who would be guarding his family. Jack was told in no uncertain terms that one snide move would lead to the execution of his wife and daughter. He was asked if he understood this and he replied in the affirmative.

There followed the longest night of the Ketcher family's lives, and it was no picnic for the robbers either. All through the night Dave drummed the plan into Jack Ketcher's head until he could repeat it word for word. The next morning Jack dressed and shaved under the ever-watchful eye of Tony and his .38. He was allowed to kiss his wife and daughter goodbye before being escorted out to his car by Dave and Tony. When he was inside his car in the garage and ready to roll, Dave gave him one last warning. 'By lunch-time today you could be back in the arms of your loved ones or you could be a widower with two funerals to go to and a lifetime spent in a wheelchair to look forward to. It's entirely up to you.' Then the robbers unmasked and left to climb into their own van. As Jack pulled away and headed for the depot, the robbers' van pulled in behind him.

The drive to the depot was uneventful and Jack arrived on time. He usually met George, the second key-holder, in the car park of the depot and they would exchange pleasantries and chit-chat on their way to open up for the day. But today Jack had to tell George that his family was being held hostage by dangerous men and that he himself was wearing a bomb. At first George thought that Jack was joking, as you would, but when the latter opened his coat and showed George the red-lit device, he knew it was no joke. George suggested that they raise the alarm but Jack pleaded with him to co-operate and save his wife and daughter. George knew he was beaten and agreed to go along with the robbery under duress. The two security men went into the depot and began to load one of the company cargo vans with the cash boxes from the vault. George, ever the security-conscious company man, decided to take a chance and half-fill the van with empty boxes and then pack out the second half of the van with wage boxes, which consisted of the wage packets of various company clients. The wage boxes did not contain as much cash as normal cash boxes and this would cut down on how much the robbers managed to get away with. Jack wasn't sure about this but didn't have time to argue so he went along with it. When the van was full, Jack, following his instructions from Dave, drove it out of the depot and left it parked on the street outside with the keys in the ignition and the engine running.

Once they had the money, Dave made a phone call and the third man cut the family's bonds and slipped away. It was almost a perfect crime, and the only fly in Dave's ointment was that after counting the money, instead of the £3 million in cash they had been expecting, there was only just under £800,000. And most of it was in wage packets. It took the gang nine hours to rip open all the little brown envelopes and count the notes, and they were left with around £3,000 in loose change that nobody even wanted to pick off the carpet of the flop. At one stage the robbers were wading shin-deep through money and brown paper envelopes. They had the carve-up and left the change lying on the floor for a very rainy day, then went their separate ways. It was the third man's job to get rid of the robbery kit. He was supposed to burn the masks, gloves and clothing and the remote-control unit used on the robbery so as to leave no forensic trace, but now that he had a few quid in his sky he was in too much of a hurry to get out of the country and dumped the entire kit in a dustbin outside a house on a quiet residential street.

The depot robbery had been a success but not so good that Dave could afford to retire on the proceeds, and he knew he was going to have to plan another one. He was toying with another clever plan that might yet allow him to hit the Big One. One of his female relations had started going out with a likely lad named Drew. Dave liked the young man, and he seemed very clued up for his age, so he cultivated him for a little while to find out just how clued up he was. Dave took him clay-pigeon shooting and to various clubs at which the clientele consisted mainly of robbers and villains, and the kid seemed right at home. Dave knew that Drew had no previous criminal convictions and that could be more than useful for the plan he was hatching. Drew liked having money well enough but didn't seem to be able to keep a job for long, and it was during one of these regular periods of unemployment that Dave suggested Drew might find himself a short but very lucrative career in the security business. So after some discussion, Drew applied for a job as a driver with one of the major cash-in-transit companies and was accepted as a trainee guard.

Drew had been thoroughly security-checked by the firm, but they had not turned up his tenuous link to Dave, and even if they had, Dave only had a couple of petty convictions which were a quarter of a century old. So, as far as anyone at the firm was concerned, he was squeaky-clean. The money as a guard was shit and the hours seemed endless but Drew, with Dave's encouragement and the promise of a massive payday, stuck at it. He graduated from mooching around the depot loading the cash vans to walking pony-bags across the pavement. For Drew, who by now was eager to get his hands on some cash and start enjoying the good life which Dave had been promising him, every day was a massive temptation. Every evening he would report to Dave on how much money he had seen, where it was kept and what security precautions were being taken. Drew photographed everything inside the depot, from the vault to the interiors of the security vans, with a tiny camera Dave had supplied. In one year Dave amassed more information on the workings of this depot than most criminals get their hands on in a lifetime. For Dave, this was going to be his Big One, and he was in no rush.

Dave's eventual plan was to rob the whole depot of its eight- to ten-million-pound weekly load, and with his man on the inside any plan of this kind was eminently feasible. But while he was working on the finer details of this job, Drew told him of something else that was unmissable. Every Thursday a security van was detailed to do what was known as the Northern Run. The Northern Run was hated by the security guards because it involved an overnight stay in another depot in Liverpool and many hours cooped up in the van on the journey there and back. Its purpose was to distribute excess cash and even bullion to the sister depot for northern clients. Drew said there was never less than £3 million on the van and sometimes as much as £5 million. Each week three different guards were detailed to escort the money or gold on the Northern Run, and they would take one of four different routes. As a further precaution, the guards were not informed they were going until they got to the depot on the morning of the run; then they would leave in the van an hour later. The big flaw in the firm's security was that on each of the four possible routes the guards themselves had a spot where they would stop for a cup of tea and something to eat, and the company didn't know it. Dave was very interested in this and thought it might make an interesting appetizer to the main meal of the depot, so he started working on the logistics of it.

But there was big trouble on Dave's horizon, and it involved Tony. One night at a boxing dinner in the West End, where all the top faces would gather in their too-tight tuxedos to smoke foot-long cigars, barely watch the boxing and gossip among themselves about who was having it off and who was doing bundles of bird, Dave was approached by a face who had been convicted of the Great Train Robbery of 1963. The man asked him what he was doing working with Tony, as he was a well-known supergrass. Dave was shocked and told the face he must be mistaken, but several other of the old villains confirmed it. Dave had grown to like Tony and he was certainly a good and reliable worker so he sought advice from the man who had first brought Tony into his company. The man admitted he had known that Tony had been a supergrass, but his comment was, 'I hardly think he's going to turn supergrass a second time, do you? I mean, it's never been fucking known in the history of crime! He made a mistake and now he's back on the right side.' Dave was reassured by this but wanted to know the full story on Tony so as to judge for himself.

It turned out that in the sixties and early seventies Tony had been a professional robber known as 'Crazy Horse' due to his wild ways and antics. He had been one of the notorious Wembley Mob, also known as the Frighteners, who had been hitting banks all over the country at that time and taking massive amounts of money. Their MO was to drive an old van right up on to the pavement outside the target bank and then to crash through the doors into the banking hall, masked and wearing heavy clothing so as to look even bigger. They would immediately fire a shot into the ceiling of the bank, the cartridge containing rock salt or rice, for effect, and then set to work on the internal door with sledgehammers. In seconds they would be behind the counter with access to the usually open vault, then, whooping like Red Indians, they would load up the cash in bags and retreat to a couple of high-performance cars that would pull up at the kerb on their exit. In one bank job alone the gang took £225,000 in cash in less than four minutes. In the world of armed robbery, these boys were classed as the mutt's nuts. It was after they robbed Barclay's Bank on Wembley High Street of £138,000 in cash in 1969 that the Metropolitan Police took the step of forming a special robbery squad whose brief it was to tackle only armed robbery in the capital. This was the birth of the modern Flying Squad, who even today are still the scourge and nemesis of every armed robber operating in London.

One member of the Wembley Mob with whom Crazy Horse was good pals was the infamous Bertie Smalls, who would eventually give evidence against fifty-three London robbers and go down in criminal history as the original supergrass. It was on a job with Smalls and another man in 1971 that Crazy Horse was nicked. Smalls and the other man convinced Crazy Horse that the case was hopeless and that they should all stick their hands up for a reduced sentence, but when Crazy Horse changed his statement to admit his guilt, the other two reneged on the deal and pleaded not guilty. Smalls and his mate walked out of court free men and Crazy Horse was sentenced to twelve years' imprisonment. Embittered by this, Crazy Horse requested a visit from a DI from the newly formed Flying Squad and spilled everything he knew about Smalls and the rest of the Wembley Mob. He later withdrew his statements after Smalls himself coughed the lot about everything, but Crazy Horse was still labelled as a supergrass and had to lie low for many years.

Dave, after hearing all this, decided to give Tony the benefit of the doubt and carry on working with him. There are those in the underworld who swear to this day that they would never have carried on working with Tony after finding this out, but maybe they are speaking with that miraculous gift of hindsight. The Guardian Security depot job was featured heavily on BBC's *Crimewatch UK* and replicas of the old-man masks and remote control were shown. It turned out that a couple of nosy schoolboys had found the real ones dumped in the bin and had them in their house. The boys' parents immediately informed the police. The items were forensically examined and, inside one of the latex masks, a fingerprint was found. This turned out to belong to a convicted armed robber from the seventies known as Crazy Horse, and the police were not shy about picking him up for questioning. Crazy Horse was no longer so crazy, he was getting on, in his fifties now, and he knew that a twenty-stretch behind bars would probably be the death of him, so when the police threatened to charge him with the depot robbery, he offered them a deal. He could deliver the depot crew in the commission of a £3 million blag – signed, sealed, delivered, they're yours. So Crazy Horse did the unthinkable – he became a supergrass for the second time in one life.

One sunny winter's morning at a service station just outside Luton a security van pulled in and Drew jumped out of the passenger seat to go and get the coffee for the other guards. Dave and Tony watched from a nearby BMW in which they had followed after getting Drew's phone call from the depot earlier that morning. As Drew made his way back with the Styrofoam cups he was joined by Dave and Tony, now masked and carrying revolvers, and implored his mates inside, with plenty of tears, that if they didn't open the van he would be killed. The guards, having grown to like their young workmate, complied. Inside the van were precious stones, gold Kruger-rands, platinum, gold, and silver bullion to the value of £3.7 million. The wheelman backed up to the van in a pick-up truck for the transfer but before they could lay a hand on any of the loot, a couple of dozen flak-jacketed and sub-machine-gun-toting members of the Flying Squad and the regional crime squad leapt from their vehicles and surrounded the robbers. Dave, thinking at first that this was another robbery firm trying to claim their booty, put up a fight and ended up rolling around on the ground with two burly Flying Squad officers before he was subdued by a crack on the head from a gun butt.

For Deadly Dave, his long run was over. When he found out that Tony had dropped him in it and set the whole arrest up he was devastated. With the weight of evidence against him, there was nothing to do but plead guilty and hope for the best. At the Old Bailey Dave was sentenced to twenty-four years' imprisonment on various robbery and firearms charges. The wheelman got fourteen years, Drew got nine, and Tony/Crazy Horse got a token five-year sentence, of which he served less than two, in a cushy police protection suite.

Almost fifteen years later Deadly Dave was released from prison with a £48 discharge grant and the clothes he stood up in. Whatever property and goods the police hadn't seized as proceeds of crime Dave had given to his now ex-wife. He was fifty-seven years old, and all he had left were his criminal contacts. In order to earn some quick cash, he teamed up with another old villain and took a job from a millionaire property tycoon. They were to rough up and put the frighteners on a man who owed him money, and for this they would be paid £25,000. In the event the man they were roughing up died of his injuries. Dave was sentenced to life imprisonment with a recommendation that he serve a minimum of twenty-five years before being considered for parole. Today he whiles away his days in a top-security prison, surrounded by cocky young criminals who can only dream of what he once had in his grasp. Crazy Horse, with no shame at all, occasionally makes an appearance, his features obscured, on gratuitous television documentaries about crime in the old days. Sometimes, there really is no honour among thieves.

14. Double Header: Mental Micky and Machine-Gun Steve

I have never met a man who looked less like an armed robber than Mental Micky. He was a Scotsman who personified the word 'dour', and the miserable cast of his features made him look like that old cartoon dog Droopy, only a lot uglier. He had thick fish-like lips that always seemed wet, a bulbous nose and, to top it all off, he wore thick-lensed National Health glasses. He minced rather than walked and looked like the kind of man who would be more at home stealing Y-fronts from a washing line than holding up security vans. But when I got to know him I found Micky to be a nice geezer and more intelligent than a herd of MENSA candidates. He may have been most unfortunate when getting kitted out in the looks department, but he hadn't stinted at the IQ counter. Unfortunately, he chose to use his considerable brain power to become a robber. For a while back in the late eighties Mental Micky was never off the front pages of the national newspapers. Not pictures of him – unless you count police photofits – but reams of copy about his ruthless personality and the need to catch him before he murdered somebody – though, having lived in close proximity to Micky in a couple of top-security prisons, in my opinion, murder would be the last thing on his mind. He got himself caught up in a sticky situation and reacted badly. It could have happened to anybody. Well, anybody who ventures on to the streets of London carrying a pump-action shotgun with the intention of relieving security vans of their cargo. In some ways Micky was a victim of his own smartness, and that caused him to leave at least one other victim in his wake. Forget what you may have read in the newspapers at the time, if you can remember that far back, because this is what really happened.

Mental Micky left his native Scotland for the bright lights of London just as soon as he was old enough to travel on his own. Once he had discovered that he preferred the company of bonnie laddies over the company of bonnie lassies, he decided that Scotland was never going to be the gay capital of the world and that London might be a better prospect. In London Micky found that he preferred a particular type of boy. Ideally they would be slim, winsome and Oriental. He spent a lot of time and money searching the streets of the Smoke for his dream boy, and though he thought he might have found him on several occasions, things never really worked out. Micky had a tendency to live beyond his means and tried leading a champagne lifestyle on a Coca-Cola salary but, obviously, this didn't work out too well and he took to a bit of petty thieving in order to fund his expensive rent-boy habit. Then, one day in Soho, he met the love of his life. Ki was everything Micky wanted and soon the pair had set up home in a bedsit in Hackney. Life was good for Micky now, but Ki wanted much more. He wanted to be wined and dined in top hotels, to snort cocaine through £50 notes and to be able to go shopping in the West End and buy all those lovely clothes he truly deserved. Micky, fearful of losing Ki to some rich sugar-daddy, knew he would have to up his game in some way in order to keep his boy in the manner to which he was itching to become accustomed. Deep inside, he knew that Ki would only stay with him if the money kept flowing – after all, he was hardly the best-looking man in London, nor even in his own bedsit. But he really loved Ki and resolved to do whatever it took to keep him hanging on and happy. So he bought himself a gun.

For a while Micky would cycle around London on his mountain bike keeping an eye on the routines of the dozens of cash-in-transit security vans that ply their trade in the capital every day. He watched closely and took notes of every move the guards made because he planned to rob at least one of them. Micky knew that some of the security firms put devices into the money bags – exploding dye-packs, alarms or tracking devices – and he needed to find out the best way of neutralizing them before making his move. He had a friend who was a bit of a wide boy and hung around with serious criminals, so Micky picked his brains for anything he might use and was surprised to find out that the information on how to deal with security devices was almost common knowledge among the criminal fraternity. Armed with everything he needed, Micky put his plan into action. He had singled out a security van that picked up from a bank near Finsbury Park, in north London, and cycled over there at the appointed day and hour of business. He carefully chained his mountain bike to a lamp-post around the corner from the work, lest it be half-inched by some sticky-fingered bike thief while Micky himself was thieving from others, and carried his pump-action shotgun in a duffel bag over his shoulder. Micky, never having done anything like this before, waited in full view outside the bank for the security van to turn up. It was lucky for him that no one mistook his ugly features for a latex mask and found his twitching and constant glances at his watch suspicious. His very obviousness worked in his favour. The van turned up about five minutes late, but as soon as the guard picked up the cash box from the security chute, Micky got to work. He extracted his shotgun from his duffel bag and drew down on the guard, threatening to blow his legs off if he didn't set the box on the pavement and open it up immediately. The guard, seeing a hideous-looking creature with a big gun, complied. Once the box was open, Micky handed the guard a Stanley knife and told him to slit open the interior cloth money bag and remove the security devices, which the guard did. Micky then handed him the duffel bag and ordered him to put the money inside. When the guard had loaded Micky's bag with cash he was ordered to roll underneath his own security van and stay there.

Micky was very lucky not to be caught on that first job as he was slower than a week in Dartmoor punishment block. In the normal course of events, you would want to be in and out of a robbery situation in six minutes maximum as police response times are very fast. Uniformed coppers love an armed-robbery call over their radios because it might be their chance to shine and get a leg-up to the CID. There's nothing like a bravery award for tackling a gunman on a copper's record for easing a path to the top. And, fair play, most of them have got more bollocks than brains and will put themselves in harm's way at the drop of a truncheon. So Micky was very fortunate as his routine ran close to nine minutes without a police response. After getting his bag back from the guard, he jogged around the corner and wasted another precious couple of minutes unlocking his bike before riding away.

Micky was flushed with the success of pulling off his first job, and he and Ki hit the West End to celebrate. He had got away with over £20,000, and the next few weeks were a round of top hotels and shopping. But money doesn't last for ever and pretty soon Micky was making plans to go again. This time, realizing he had been a tad slow on the first job, he chose a van that made a stop well away from the street. It was a cash pick-up from the South Bank next to the Thames, and the security van had to pull into an underground car park. Micky figured he could be well away before the alarm was raised and the police would have to negotiate the subterranean complex. In the gloomy bowels of the South Bank, at Waterloo, there existed at that time a shanty-town of homeless dwellings constructed mainly of cardboard boxes. Known as Cardboard City, it was the home of the mentally ill, the perpetually drunk and stoned, and penniless mendicants who had been shoved to one side by a Tory government whose leader insisted there was no such thing as 'society' and that greed and looking after number one were the order of the day. During daylight hours most of the denizens of Cardboard City would be out on the streets begging, stealing and busking in order to get the money for their next slice of bread, bottle of wine or heroin fix, so the spot where Micky planned to hit the security van would be pretty empty. He watched the pick-up several times and was happy that he would have no trouble working his routine.

On the day of the robbery Micky parked up his bike, chained it to one of the central pillars in the car park and waited for the van. It arrived on time, and he watched as the guard walked into the building and emerged some minutes later with the cash box. Micky, just as before, pulled his gun and forced the guard to remove the security devices before handing it over. But he soon realized that he was being watched. About fifty yards away, walking through the car park and sharing a bottle of cider, were three young homeless men. When they spotted what was going on, they decided to move closer and made their way across the car park until they were only a few feet from the van. The men were drunk, but when they saw the guard transferring wads of cash into Micky's duffel bag their eyes lit up, imagining how much Special Brew they could buy with just a fraction of the money. Micky made the guard roll under his van and then began to make his way towards the get-away bike. The dossers followed, calling out for him to throw them some of the money. At first Micky ignored them, and the men started to get more vocal and demanding. 'Come on, you tight cunt, just give us a few fucking quid, will you?' they shouted from less than six feet behind him as he ran. Micky was starting to get very nervous.

Micky found his bike and crouched down to undo the lock, still ignoring the threats and exhortations of the three men. It was then that the men decided that the vocal approach was not going to work and that they should physically take the money. One of them threw the cider bottle at Micky's head. It missed but shattered on the concrete column and showered him in broken glass. Micky, deciding that a play's all right but this was turning into a fucking pantomime, decided to throw a scare into the men. He stood up and slipped his pump-action shotgun from his coat and turned on them. At first the three men moved back, but when Micky crouched once more to unlock his bike they moved forwards again, and one picked up an empty beer can and threw it. This time the missile hit Micky full in the face, cutting his lip and knocking his glasses askew. 'Fuck off!' Micky roared, threatening them with the gun once more. Again they backed off, but as soon as he resumed his business with the bike he was hit on the head by another thrown can. This was the last straw, and Micky knew he was going to have to fire off the gun in order to get rid of them. He stood up and faced the men, who were now ducked behind another concrete pillar. 'If you don't fuck off I will shoot you!' Micky yelled at the men. 'Give us some of that money and we'll go!' was the reply he received. So Micky aimed at the concrete pillar they were hiding behind and pulled the trigger of his shotgun.

Micky told me years later, and I had no reason to disbelieve him, that he wasn't aiming directly at any of the men and only wanted to scare them. But his shot glanced off the concrete pillar and found the head of one of them. Micky quickly unlocked his bike and then rode like the wind for the exit. The delay in his escape meant that the police were already making their way into the centre as he was making his way out, but they were expecting the traditional tyre-screeching motorized-vehicle get-away from the robbery and drove right past Micky on his bike without a second glance. Micky had got away with the cash, but the sight of the man's head exploding in a shower of blood and bone fragments would not leave him. He guessed the man must be dead, and the thought of being a murderer sickened Micky to his stomach. He went and had a few stiff drinks and laid low until the following day when he could get his hands on a newspaper and see exactly how bad his situation had become. The next morning he saw in the papers that the man he had shot was not dead but in a coma, and Micky fervently hoped that he would pull through.

For the next few days Micky fretted over the shooting, but there was nothing practical he could do about it. He thought about handing himself in to the police and trying to explain that it had been an accident, but he knew that, even if they believed him and the man didn't die, he would be looking at twenty years in prison – and Micky had never even spent the night in a police station up to then. He decided to sit tight and hope for the best. Then some enterprising tabloid reporter picked up on the story of the shooting and decided to give it his own twist in order to titillate the public and sell a few more newspapers. He interviewed the two dossers who had not been shot, bought them a few drinks and then fed them a story that they could feed back to him as gospel. The story was that, far from being lowlives who had set out to rob a robber, they were in fact heroes who had tried to help the security guard and return the money to its rightful owners, and one of their gallant number had been shot for his trouble. They claimed, in the words of the reporter, that though they might have been marginalized and all but forgotten by their country, they were still patriots who would do their duty unto death when called upon. Even as they dodged the hail of hot lead from the gun of the leering law-breaker, they had fortified each other's courage with cries of 'Let's do it for England!' – and that was the headline in the newspaper the next morning: HOMELESS HEROES 'DID IT FOR ENGLAND'!

When Micky read this, he became incensed. Not only was

it a pack of lies but it also guaranteed that, were he caught, he would stand little chance of being believed. He stewed on it for a couple of days and was even more annoyed when other newspapers picked up on the story of the heroic dossers and began reporting the story as though it were true. Though an armed robber on the surface, at heart Micky was a middle-class academic, and his only natural course of action to try and get his own version across was to write a letter to *The Times*. In his letter he explained exactly what had led up to the shooting and expressed a view that any member of the public who would try to tackle an armed man must be foolish in the extreme and undeserving of the tag 'hero', which should be reserved for the many people who did commit heroic deeds in the course of their daily lives. He did not sign the letter but it contained enough detail about the events to be accepted as genuine, so the newspaper published it on the front page the next morning.

Writing to *The Times* was a step too far for the police and the security firm, and they offered a reward for Micky's capture. Then one of the tabloids, sick that it had not got exclusive access to the *Times* letter, weighed in with a substantial reward of its own, and Micky's days of freedom were numbered on Ki's itchy telephone fingers. Once the proceeds from the South Bank robbery had run out and Micky was showing a natural reluctance to go out and rob another van, Ki decided it was time he collected the reward. He phoned the police hotline and gave them chapter, verse and full stop on his lover. The police burst in on Micky early one morning as he slept a fitful sleep full of nightmares about exploding heads. He was charged with armed robbery, attempted murder and possession of firearms. He pleaded not guilty to the charge of attempted murder but was found guilty by the jury when the two newly scrubbed, shorn and besuited dossers turned up in court and once more recounted their finest hour. The third man had come out of his coma after several months but was so brain-damaged he could not leave his hospital bed and would need constant medical care for the rest of his life. Micky, due to his previous good character and lack of a single criminal conviction to his name, was sentenced to twenty-three years' imprisonment.

Micky did his time without a murmur, and at the time of writing is still doing it. He never meant to shoot anybody but accepts that if you carry a gun bad things can happen. The man who was shot was awarded £1.7 million in compensation, but it is no good to him other than to pay for his medical care. The other two 'heroes' have not been heard of since.

Machine-Gun Steve was way out of his depth as an armed robber. A tall, good-looking, well-educated middle-class kid from a good family, he was like a strawberry in a gooseberry barrel among the population of a top-security prison. But Steve earned his own unique place in British criminal history, and paid the price for it. His old man had been an avid gun-collector and Steve could hit a target with a .357 Magnum almost before he could crawl. He grew up around guns and was very confident with them, able to strip and reassemble an AK47 by the age of ten, blindfold. But when he started using guns to commit armed robberies, his competence and confidence around firearms were to get him into a lot of trouble. At heart he was a good and decent kid, but he took his sense of adventure just that little bit too far.

Steve had a good pal called Zee, and the two lads were almost inseparable. They grew up together, went to the same schools and were always in and out of each other's houses. As a result, Zee also became very comfortable and proficient around firearms, and the two boys would often go target-shooting together. When he hit his teens Steve started his own gun collection and was able to purchase them by using his father's licence, with his father's consent of course. Steve had some very interesting guns, the kind of firepower most criminals would sell their in-laws just to get their hands on, but he was a straight-goer and had the paperwork to prove it. He didn't mix in criminal circles, and the closest he came was when he was watching gangster videos with Zee. The boys loved what they perceived as the glamour of the criminal lifestyle and sometimes discussed the idea of becoming gangsters themselves. They took to going out with guns concealed on their persons, in shoulder and ankle holsters, pretending they were hitmen or robbers. I'm no psychiatrist but even I can see that it was only a matter of time before the lads might act on these fantasies. It took a couple of girls entering the mix to make this happen.

The two lads fell in love with a couple of lovelies around the same time, and to impress them, they played up their gangster fantasy, adding an air of danger to their otherwise mundane middle-class lives. They hinted broadly that they robbed security vans for a living and then, in an effort to prove it, spent every penny that they possessed on wining and dining the girls in all the top restaurants. Pretty soon the two boys were flat broke and Zee suggested that maybe it was time they really did rob a security van. He reasoned that they already had all the firepower they would need and they had picked up enough hints about what to do from crime videos and documentaries. How hard could it actually be to rob a security van when it was a regular job for some of the uneducated, sloping-browed, knuckle-dragging crowd? Steve agreed, but only on the proviso that it would be just the once and no more. He didn't want to make a career of it, just one go to see if they could really pull it off.

The lads took a look at the routines of security vans and picked one at random. Armed with enough firepower to mount a coup in some Third World countries, the boys set about their work with gusto. Steve was carrying a Skorpion machine pistol with a thirty-two-round magazine, had a .357 Magnum revolver in a shoulder holster on one side of his body, a .45 Browning automatic pistol on the other side, a Charter Arms snub-nose .38 revolver in his waistband and a Star .32 automatic pistol in an ankle holster. And Zee was similarly kitted out. The boys wanted to be ready for any eventuality, though what they were expecting to occur that could only be solved by letting off a couple of hundred rounds of ammunition, I dread to think. Plus, in their get-away car they had four shotguns, including a Savage pump-action and a Remington Magnum automatic, as well as extra ammunition for all the guns. The word 'overkill' springs readily to mind. But they were young and they were amateurs. And boys will be boys.

More by luck than anything else, their first job was a success. They drew down on a guard outside a high street bank, and without having to fire a shot nabbed themselves a pony-bag. The boys made a clean get-away and with the £17,000 they found in the bag they thought they were the dog's bollocks. They spent most of the money on their girls, even taking them both off for a Caribbean holiday, but their real buzz was in knowing that they were now genuine armed robbers and wanted men. This added a certain spice to their lives that had hitherto been missing and they milked it, becoming very serious about their gangster status and going nowhere without a concealed gun. They told each other that the cops would never take them alive, and other Cagney-ish clichés. For this dynamic duo, the world had suddenly opened up and they were going to live every day like it was their last.

Their next van robbery also went off perfectly, and this time they got away with £25,000, which they once again spent impressing the girls. Steve bought his sweetheart a £6,000 diamond ring for their engagement. She must have thought all her Christmases had come at once. What other nineteen-year-old kid can buy his bird a six-grand ring? The Flying Squad was baffled: these two well-armed and well-spoken robbers who had suddenly appeared on the scene were a complete mystery. There were no whispers about them from the snitches in the underworld, no recognition by any serving copper, and they left no traces behind. Their MO was pretty standard, almost textbook, as though they had learnt it from an armed-robbery manual. Even their demands were couched in clichés – 'Give me the money or I'll blow your head off.' None of this left the police much to go on. One thing the police were sure of was that anyone who would take a couple of machine guns to rob a pony-bag was not the sort of person who would take kindly to a refusal to hand over the prize. These men were classed as extremely dangerous and the Squad poured plenty of resources into getting a lead on them.

In the meantime the boys hit another van for £25,000 and began to think they were invincible. With this came arrogance – they seemed unable to keep their mouths shut about what they were up to. At a party they told an old schoolfriend that they were now in the security business and then laughed as they explained they were actually relieving the security companies of their excess cash. Knowing about Steve's firearms collection, the friend became worried enough to phone the police and tell them of his suspicions. The cops get these kind of calls all the time – wives who suspect their husbands might be the Peckham Pouncer, girlfriends who suspect their boyfriends of being Lord Lucan and kids who think their mothers may have been feeding them Shergar in pie form – so they just logged the call and eventually it made its way to the offices of the Flying Squad. It was over a month before anyone actually looked at it, and the boys had hit another security van by then.

On this job the boys had got careless and waited for the security van on a street that was covered by CCTV. In those early days the quality of CCTV footage wasn't up to much – nowadays it's crystal clear and able to spot a pimple on a flea's bollocks from three miles away – but the police at least had a bit of grainy footage to work on. Fortunately for the police, Steve was almost six foot five and towered head and shoulders above most of the crowd on the street. Zee was of more average height but was easily spottable standing next to Steve. The pictures were not good enough to make out any facial features or to use as evidence in a court of law, but at least they offered the robbers' rough dimensions, and that was a start. Finally getting around to the telephone call from Steve and Zee's pal, a police constable was sent to interview him. The witness repeated the conversation he'd had with the boys and the fact that they were both very familiar with firearms, and when he described Steve alarm bells began to ring in the copper's pointy little head. The Flying Squad decided to put Steve and Zee under surveillance.

Over the next couple of months, as the two boys went about researching future robbery jobs, they were followed, photographed from every angle and had their phones tapped by the surveillance squad. It wasn't very long before the police realized that this was definitely the team they were after. They only had to see them sitting in their car watching the routines of the guards to know that they were on to a win-double. But for the Flying Squad, conspiracy to rob or possession of firearms are not enough: they want to catch the robbers in the act every time. A clever brief could make mincemeat of most conspiracy charges – after all, nothing has actually been done – and even on the robberies the boys had already committed they had left behind no evidence. Unless they were going to stick their hands up, they would walk. It's standard operating procedure for the Flying Squad to allow a robbery to be carried out and then arrest the perpetrator in possession of the gun and the money on the spot. Get out of that one – as they are fond of saying at the moment of arrest. So they let the boys run for a while and bided their time.

Steve and Zee now classed themselves as full-time professional armed robbers, and why not? They had already pulled off a string of successful blags. Now they were looking for their next target, unaware that the police were watching them closely, but they had a difference of opinion. Steve wanted to rob a van at Plumstead and Zee fancied one at Blackheath. They watched both jobs closely for a couple of weeks, alternating between one and the other. Both vans were delivering on the same day, and the problem for the watching police was that they didn't know which job the boys were actually going to do. They were helped out in this when they saw the boys mooching around the Plumstead site on the evening before the robbery was due. Plumstead it was. The Flying Squad briefing took place at Plumstead police station in the early hours of the morning of the robbery, and the DI in charge stressed the fact that these robbers were heavily armed and might decide to shoot it out, and on a crowded shopping parade that was not an option. The Squad would have the element of surprise on their side, but if things looked like they were going pear-shaped, then their brief was to take the robbers down in any way they could, up to and including lethal force.

By ten that morning, an hour before the security van was due to arrive, the police ambush was in place and discreetly armed police were mingling with shoppers, sweeping the street in council donkey-jackets and browsing in the windows of a mucky bookshop. Unfortunately for them, the boys had changed their minds and were hitting the Blackheath target. As a precaution the Flying Squad DI had posted a lone car at Blackheath containing two DCs and a Detective Sergeant. They were only there to keep an eye open on the off chance. So you can imagine their surprise when the van turned up right on time and so did the robbers. There was no mistaking the distinctively tall figure of Steve as he loped through the crowd and drew down on the guard with his machine pistol, and there was Zee standing in front of the van, his gun aimed at the windscreen. The DS ordered one of the DCs to follow him as he exited the unmarked car and began to run across the main road, drawing his Smith & Wesson Model 10 revolver as he ran.

Some people might think it was awfully brave of the DS to tackle the robbers, going up against machine guns with a five-shot revolver and two speed-loaders but, personally, I think it was the height of stupidity. One thing is sure, by the end of that day he would be sorely regretting his actions. As the ambush team decamped from Plumstead and boarded their vehicles to rush to Blackheath, Steve and Zee had already collared the cash bag and were heading for their get-away car. As they legged it along the pavement, they were suddenly confronted by the DS, in classic shooting stance, feet apart and spare hand braced on the wrist of his trigger hand, and a DC carrying a baton. 'Halt! Armed police!' the DS commanded. But the boys didn't even slow down – they simply changed the direction of their run in mid-stride and headed out into the traffic. Unable to get a clear shot as they dodged through fast-flowing traffic, the DS and DC followed instead. The boys, panicking now, ran into a residential sidestreet and, spotting a man just about to get into his car, they stuck their guns in his face, snatched the keys and jumped in themselves. They started the car, but as they went to go forward the unmarked police car, now with the DS and the second DC on board, came screeching around the corner and blocked their way. The DS jumped out of the police car and once again got into a shooting position behind the car door. By now Steve was desperate to get away and leant out of the open passenger window of the hijacked car and fired off a full clip from his machine pistol. He claimed later that he aimed at the road in front of the police car, and this was accepted by the prosecution, but the Skorpion holds thirty-two rounds and one was bound to find a target.

Over the noise of the discharging machine gun the DS's scream of pain was clearly heard as one of Steve's bullets found his skull. He collapsed in a spray of blood and Steve pulled another ammunition clip from his waistband and reloaded. Zee, finally coming to his senses, threw the car into reverse and put his foot down. Half-way down the road, he pulled the handbrake on, threw a 360 and off they went, leaving behind a bullet-riddled residential street and a head-shot Flying Squad sergeant. The ambush squad rushing from Plumstead heard over their radios that an officer was down, but they knew exactly where the robbers were going from their weeks of surveillance, so that's where they headed. When Steve and Zee dumped their hijacked car a couple of streets away from their flop, they thought they were free and clear. But as they walked on to the street, they suddenly heard the cocking of many firearms in the unnaturally still summer morning air, and a cry of 'Armed police! Don't move a muscle!' The gig was up for Steve and Zee, and they knew it. They dropped their guns and lay face down on the road as ordered. By this time the Flying Squad officers had heard that their injured colleague was on the critical list and not expected to last the night, so the restraint they showed in not shooting the boys was admirable. But any false move by Steve and Zee and all bets would have been off.

The boys were charged with armed robbery, possession of firearms and the attempted murder of a police officer. The DS eventually pulled through and was awarded a bravery medal for his actions. He was lucky, as he had actually been hit by a spent bullet that ricocheted off the road and lodged in his temple. I was at Highdown prison on the day that Steve was remanded there and put in the cell next door to me. I had heard on the radio about the copper being shot, and having had my own trouble with the Flying Squad, I was the first one to shake Steve's hand when the cells were opened later that evening. I had a pretty skewed sense of criminal values in those days. But I noticed that he was no more than a big, scared kid. He and Zee pleaded guilty and were given eighteen and sixteen years' imprisonment respectively. The last time I saw Steve was at Whitemoor prison three years ago. He was still category A and had just been refused his second parole. He was nineteen when he was nicked and is now twenty-nine and no longer believes there is any glamour in a life of crime. To date, his only 'achievement' is to go down in British criminal history as the first man to fire a machine gun at police in the course of their duties. And that's something he no longer wants to talk about.

15. Gangs and Crews

Many armed robbers work in gangs, usually with a minimum of three members: one to do the scary stuff – shouting threats, waving the gun around and generally terrifying people into compliance – one to gather the money and also as back-up for the first man, and the third to drive the get-away car. Sometimes there are as many as six in a gang, but unless you are knocking over a security depot or the Bank of England, it's odds on you'll be working non-stop just to pay the wages. Each gang has its own MO and identifying features, such as choice of targets and working hours. For example, in the seventies there was a gang of van robbers who became known as the Thursday Mob because their favourite day for security-van robberies was a Thursday. Then there was the Crash-Bang Gang, so called because their method of robbing banks was to kick the doors in – crash – and fire a shot into the ceiling – bang. Most criminals have a superstitious streak and can point to things that are lucky or unlucky for them when committing crime. If they hit a bank that is particularly lucrative for them, they will go on hitting the same branch throughout their careers. The Chainsaw Gang hit a security van inside the Blackwall Tunnel on two different occasions because it had been such a touch the first time around. Little Andy robbed the same building society nine times until, eventually, they had to close the branch down. The Laughing Bank Robbers had a penchant for the old Midland Banks, before they were taken over by the Chinese. A lot of the time it's just a luck thing which tends to become ritual for the robbers. And it always comes as a shock when the luck runs out. There have been some strange old gangs and crews over the years – and here are some of them.

The Cash and Carry Crew was a black gang out of Harlesden led by a stocky, ferocious robber named Bulldog. The gang was ruthless when it came to robbing and would hit anywhere that might contain a prize, but its favourite targets were cash and carry warehouses, where the members would not only empty the safe of cash but also load up a van with spirits and cigarettes before making their get-away. Having a load-up on highly saleable goods sometimes tripled their take, and the boys were in clover every time they hit a cash and carry. As well as Bulldog there were two other members of the gang: Yellow was a big, mean-looking half-caste who carried a 9mm Glock pistol even when not working and had been known to fire it off if the mood took him, and Crispy would just do whatever Bulldog told him to do because he was as thick as two short planks. They were a formidable crew and had some nice little touches before it all came on top for them.

Their last job was a cash and carry on an industrial estate close to the M25. It was owned and run by an Asian family who had built it up from scratch; all of them worked in the business, even their ten-year-old son. Bulldog's crew had never had any agg on their jobs – they were always heavily armed and even a blind man could see that these boys meant business, so it was best not to fuck about with them. They would enter the premises masked up and quickly round up the workers at gunpoint before holding them all in a central location, usually the office, as the crew went about its work. The gang would single out the manager and force him to open the safe, either through threats, or a pistol-whipping if he proved reluctant. Then they would force the staff to load their Transit van, which Crispy would have driven up to the entrance. In effect, they were take-over robbers who were confident enough in their own abilities of control to hang around on a job for as long as it took. Obviously, they would neutralize any alarm system before they started.

On this particular job they gathered the five members of the family together in the office, as usual, and told the father, who was also the manager, to open the safe. He refused, and Yellow gave him a few whacks with his Glock. Bloodied but unbowed, the man still refused to open the safe or tell the gang where the key might be hidden. Bulldog, seeing the stubbornness in his eyes, ordered Yellow and Crispy to search all those present for the key. After a couple of minutes it became apparent that the key was not on any of them, so he then ordered a search of the office – and still there was no sign of a key. Bulldog was not going to leave the job without the cash so he ordered Yellow to rough up the man some more. In the end Yellow's arm grew tired of hitting before the man grew tired of refusing to comply. The man was a mess, blood pouring from his head and face, but there was no way he was giving up his hard-earned cash to these robbers. The rest of the family, his wife, brother, sister-in-law and young son, stood stony-faced throughout this beating. Realizing they were getting nowhere slowly, Bulldog called Yellow aside and had a whispered conversation with him. Then Bulldog told the manager that if he didn't start co-operating immediately, Yellow was going to take his son into the next room and shoot him.

You would think that this kind of threat from what were obviously ruthless and violent men would be enough to make any father's blood run cold and force co-operation. After all, who could value money over the life of their child? But the manager was made of rock. He said something in Urdu to his son and then refused to say another word. Bulldog gave Yellow the nod and the half-caste, with an evil smile on his face, pulled the boy out of line and marched him into the next room. Bulldog faced the manager once more and gave him the ultimatum again – give us the money or your son dies. The man closed his eyes slowly and kept his mouth firmly shut. The boy's mother was crying, wailing and wringing her hands, but her husband was in a zone of his own. Incensed by the man's refusal even to acknowledge him, Bulldog shouted the order and there was the sound of a gunshot from the next room. The mother and sister-in-law collapsed into each other's arms in a cacophony of screeching and crying, but the father remained impassive. Bulldog now told the man that if he didn't shake a leg and get that safe open, the next one to go would be his wife, and then each member of his family until he was the only one left. The man opened his eyes and looked directly at Bulldog. 'You have taken my only son,' he said slowly. 'There is nothing more you can do to me.'

At that moment Bulldog realized that they could shoot the whole family in front of him but the man was never going to open the safe. He mentally shrugged and knew he was on a loser, so he decided to cut his losses and just load up the van and go. He called Yellow in from the other room and he entered, pulling the boy, very much alive but with a piece of tape over his mouth to stop him crying out and giving the game away. Yellow had discharged his pistol into the air as he had been instructed by Bulldog. Yes, the Cash and Carry Crew were ruthless, violent men, but even they drew the line at killing a ten-year-old kid. The boy was reunited with the rest of the family, who were all over him, hugging, kissing and crying, except for the father, who remained still and stony. Crispy went out and brought the van around and Bulldog ordered the family to start loading, but when they moved to do it the father shouted an order in Urdu and they all moved back into line and refused to move. Bulldog was exasperated but, not willing to go through any more of this, he ordered Yellow and Crispy to load the van while he covered the family with his shotgun. With a bit of grumbling about how they might as well give up crime and go to work on a building site if they had to do the donkey work themselves, the boys set about their task.

What Bulldog and his crew didn't know but were about to find out was that, as they had made their entry into the building, the father had spotted them and had had time to press a silent alarm that led directly to a security firm twenty miles away. The firm had received the alarm and informed the nearest police station, who mobilized an armed team on the off chance that it wasn't a false alarm. The first Bulldog knew of this was when he glanced at a CCTV monitor in the office linked to a camera which covered the yard and saw several flak-jacketed coppers advancing silently on the building holding Heckler & Koch MP5s as though they meant business. Bulldog warned the rest of the gang that it was on top and then ran from the office and headed towards the rear entrance of the building. Yellow and Crispy legged it out of the front door and ran slap-bang into the police. They put up a bit of a struggle but were soon overpowered. Bulldog managed to get out of the building and vaulted a fence that led down to the motorway. Followed closely by three armed coppers who were ordering him to drop his gun or be shot, Bulldog kept running but threw his shotgun back at them. There was no way he was going to engage in a shoot-out with police marksmen, and he figured that if he didn't have a gun they wouldn't shoot him. That's a gamble many robbers have lost in the past but Bulldog was lucky that the cops who were chasing him were not the cowboy kind who shoot first and make up cover stories later.

Bulldog made it to the motorway and managed to get across three lanes to the central reservation before realizing the reckless futility of his flight and sticking his hands up. The police brought the fast-moving traffic to a halt and Bulldog was taken into custody. And that was the end of the Cash and Carry Crew. At their subsequent trial they were found guilty. Bulldog received sixteen years, Yellow fifteen and Crispy fourteen. The father who had stood up to the robbers and who would have let his young son be executed rather than hand over the money in the safe was congratulated by the trial judge for 'bravery and fortitude in the face of extreme peril'. Personally, I wouldn't mind this fella guarding my money but I'm glad he's not my dad. The Cash and Carry Crew served their sentences, were released and are now all back in prison serving longer sentences for crimes they further committed as individuals.

The Maggie Thatchers was a team of Islington bank robbers who, quite by accident, hit on a gimmick. It was the only thing that made them stand out from other such bread-and-butter robbery teams of the time. In the eighties, at the height of Conservatism and the armed-robbery boom, some shops began selling joke masks of the most infamous politicians of the day. The masks were funny caricatures of the likes of Margaret Thatcher and Ronald Reagan and were much loved by students and protesters alike. One afternoon in the winter of 1986 four men entered a bank in Camden Town with intent to rob. They were dressed in identical blue boiler suits, carrying various firearms, from sawn-off shotguns to a Russian Tokarov pistol, and they were all wearing Margaret Thatcher masks. This quartet of 'iron ladies' demanded the cash, and within three minutes had slipped out the door £20,000 richer – proving that free enterprise really was working under the Tories. The robbery was reported in the local papers, but I think the national dailies really missed a trick in not picking up on it.

The Maggie Thatchers, as the gang became known, was led by an experienced bank robber from Holloway Road named Red. Red had already served ten years for armed robbery and was now out and back in business with a new team. He had chosen the Margaret Thatcher masks for the job not as some kind of political statement but because they were cheap and available. But when he read of the stir the masks had caused, it tickled his funny bone and he decided to milk the situation for laughs. Just because you go around pointing guns at people and growling for a living doesn't necessarily mean you don't have a sense of humour, and Red had one. On the gang's next bank job Red, in Thatcher mask, told the assembled staff and customers that he was 'merely seeking to strike a blow for first-time buyers by lowering interest rates!' This was a hoot and went down a storm with his terrified victims, who thought the gang might actually be terrorists come to murder them. One old woman fainted on the spot.

The Maggie Thatchers did a couple more robberies, including one in Kensal Rise during which Red suddenly shouted, 'The lady is not for turning!' in the middle of the quiet banking hall, scaring not only the victims of the robbery but the rest of his own team. Red thought his antics were highly amusing but the rest of the gang grew tired of the political bullshit and began to drift into other gangs as Red started watching *Newsnight* regularly and taking an unhealthy interest in Margaret Thatcher herself. The last straw came when one member of the gang turned up for a job with a Ronald Reagan mask and Red suggested they enter the bank holding hands. After that no one would work with Red, as he was classed as a loon. Realizing that he had got a bit carried away with it, Red abandoned the political satire and formed another, more conventional crew, having some success before being ambushed on a bit of work by the Flying Squad and PT17, the specialist firearms squad. Red is presently serving twenty years.

The Celtic Acid Gang was made up of four Celtic football supporters, two Scottish and two Irish, who were big into the acid-house music scene. They were all living in east London and met up on their way up to Scotland for the football and then again at illegal raves in the barns and fields of south-east

England. They all had previous convictions for various crimes, from illegal possession of drugs and offensive weapons to GBH, but none had a conviction for armed robbery before they teamed up and decided to hit a few banks for the craic and the money. Chucky, the leader of the gang, had spent three years in the French Foreign Legion before deserting and going to live in Amsterdam. While in the 'Dam he became involved in the smuggling and distribution of hash, LSD and Ecstasy tablets into the UK. He had to leave Holland after the drug operation was taken down by Dutch police and Interpol, and he slipped into England on a false passport.

Having met up with the three other likely lads, Chucky put it to them one day that if they wanted to make good money they should form a gang and rob a few banks. The boys, having nothing much else to do, were amenable to this suggestion, so Chucky, using his Dutch contacts, arranged for suitable fire-arms to come across from the continent hidden in boxes of fresh tulips. Chucky was the paranoid type, which came from knowing that not only was he a Foreign Legion deserter but he was also classified as an international criminal and had an Interpol warrant hanging over him, and he wanted to amass enough money to flee Europe for the more unreachable environs of South America, where he might bribe government officials into allowing him citizenship. He never told the other lads what he needed the money for and they never even knew his real name. Chucky knew his way around a gun and had been trained in unarmed combat and knife-fighting in the Legion, so he was a bit tasty and no one objected when he became the leader of their little gang.

Chucky may have been the big cheese when it came to rucking and drug distribution, but he was an amateur when it came to robbery, and he made a few fundamental mistakes. If they were robbing banks four-handed, then he should have realized they were never going to clear enough money to get too far ahead in the game. Taking till money is no good for a big gang, and there has to be some technique for getting behind the counter and at the vault or robbing the reserve on, or soon after, delivery. Just walking in off the street is a mug's game unless you are happy with survival money. But Chucky just kept plugging away at it, sometimes walking out with as little as five grand, which is OK for a lone robber but, split four ways, meant they had to go to work twice a week in order to make it worthwhile. But one refinement Chucky did come up with was very clever, if a little after the fact.

Chucky supplied the gang with LSD microdot tablets, which they would carry into their bank robberies and swallow as they were leaving the bank. The idea behind this innovation was that if things went very wrong and the police were waiting outside a jug for them, or one of their number got separated and happened to get captured, then they would have a ready-made defence. They would demand a doctor on reaching the police station and request blood samples be drawn. Once the blood had been analysed and entered into evidence they could then claim at court that either they had been administered a hallucinogenic substance against their will and had been forced to rob the bank for some higher controlling force, or that they had no idea what they were doing due to the influence of the drug. Either way it would surely be enough to throw a shadow of doubt into most jurors' minds and maybe lead to an acquittal. It was a clever ploy and may have worked, in ideal circumstances, but the Celtic Acid Gang fucked up.

On their fifth bank job things started to go very wrong for the gang. Unknown to them, Chucky had 'crossed targets' with a notorious robber who was being watched by the Flying Squad. Crossing targets is when one criminal unknowingly wanders into the sphere of another criminal who is under surveillance by the police. When the police target a criminal for surveillance, they follow him everywhere, noting his every movement and taking photos of every single person he meets with or talks to, sometimes for months on end. If a 'strange' face turns up in any of the photographic evidence, then copies are made and distributed to all law agencies to see if anyone can identify the face and put a name to it. Chucky had met with this particular watched man seeking a bit of advice on how to hit the big money and was photographed. Chucky was pinned by Scotland Yard as having an outstanding Interpol warrant for drug distribution, but someone wondered what he was doing talking to a top-of-the-range armed robber, so it was decided that, rather than just pick him up from the flat a couple of the surveillance team had followed him to, they would put a small team on Chucky and see what he was up to.

The police watched Chucky and soon picked up the rest of the gang. Within a couple of weeks they knew all the gang's addresses, haunts and habits and the location of the lock-up where they kept their robbery kit and stolen get-away cars. The case was handed to the Flying Squad, who, as is their wont, decided to follow them to their next job and then mount an ambush. The gang decided to rob a bank in East Ham, but this was to be their last bank job, as Chucky had received enough tips from his robbery contact to start planning a few security-van jobs and get hold of the big money. They went into the bank as usual, Chucky wearing his trademark disguise of motorcycle leathers and a full-faced crash helmet with a tinted visor. Once inside the banking hall, they pulled their guns and proceeded to rob the gaff. But Chucky ran into his first bit of trouble when he pushed to the front of the queue and got to the jump. There was an old woman being served, and thinking that Chucky was there to take her pension money, she refused to budge. She later told newspaper reporters that, far from being scared, she was more furious than anything else. 'I lived through the bleeding Blitz, you know, and no young tearaway with a shotgun was taking my pension money!'

As Chucky made to move her aside so he could address the cashier, the old woman hit him over the head with her handbag.

Chucky wasn't hurt by the handbag blows – he was wearing a crash helmet, after all – but he did find it annoying and embarrassing. He was an ex-Foreign Legion killer and now armed robber, having the crap bashed out of him by an eighty-year-old woman with a handbag. He gently moved the woman to one side and told her to calm down, which she did when she saw he wasn't after her pension after all, and he trained his shotgun on the cashier. Then the gang proceeded to rob the bank. Meanwhile, outside, the police ambush squad had got into place and stopped the traffic by means of a roadblock at either end of the normally busy road. The gang, once it had finished its business, popped the acid tabs and went to leave the bank. Chucky was first, and as he reached the top step leading down to the street, he noticed the lack of traffic and immediately smelled a rat, or several. He ordered the gang to retreat back into the bank and the police cursed their luck as they saw the door closing on them.

As siege situations go, it was pretty much a damp squib. The gang held out for an hour inside the bank before coming to the conclusion that there was no way out but to surrender. They were all tripping heavily from the LSD tabs but, luckily, no one had a bad trip and decided to shoot his way out or start executing hostages to see the pretty colours their heads would make as the bullets passed through. The boys laid down their guns and walked out of the bank, their hands on their heads, one at a time. To Chucky's eternal shame, the picture the newspapers seized on from the CCTV footage inside the bank was the one of him taking a handbag in the crash helmet from a frail pensioner. Some papers ran it under the headline SUPERGRAN! At trial a year later, the gang's acid defence cut no ice with the jury and they were each jailed for fifteen years. When Chucky had served his sentence he was extradited to

Holland on the Interpol warrant and received another ten years for his drug charges. The Celtic Acid Gang earned about as much money as they would have done if they had spent their days working at straight jobs instead of robbing banks. As far as I know they have never gone back to armed robbery.

One gang that will certainly go down in British criminal history was known as the Dirty Dozen. It was so named by the Flying Squad, because of the loose connection between the twelve main members, though they never actually went on any one job twelve-handed. The gang was from the Kilburn and Cricklewood areas and its members were mainly of Irish descent, though second generation, having grown up in London. The gang had access to plenty of firearms from their teens as their part of London had more than its share of drug dealing, and where there are drugs, firearms naturally make an appearance. The main nucleus of the gang began their robbery careers around 1980, led by a charismatic leader known as Gentleman Jimmy. They rinsed their corner of London, robbing every likely target at least twice before branching out to other parts of London and the suburbs. They were voracious robbers, sometimes hitting two or three targets a week, and spent their money on clothes, jewellery, fast cars and cocaine. Throughout the eighties and nineties the Dirty Dozen was top of the Flying Squad's 'Most Wanted' list, but the cops could only rend their garments and gnash their teeth in frustration as the gang was too smart to walk into an ambush. The Dirty Dozen pioneered the use of scanners to monitor the police airwaves in their part of the city, and they always seemed to be one step ahead of the frustrated police.

Then, in the early nineties, the police got lucky and managed to ambush Gentleman Jimmy and his gang as it made a hit on a security van. Jimmy and his firm were nicked without a shot being fired, and after a long trial at the Old Bailey were jailed for many years, Gentleman Jimmy receiving the longest sentence, as befitted the ringleader, of twenty-four years. Five years into his sentence Gentleman Jimmy escaped from a prison escort and has not been seen or heard of by the authorities to this day. The police didn't get all the gang members in their original swoop, and those that were left carried on with their robbery careers with varying degrees of success. Until, one by one, these gang members started getting nicked and jailed for lumps of bird. Old Bill were over the lunar orb with their apparent success in wiping out the Dirty Dozen, but they were later to realize that, as they took out the top men in the gang, new, younger members would step up to take their places. By 1992 a whole new generation of the Dirty Dozen were at it and the financial institutions of the capital were still taking heavy hits.

The men who had now taken on Gentleman Jimmy's mantle were brothers from Harlesden called Finbar and Danny. Finbar was particularly violent and had a reputation as a hard bastard around the manor. He had once beaten and glassed a man in his local pub because there was a rumour that the man had committed a rape on a young girl who he vaguely knew. He also wasn't shy about pulling loaded guns on people for any real, or perceived, slight. Plenty of people were afraid of Finbar, but everyone loved Danny. Danny was calm and friendly and, though not averse to a bit of violence if the situation really called for it, had a great personality and sense of humour. The boys, along with the rest of their gang, were working robbers, and hardly a week went by when they weren't either looking at a job or out committing one. Though they all lived in council flats, where they had grown up, the gang drove top-of-the-range motors and dressed like premiership footballers. They looked after their family and friends and spent money as if they were getting it for free, which, in reality, they were.

Finbar and Danny were up for anything. One night they

were on their way for a night out at a club on Cricklewood Broadway when they spotted a security van and a guard loading a cash-machine. Though the brothers were unarmed and dressed for a night on the town, they decided this opportunity was too good to miss. With their ties wrapped around their faces as masks and a beer bottle they picked out of the gutter, they jumped the guards. Holding the broken bottle up to the guard's throat and threatening to stick it in him, Finbar made him open the box and take out the security devices. Then, with Danny carrying the cash box, they legged it through the backstreets and got clean away with £60,000 in cash. This was how cool and on the ball the boys were, ready to rock 'n' roll at the drop of a hat.

Another time, the brothers drew down on a post-office security van and the guard who was carrying the cash box managed to get inside the post office and lock the door behind him. The boys simply blew the glass out of the door with a shotgun blast, calmly walked in and took the box from the cowering guard. The police knew all about Finbar and Danny, but there was fuck all they could do without any solid evidence so it became another waiting game. But then the boys were unlucky enough to be spotted by a passing police patrol car as they exited a just-robbed bank. The uniformed cops followed them to their get-away vehicles – a car and a powerful motor-bike so they could split up immediately – and confronted the masked men. Finbar pulled his .45 Browning automatic pistol from his leather jacket and walked towards the two unarmed officers as Danny made his get-away on the motorbike. When Finbar was less than three feet away from the coppers he cocked the gun and pulled the trigger. Both cops dived out of the way and scurried beneath their car while Finbar looked at the pistol quizzically. He jacked the slide to see if a round had been caught in the mechanism, but it was clear. He cocked the gun once again and aimed under the car at the quivering coppers. He pulled the trigger and nothing happened. With a shrug he walked back to his car and drove off.

Though the boys had been masked, the bank had fitted their MO and the police were sure that Finbar and Danny were the robbers. The fact that Finbar had attempted to kill two police officers put them right at the top of the police target list and they renewed their efforts to catch these dangerous and arrogant criminals. When Finbar later test-fired the Browning it went off no problem, but he sold it on anyway and bought a revolver. One of the robbery gang, and probably the only person more gratuitously violent than Finbar, was Slimy Steven. Steven's *raison d'être* was coshing guards and spraying ammonia in their faces, even after they had handed over the prize. It was heavily rumoured that Steven had killed a drug-dealer to whom he owed £25,000. The man was found shot to death in his own car soon after a meeting with him.

Steven had fallen out with Finbar and Danny over a girl but swallowed his hatred and kept working with them because they were great earners. The police suspected Slimy Steven of a bank robbery committed by a lone gunman, so they raided his home early one morning and discovered a sawn-off shotgun and a box of cartridges for the gun. He was arrested and, at the police station, knowing he would be going to prison for a fair old while and figuring he'd had a good run, he offered to turn supergrass on the rest of the Dirty Dozen and Finbar and Danny in particular. The Flying Squad had had the gang under intermittent surveillance for over five years without ever getting a sniff of evidence on them, so they jumped at Slimy Steven's offer. In return for a token sentence of five years and for moving him and his entire family into the witness protection scheme, rehousing them all and giving them thousands of pounds of taxpayers' money as resettlement funds, Steven gave the police details of over a hundred robberies the gang had been involved in.

He gave evidence at the Old Bailey against Finbar and Danny and smiled as they were convicted of over fifty armed robberies between them, the record number of convictions for that crime. Finbar went down for life and Danny for twenty-four years. The rest of the Dirty Dozen received various sentences for their deeds. Slimy Steven, perhaps the most guilty of all the robbers, having admitted to over five hundred crimes, many of them violent, did less than two years of jail time and is now living somewhere far away where nobody knows him. It is rumoured that he's writing a book about his exploits as a supergrass. Who knows, if it becomes a bestseller, he might get a visit from the ever-elusive Gentleman Jimmy looking for a signed copy from the man who eventually brought his gang down. Stranger things have happened.

16. Amateurs

With the rise in illegal-drug addiction in British society there has come a whole generation of desperate criminals, people who, without the need to feed an expensive drug habit and without the false sense of confidence and ability that comes as part of a drug-induced episode, would never previously have dreamed of attempting to commit crimes – or, at least, crimes that are way out of their league in terms of their scale of seriousness. No matter what you may think about the men who commit serious armed robbery for a living, and though I myself used to be one of those men and now find their actions reprehensible, they do possess certain qualities that, in other situations and circumstances – say, big business or war – would be entirely laudable. It takes nerves of steel and supreme confidence to do a job where you know that one mistake, one missed detail or wrong move can see you shot dead by armed police officers or deprived of your liberty for at least a decade. Yes, armed robbers are lazy, greedy parasites who cause untold fear and misery, but junkie amateurs are worse.

In the late eighties and early nineties there sprang up a crop of amateur, some might say bungling, robbers with a penchant for robbing banks and building societies with fruit and veg instead of firearms. Of course, these men were so low down the criminal food chain or so erratic in their habits that no self-respecting criminal would even contemplate supplying them with a real gun. Criminals, no matter how ruthless, still have innocent friends and family members who use financial institutions and they would not like to see them gunned down by a clucking skag-head who's just had a refusal over the jump.

There are criminals who really don't give a toss who they deal with – drug-dealers, for instance – but in my experience the armed-robbery set are usually men of twisted morals but morals none the less, and giving a gun to some numpty who might shoot his own foot off or, worse, some innocent person's head, is a no-no. There is also the fact that such a div might grass you up in a hot second and you could find yourself standing next to him in the dock as the judge gets ready to piss a few decades down the toilet of incarceration. Anyway, most of these clowns have to resort to gun-like objects in their quest for easy money.

On occasion, and at a push, I myself have resorted to imitation firearms when the real thing wasn't available. I have also had real guns that had no ammunition on robberies, and I once emptied every till drawer in a bank with no more than my fingers inside a brown paper bag – though I wouldn't recommend this to anyone of a nervous disposition. But as the vast majority of robbers never actually fire a shot on a robbery, it could be argued that guns are actually surplus to requirements. In reality they are a frightener – and, as a very last resort, a means of escape. Few people will confront or tackle a man with a gun, though there are some fuckwits who will, just like there are some people who have to put their hand in the fire to see if it really burns. For me, and others, there is also the comfort of knowing that a shot into the ceiling or into the air is an attention-getter *par excellence* when things start getting a bit warm. But I can honestly say that I never had to fire a shot in the commission of any of the hundred-plus robberies I committed during my career as a robber. Some of the following characters could have the same feeble boast, but that was only because most of them didn't have a gun.

Dodgy Derek was a young kid who needed cash for his crack habit and decided to hit a couple of building societies. He had few criminal contacts and the only time he had ever seen a real gun was on a school trip to the Imperial War Museum when he was twelve years old, so he was a bit stumped as to what he would use as a weapon. He considered going in with a knife and holding it up to a customer's throat but wasn't sure if this would be enough to get the cashiers to hand over the dosh. He was right in this thought, as I explained in an earlier chapter. Besides, knives are messy and way too personal. With a gun, or something that looks like one, you can keep people at arm's length and that's a must when you may be dealing with a crowd of terrified people. So Derek decided that a large banana in a plastic bag would be just the job.

Derek entered a small branch of a well-known building society and nervously approached the counter. With his coat collar up and his baseball cap pulled low over his eyes he took his bag-covered fruit from his pocket and mumbled, 'Give me all the money, or I'll shoot.' Maybe the cashier was brand-new in the job or a bit short-sighted, but she gasped in shock and emptied the money from her cash-drawer, placing the notes in the till-well. Derek couldn't believe his luck and scooped up the £1,300 and stuffed it into his pocket. Without bothering to get the rest of the tills he turned on his heel and quickly left the building. There were several customers and at least two other staff serving at the counter but nobody even knew a robbery had been committed until the cashier fainted just after Derek left. The robbery had gone without a hitch and Derek was in crack-heaven for a couple of days, until the cash ran out or, rather, was blown out of Derek's crack pipe. As is always the case, this taste of easy money had Derek hooked not only on class A product but on the means of getting it. He hit another two building societies in quick succession. Though the cashiers on both jobs handed over the cash, they both confided that the 'gun' the robber was using looked remarkably like a banana. The local papers picked up on this fact and nicknamed the robber 'Banana Man' after the children's cartoon character, and basically lampooned and ridiculed him in print.

Derek didn't care about all the publicity – he was too busy scratching himself and staring glaze-eyed into the middle distance in some stinking crack den in Woolwich – but a lot of building-society cashiers read it and kept a look-out for anyone who might try to hold them up with some yellow fruit. So it was that when Derek walked into his next robbery and flashed the plastic-covered banana, the cashier merely smiled and pressed the silent alarm. She delayed him by insisting that she count out the notes individually, but even Dodgy Derek wasn't stupid enough to stand for too much of that: as she reached £640, he told her to just throw the rest into the till-well and he would count it himself. Derek got out of the gaff about thirty seconds in front of the police, and as he ran full pelt through the streets chased by several large coppers, he managed to stash the money into his Y-fronts and also to peel and partially eat his gun. But it was all in vain, as he was rugby-tackled by a sixteen-stone uniform and brought down in a flurry of banknotes and banana bits. At Woolwich Crown Court some months later he pleaded guilty to armed robbery and possession of an imitation firearm and was jailed for nine years.

Another chancer who was to fall foul of the law and end up eating his gun was an East End tearaway and junkie named Ernie. Ernie, needing to feed a voracious heroin addiction picked up in prison, where he had been serving time for petty theft, decided to hit the same robbery trail taken by his opposite number south of the river. Though Ernie had never heard of Banana Man, he had heard of blagging and, just like infamous American bank robber Willie Sutton, Ernie chose banks because 'that's where the money was'. Looking for something that resembled a gun, Ernie was drawn to the veg counter of a supermarket where he did most of his hoisting. Spotting a rather large cucumber, Ernie was stunned by its resemblance to a shotgun, particularly when he wrapped it up in brown paper. So he slipped the length of veg into his voluminous shoplifting coat and headed for home. Ernie considered actually carving the cucumber with a knife so that it looked even more like a gun. He realized that with a few strokes of the blade he could give it a trigger-guard and a double barrel, maybe even a bit of engraving on the side like a real classy Purdey. But in the end he couldn't be bothered. He needed cash for drugs not a hobby as a veg-whittler. So off he went.

Given the obvious monicker of the Cucumber Kid by the police and the press, Ernie went on to have a short-run but pretty effective career as an armed robber. He hit six banks in quick succession and cleared around £20,000, which is not bad for a man armed only with the fruit of the *Cucumis sativus*. After each job Ernie would carve up his cucumber and eat it with fish-paste sandwiches. Then he would nip down to the supermarket and nick another likely-looking weapon. He believed that thieving the cucumbers added to his luck, even though he could now afford to buy them. But it wasn't long before Ernie got his collar felt by Old Bill. The trouble with skag-heads is that once they get a bit of the old powder in their veins they can't keep their mouths shut, and Ernie started boasting about his vegetable antics to the wrong people. Once again our amateur was charged with armed robbery and possession of an imitation firearm, and was sentenced to seven years' imprisonment. His story warranted a small column on page five of the *Sun*, and that was the last that was heard of the Cucumber Kid.

Quite apart from fruit and veg, some amateurs are willing to use anything to give the appearance of a gun in order to hold up jugs. One lunatic from the north-east of England, who

I met in my prison travels, had his own unique gun substitute. Geordie Keith, as he was known, did not one but two separate series of bank robberies using the metal pipe section from a Henry hoover. But Geordie Keith did not confine his shenanigans to armed robbery. He was pretty much an expert bungler at most other crimes as well, ram-raiding being one of his favourites. Ram-raiding is the process of driving a stolen car through the front of a shop or warehouse and then loading it with as much loot as you can before driving away. Sometimes, after breaking in, ram-raiders load several vehicles before making their get-away. This crime started in the north of England in the early nineties and quickly spread across the whole country.

Geordie Keith never really had much luck with ram-raiding, though it wasn't for want of trying. One night he and a mate of his thought they might do a jeweller's and nicked a couple of old Fords for the job. The reason they chose the Ford marque for their vehicles was nothing to do with preference or suitability for the job in hand but more to do with the fact that these were the only cars they were capable of nicking. Unless you counted Morris Minors – and most of those couldn't build up enough speed to smash through a wet paper bag. Ford motor vehicles used to be notoriously easy to nick as their doors could be opened with a pair of household scissors and the ignition started with a screwdriver. They are the favourite make for kids and joyriders. The fella Geordie Keith chose to work with was a gadgee named Biff, who wore thick, bottle-bottomed specs and was still blind as a bat even with two inches of refracted glass in front of his piggy eyes. Biff classed himself as a bit of a wheelman but he could barely see the windscreen let alone the road in front of him. He lined his hot Ford Fiesta up to the front of the jewellery shop and slammed his foot on the accelerator. The car shot forward in a cloud of smoking tyres, mounted the pavement and veered off, crashing cleanly through the plate-glass window of the Cancer Research charity shop next door to the jeweller's.

Gutted that they had missed their target but unable to resist the possibility of nicking something, anything, Geordie Keith legged it through the ruined front of the charity shop and grabbed two armfuls of second-hand men's suits and moth-eaten overcoats before racing to the get-away car. The job was a bit of a disappointment to the clueless twosome but for a while they were the best-dressed Geordies in Wallsend. Not put off by their poor show at the old ram-raiding game, they started planning their next job. Biff claimed some electrical knowledge, but it was mostly to do with the fact that he could change a thirteen-amp fuse, and he claimed that he had been told it was possible to cut the alarm systems of a row of shops if you jemmied open one of those green metal boxes that sometimes sit at road junctions. Geordie Keith told him that he thought these boxes contained only telephone wires as he had sometimes seen British Telecom workers fiddling with them. Biff nodded sagely and put a grubby finger to the side of his nose. 'Aye, bonnie lad, but shop alarms run off phone lines, d'ya see?' Geordie Keith could only bow to the superior knowledge of his myopic mate, as he didn't really have a clue when it came to technical gear. His bedsit had been in darkness for a month because he didn't know how to change a bulb.

In the dead of night the gruesome twosome jemmied open a green telephone junction box just up the road from a row of sports, jewellery and clothes shops. The idea was to cut the alarms and then ram-raid at least three of the lucrative premises at their leisure. Wearing wellies, and rubber gloves up to his elbows and wielding a pair of rubber-handled bolt-croppers, just in case he got an electric shock, Biff looked at the jumble of hundreds of different-coloured wires inside the box as Geordie Keith kept watch on the silent street. Having not a clue what he was doing but not wanting to appear stupid in front of his equally stupid compadre, Biff just grabbed a bunch of wires and, turning his face away in case of an explosion, cut through them with the bolt-croppers. There was no outward sign of anything happening so Biff assumed he had done good. He gave Geordie Keith the thumbs-up and they jogged back to their waiting Ford battering ram and drove slowly to their targets.

The boys lined their car up on the window of a shop selling leather coats and then let her blow. The car mounted the kerb, shot across the pavement and into the front of the shop with a loud crash. For a split second there was only the sound of rending metal, splintering wood and falling glass, then the loud whoop of the burglar alarm filled the night air. The boys were also stuck, their car wedged firmly into the shopfront, as the broken building had collapsed down on to their bonnet. The engine had stalled so Biff started it up again and tried going forward, but all this did was jam the front half of the car further into the building. He threw the gear stick in reverse and the tyres threw up a cloud of noxious-smelling smoke as they slid and skidded on the pavement, unable to find a grip. The alarm was still wailing and, to make it worse, the boys couldn't open any of the doors as they were blocked by debris. They had to scramble into the back seat and take it in turns to kick the back windscreen until it collapsed outwards and they were able to clamber from the car. They ran across the street to their get-away car and discovered that Biff had left the screwdriver in the ignition of the car trapped in the front of the shop. They had no choice but to make their get-away on foot. Empty-handed.

The boys had one more try at ram-raiding before they gave it up as a lost cause. This time they crashed through the front of a supermarket and legged it up the long aisles to the back of the shop where the cigarettes and alcohol were kept. It was a big building, and by the time they got back down the aisles with what was to be their first load, they could hear the sound of police sirens even over the sound of the shop's alarm. They jumped into their car and lit out with what they had. When they examined their loot later, Geordie Keith had nicked a twenty-four-can case of cheap lager and Biff, inexplicably, had grabbed a box of Cadbury's Bourneville chocolate bars. 'Eee, it's better than that milk shite,' was all he would say by way of explanation.

Realizing he was never going to make his criminal fortune with Biff, or from ram-raiding, Geordie Keith decided to go it alone. He dreamed of being a real villain, having loads of money, flash cars and gorgeous women hanging off his arm, and he knew, from watching gangster films and documentaries, that the only way to get all this was by becoming a bank robber. He began to ask around for a gun, but a melt like Keith was not going to be trusted with a shooter, so he came up blank in all directions. In desperation, he ripped the pipes from the Henry hoover he had in his bedsit and lashed two lengths together with a bit of tape. He figured that as long as he kept most of the 'gun' concealed under a bag he might just get away with it.

Surprisingly, the cashiers at the first bank that Geordie Keith tried didn't think he was a cleaner come to hoover the carpets but accepted him as the genuine article and handed over the cash sweet as a nut. Even Geordie Keith himself could hardly credit it, but the old hoover-pipes-in-a-bag coup really worked. He didn't steal massive amounts, just over £6,000 in all of his robberies, but it was good money for a man whose previous biggest score had been a stack of second-hand suits and a case of cheapo lager. Geordie Keith was living the dream and money was no object: sometimes he would have both chicken-and-mushroom and steak-and-kidney pies when he walked into his local chip shop. But, inevitably, he ended up nicked for something silly, and in order to clear the books for a new start when he got out of prison he coughed the lot about his hoover robberies. At court the psychiatrists' reports said that though Keith wasn't technically mad he was one sandwich short of the picnic and a little slow on the uptake. The judge took this into account and sentenced him to six years in total for the hoover jobs and everything else he had admitted.

That should really have been the end of the Geordie Keith story – he went away and did his bit of bird without incident – but it turns out he was a real card-carrying recidivist. After getting out of jail and going back to his manor, Geordie Keith once again heard the siren song of crime calling him. I suppose it's understandable really – not defensible but understandable – he was a poorly educated, slightly backward man from the slums of what was then probably one of the most poverty-ridden areas of the country with massive unemployment and a crumbling infrastructure. What else was he going to do? Go on the dole? Anyway, Geordie Keith cut out the ram-raiding this time and went straight for the hoover pipes. He robbed three more banks of moderate amounts of money before he was caught. This time the world had moved on and the judge was not so understanding. Geordie Keith now fell under the auspices of the Two Strikes Act pioneered by Michael Howard. Geordie Keith was sentenced to life imprisonment as a second-time 'violent offender'. At the time of writing he has served almost nine years and probably has another nine to do. Like the hoover he once used as a firearm, all he can do is suck it up and keep going.

Another amateur who really was dangerous, though mostly to himself, was a robber who became known as Limpy. Limpy managed to get his hands on a real double-barrelled shotgun and ammunition for it. His game was robbing railway-station ticket kiosks which, before the influx of ticket machines, was a fairly lucrative business. His MO was to wait until the station was quiet then force the ticket clerk to open the door to the kiosk by showing him the sawn-off and threatening to blow his head off if he didn't do as he was told. Once inside, he would nick the money from the safe, lay the ticket clerk on the deck and walk briskly away with another week's heroin money. Nice work if you can get it, and as Limpy worked alone, the few thousand pounds' take was all his own.

I learnt many years ago that when dealing with loaded firearms you have to be very careful and always respect the fact that what you are handling is a lethal weapon. If the weapon is a hammer-cock model you should never cock the hammer unless you are about to shoot, and you should always be aware of the position of the safety-catch. Unfortunately for Limpy, he didn't get to know his gun before setting out on his crime spree. One afternoon he robbed the railway station at Crystal Palace, in south London, and in order to impress his seriousness on a reluctant ticket clerk, he cocked the hammer on his gun. After he had the cash and was on his way out, he slipped the sawn-off into the waistband of his trousers, forgetting the gun was still cocked, and it went off. Limpy blew his own foot off and was arrested at the scene as he rolled in agony on the station concourse. Amateurs – if they weren't so fucking dangerous they'd be funny.

Perhaps the most bungling of all amateur robbers I have ever met were Pip and Squeak, a pair of south London bandits who were either the most stupid, or unlucky, men alive. Pip and Squeak were a couple of commercial burglars who really got into armed robbery almost by accident and opportunity than planning and design. One night, as they were burgling a unit on an industrial estate in Wandsworth, they came across an unexpected bonus in a semi-automatic .225 rifle. It was hidden under a desk in the unit, which held two gross of boxed car stereos that the boys had targeted. They cleared the unit and also took the rifle. The gun wasn't loaded and there was no ammunition in the unit, but they figured it would be worth a few quid when sold on the black market. The next evening, as the boys sat watching *Crimewatch UK* over a fish supper in Pip's palatial bedsit in Streatham, Squeak suggested that they could probably do better than the robbers they were seeing on the TV screen, and that now they had a gun they might at least give it a try. Pip was up for it, imagining emptying bags of lovely cash on the carpet and rolling in it.

The next day Pip purchased a junior hacksaw and went to work on the barrel of the rifle. In its original length the gun was way too long to conceal under a coat. He lopped nine inches off and the gun now looked the part. The boys decided to hit a bank near Streatham Common and really enjoyed getting into the planning of it. The plan was a good one; it was just a shame that the mugs who were to put it into action were not really up to it. The bank was situated on a corner junction of the very busy high road and an equally busy left turn, and there were sets of traffic lights right outside the premises. Squeak had an idea that would ensure their get-away no matter how heavy the traffic or whether the lights were against them as they made their exit from the jug. He noticed that the pedestrian pavement outside the bank was very wide and suggested that, if they were to use a Mini for the get-away, they could drive straight up on the pavement and around the corner, thus avoiding the traffic lights and other traffic that might cause them to be blocked in. Pip thought this idea was a Brahmer and congratulated his divvy pal. They were mustard at making plans, now they just had to carry them out.

The boys had no trouble nicking a Mini. They found one in the backstreets of Brixton, keyed it up and drove off as though it was their own. On their way back to Streatham they noticed that the little car was low on fuel so they pulled into a small garage to fill it up. Pip had a bit of a temper on him so when he got into an argument with the fella behind the counter about going a penny over on the pump, he flew into a rage. He tried to go around the counter but the bloke pulled a baseball bat on him and he had to beat a temporary teeth-gnashing retreat. He climbed into the driver's seat of the stolen Mini and backed out on to the road. Then, with Squeak screaming beside him in terror, he threw the small car into gear and drove it directly at the shopfront of the petrol station, aiming for the counter where the assistant still stood with his baseball bat in his hand behind the wood and glass screen. The little car crashed straight through the shopfront and ended up at the far wall with its bonnet buried in plastic cartons of oil and brake fluid. The assistant had managed to dive to one side as the car struck and fell into a pile of steering locks. For a moment there was complete silence in the shop and then, with a loud, rending crash, the roof fell in. Pip wound down the window of the car and pointed at the dazed assistant. 'You mug!' he shouted. 'That'll fucking teach you!' He then keyed the engine, slammed the gearbox into reverse and shot backwards out of the ruined building, scattering debris all over the forecourt and the road beyond before driving off at speed. The boys had to dump the Mini – though it was barely damaged by the crash, the number plate and description would now be red-hot – and they spent another week looking for a suitable car to use on their bank job. They found one in a quiet street in Selhurst and the game was afoot once again.

On the day of the robbery Squeak was sitting in the stolen Mini, its engine running, outside the bank, while Pip, wearing a long overcoat to conceal the gun and a hat to conceal his features, marched into the bank. The bank was a big one, with a long banking hall and tiled floor, and there were several customers inside. Pip, screwing up his courage and thinking of all the loot he was about to get, stood just inside the entrance and looked around. The nearest customers were about ten feet away at the counter, and further into the bank, others were waiting patiently in the queue. He unbuttoned his overcoat and reached a hand inside to get the rifle, at the same time shouting loudly, 'This is a raid!' Unfortunately for him, when he had sawn the barrel from the gun he hadn't smoothed the edges of the remaining metal, and the burrs on the barrel had become entangled in the lining of his overcoat so, as Pip pulled the gun, he met with some resistance. By now all eyes had turned towards the sound of his shout and were watching as he seemed to be either struggling with something inside his coat or putting on an impromptu break-dancing display. In a panic now, Pip gave a hard pull and the fabric inside the coat ripped and released the rifle. But due to the sweat on his hand and the sudden release, the gun flew from his grip and tumbled through the air. Hitting the polished tile floor, it slid along for what seemed like an age before coming to rest at the feet of a middle-aged man in the queue.

For a moment there was complete silence inside the banking hall, but if the staff and customers had strained their ears they might have been able to hear the slight sizzle as Pip's features began to burn with embarrassment. In panic Pip shouted, 'Nobody move! Put your hands up! All of you!' The customers, slightly nonplussed by the strange tableau unfolding before them and not really sure what was going on, politely complied and put their hands up. Pip took a few nervous steps towards his downed gun but was still a good ten feet away from the inert firearm. He pointed at the man whose feet were set closest to the gun. 'You!' he shouted. 'Kick that gun back to me.' The man shrugged slightly and then put his foot on the rifle and slid it back up the hall. Pip quickly snapped it up and, more confident now, pointed it at the customers. 'OK,' he said, relieved, 'everyone against the back wall and face it.' The customers did as they were told without a murmur and Pip turned his attention to the counter. But while he had been fucking about losing his gun, all the bank staff had quietly slipped out from behind the jump and out of sight, into the rear offices. At that moment one of them was on the phone to the police. There was nothing to do but try and at least make a dignified exit. But Pip couldn't even manage this. As he reached the outside door he caught his foot on a mat and tumbled out of the bank and on to the pavement. The rifle flew from his hands and skidded across the pavement and down the kerb to end up under the waiting get-away car. Watched by puzzled passers-by, Pip scrambled to his feet and ran to the Mini. He got down on his hands and knees and tried to reach under the car to retrieve the gun, but he couldn't reach it.

By now the police were on their way and announcing it by use of sirens, so Pip had to abandon his gun and jumped into the passenger seat of the Mini shouting, 'Go, Go, Go!' at Squeak, who didn't need telling twice, let alone in triplicate. He drove the car up on to the pavement, shot past the entrance to the unrobbed bank and down the kerb at the other side – and straight into a bus. The car hit the big red bus pretty hard and both Pip and Squeak were stunned and shaken by the impact. They were still sitting in the car when the cops arrived and swarmed all over them like a blue-serge plague of biblical proportions. The police recovered the sawn-off rifle from where it lay in the road and soon had Pip and Squeak cuffed and in custody. At their subsequent court appearance they pleaded guilty to attempted armed robbery and possession of a firearm with intent. They were each jailed for ten years.

The antics of amateur robbers can be amusing when viewed from a safe distance, but make no mistake, all these men, no matter how feeble their attempts at terror for financial gain, left traumatized victims in their uneven wake. But they paid the price, and that should be a warning to anyone who might be thinking that armed robbery is a bit of a laugh.

17. The Scarface Cartel

It was my fate to spend some months next door to Betty in HMP Wandsworth's notorious D wing back in the late eighties. He was a funny character who came from the Bethnal Green area of east London, not too far from where the Kray brothers set out on their own now legendary lives of crime, and like the infamous siblings, he was to spend a lot of his life behind bars. Betty was a very professional robber and a good fella, but he was an incurable gossip, and this was to get him into trouble. He would slag everyone behind their backs and foster an atmosphere of paranoia wherever he went. In the outside world Betty's malicious gossiping went largely unnoticed or ignored, but in the tight confines of a top-security prison full of hair-trigger lunatics who would slash a man for yawning in their general direction he was a fucking liability. Betty's saving grace was that he had pulled off some terrific bits of work and was on friendly terms with a lot of the criminal faces, but his acid tongue was always going to get him into trouble at some stage. More about that later.

Betty, as well as being a top-notch solo robber, was also a member of a loose gang of blaggers known as the Scarface Cartel, because the link between them all was a violent south London robber called Scarface. Scarface was a brutal man without a shred of conscience and, as it turned out, he was a bit short on loyalty and integrity as well. He came from a traditional criminal background, both his father and older brother being heavily involved in crime before him. But to Scarface's eternal shame, his own father rolled over and turned supergrass in the seventies after he was captured on a heavy bit of work. He dobbed all his confederates in and had to do the disappearing act off the manor – about ten minutes in front of the contract killer who had been hired to wipe him out. So, as a teenager heavily into crime himself when it happened, Scarface had to carry the stigma. In a culture where even talking to 'the other people' in a polite manner was frowned upon, having a father who had given up his own pals to save himself from incarceration was a heavy load for anyone to carry. In order to prove he was nothing like his old man, Scarface became a 'supercriminal'.

A lot of people would mention how 'staunch' Scarface was but in the same breath they would mutter about his over-zealousness when it came to anyone who might be even slightly suspect. Scarface was the terror of whatever prison he happened to be in. He was a big, violent man who never ducked a fight and battled the system, in the shape of knocking out its uniformed foot soldiers at every opportunity, but he saved his most terrible violence and venom for anyone who might be suspected of being a grass. While serving an eight-year sentence for armed robbery at HMP Albany in the mid-eighties Scarface became the pioneer of the early morning call. If he suspected that an inmate might be a grass, or even too friendly with the screws, or someone whispered in his ear that so-and-so was a bit dodgy, he would burst into their cell as soon as the cell doors were opened in the morning and stab, slash or beat them, usually while they were still in their beds. Scarface didn't fuck about – if he went to do you, it was hospital time for the next couple of months. When it came to suspected informers, Scarface was like some modern-day Witchfinder General, and would become judge, jury and executioner. His dad's traitorous actions coloured his attitudes and led to many innocent men being accused and then stabbed or beaten.

Being on a wing with Scarface was a bit of a nerve-racking experience for some characters. If he didn't like the cut of your jib or the way you combed your hair, he could quite easily convince himself that you were no more than a dirty grass and that your number was up. When I reached Albany, some years after he had left, it was still standard to get yourself a weapon and a wedge for your door asap, just in case anyone tried getting in first thing in the morning for a bit of wet work. Scarface certainly left a lasting impression on that jail.

There were, however, some men who met Scarface in prison and got on very well with him, though even some of these considered him a dangerous psychotic. Once he got out, Scarface kept in touch with armed robbers from all over the country, and one of these was Betty. Another was a black robber out of Camberwell named Jimmy. Jimmy was well respected on the serious-crime scene as a good worker and a money-getter, as those who steal big are known, and he went two-of-toast with an older white villain called the Beard. Scarface roamed all over the country committing various jobs with villains from Liverpool, Manchester and even Cardiff, but when he was in London he would work with Jimmy and the Beard, or Betty and another robber from east London known as the Old Boy, because he was about ten years older than the rest of his confederates. Scarface was earning bundles of money, and in his spare time he was stabbing and glassing civilians in pub and club brawls, usually started by himself. For over twenty years Scarface never stopped trying to prove how hard and staunch he was, and how unlike his father.

Then one day he got a raid from the Flying Squad, who had been after him for years, and in his five-bedroom house in Nunhead, a quiet suburb of south London, the police found several thousand pounds in marked money which had come from a security-van robbery in Deptford and a loaded revolver. Scarface was well and truly in the shit and, with his previous convictions, looking at fifteen years and up. This was when his true character came to the fore and he offered to work with the police in order to bring down other robbers in his circle. The man who had probably punished more informers and suspected informers than the Provisional IRA was now to become a supergrass himself. Just like dear old Dad. The police, knowing of some of the heavy contacts that Scarface had, jumped at this chance of getting their hands on so many slippery robbers, even if it meant that the main rat would walk away with no more than a slap on the paw. After getting clearance for the deal from the top brass the police released Scarface on bail and told him to go to work.

Scarface had developed a bit of animosity towards Betty due to a previous bit of work in which he had considered the latter's actions bordering on amateurish panic. Betty was certainly a panicker. It was part of his character: not only did he gossip about everybody but he also worried constantly that everyone was gossiping about him. It was a circle of paranoia. That was just the way he was. The job in question had been a security-van robbery in Torquay, Devon, which Scarface had set up. Essentially, the robbery was only a two-man job but Betty had been at a loose end and hanging around when Scarface approached the Old Boy with the work. Betty asked to be involved and, seeing an opportunity to get him to do the hard, dangerous part, Scarface agreed, as long as Betty would do the actual robbing. He told Betty that as the parade where the guard was to be robbed was particularly thronged with holiday-makers at that time of year, it would be best if he wore a disguise that did not include the traditional ski-mask, as the sight of that would bring the job on top straight away. 'What shall I wear?' Betty asked. 'I don't know,' Scarface replied. 'Just something that will blend in.'

The three robbers drove down to Torquay the night before the robbery and booked into a hotel for a couple of days. After the job was done they would lie low for a day before heading back to London, just in case the police had set up road blocks or vehicle checks. They spent the night drinking in the bar, and Scarface was his usual charming self, getting into an argument with a couple of holiday-makers who he thought were looking too closely at him. The Old Boy and Betty had to drag him back to his room to stop him from glassing one of the tourists and bringing the police down on them before they'd earned a penny. The next morning the three robbers emerged from their rooms, and Betty was wearing a set of snow-white overalls. 'What the fuck have you come as?' Scarface asked, shielding his bloodshot eyes from the glare that was coming off Betty's garments like a solid wave. Betty smiled. 'I'm a painter and decorator, ain't I?' he replied. 'Fair enough,' said the Old Boy. 'But you don't look as though you've ever done a stroke of work.' They piled into their hired get-away cars and headed off for the job.

The idea was that the Old Boy would be the wheelman and Betty would do the actual robbery. Scarface was surplus to requirements, but it was his work so he would sit in the get-away car with the Old Boy and intervene only if Betty got into any trouble. Betty was carrying a .38 automatic pistol and Scarface had a big old .44 Colt revolver in his pocket. After they had parked their change-over car and all piled into the one motor, the Old Boy drove them to the work. The van guard would be picking up the cash from a bank on a parade of shops near the sea front, and Scarface had information that, due to it being the tourist season, there was bundles of dosh and the guard was careless enough to carry two or three pony-bags across the pavement at a time. They sat in the car and watched as the security van turned up right on time and the guard got out and went into the bank. 'OK, Betty. Have at it,' Scarface ordered. Betty reached inside a plastic bag he had been carrying and pulled out a big ginger Ronald McDonald wig and plonked it on his head. The Old Boy almost pissed himself laughing at the sight that Betty now presented. Scarface spun in his seat to face him, mouth hanging open in astonishment. 'What the fuck is that!?' he demanded. Betty was unfazed as he pulled the wig on tight. 'It's fucking brilliant, that's what it is,' he said proudly. 'Everyone will be so busy clocking the wig and the overalls they'll never remember my face.' Scarface shook his head. But before he could reply Betty was out of the car and loping across the pavement.

Betty was waiting in the vestibule of the bank when the guard came out. Unfortunately for Betty, the guard, spotting the big ginger afro as he entered the small space, was suspicious straight away. As Betty went to draw down on him the guard swung the money bags and caught him square in the face. Betty was knocked backwards and dropped his gun, and when the guard saw this the fight was on. Brawling like a couple of drunken sailors, Betty and the guard went tumbling through the doors and on to the street. In the nearby get-away car the two waiting men saw what was happening but neither made any move to intervene. 'Oh, look at this!' commented the Old Boy. 'It's like Ronald McDonald rucking with Postman Pat. I hope no kiddies see this, they'll be scarred for life.'

Scarface, who was wearing, of all things, a deerstalker hat as a disguise, grunted. 'I suppose I'll have to go and help the cunt,' he said as it became clear that Betty was now getting the worst of the fight, the guard holding him around the throat and launching punches into his already bloody face.

Scarface, unhurriedly, climbed out of the car and walked over to Betty and the guard. Using the butt of his revolver, he hit the guard behind the ear, all but knocking him out, then picked up the money bags and walked back to the car. Betty, dazed and bloody, staggered about a bit and then snatched his ginger wig from the pavement, where it had fallen in the struggle. He jammed it on to his head and shambled over to the car. Scarface was already back in the car with the money, and when Betty approached, ginger wig askew and nose swelling on the spot, he wound down his window and said, 'Gun.' Betty, in bits and just wanting to get away, said, 'What?' Scarface sighed. 'Go and get your fucking gun,' he ordered. Betty nodded and loped back into the vestibule of the bank and picked up his gun from where it still lay on the floor. As he jogged back to the car he noticed that the security guard was climbing off the pavement and holding the back of his head. Betty stopped for a second and kicked him hard in the ribs, putting him down again. Then he jumped into the car and off they went.

All the way back to the hotel, Betty got on Scarface's nerves with his constant whining and moaning. 'We're nicked! We're nicked!' he kept saying over and over in a panicky voice, and Scarface eventually turned to the back seat and threatened to blow Betty's wig off if he didn't shut up. Back at the hotel after they had washed up, stashed the robbery kit and were counting the money, which amounted to just over £40,000, Betty explained his worries. He had a very rare blood group, which the police were aware of, and he was worried that he had left blood at the crime scene which would lead Old Bill straight to his door. Scarface and the Old Boy reassured him. 'Don't fucking worry about it. These yokel cops down here ain't going to have the brains to check the blood. Stop driving yourself, and us, mad. They probably won't even see the blood – it's not like you left a puddle behind, is it?'

Betty began to calm down and the Old Boy turned the telly on to take his mind off things. But the local news was on and it was all about the robbery. The camera panned over the outside of the bank and then closed in on an area of pavement that was marked off with yellow evidence tape. Inside that rectangle of tape the camera picked up several bright red spots of blood. And there was a white-suited forensics merchant soaking it up with a cotton bud obviously for analysis. Betty was inconsolable, and even on the way back to London the next day, he couldn't stop whingeing about it. So Scarface figured, if he was going to start somewhere on his new grassing career, it would be with the annoying, whining Betty.

Betty, despite all his crying and worrying, had never actually been tied to the Torquay job. But now Scarface decided to drop him in it as a taster to Old Bill of how useful he could actually be. He pointed the police in the direction of the incriminating forensic evidence and then towards Betty. Betty was soon remanded in custody but he was old school and gave no-comment interviews all the way, his brief in attendance. At this stage he didn't know that Scarface had put him in it and just figured they had got him with good detective work because of the blood.

Old Bill didn't want anyone knowing Scarface had turned turtle, as he was going to be very useful to them as an *agent provocateur*. Under British law nobody has the defence of *agent provocateur*, as they do in the rest of Europe. If the police themselves, or someone in their pay or control, encourage you to commit a crime you would otherwise not have committed, you cannot use this as a defence at your trial. So, in theory, and sometimes very much in practice, an undercover agent of the state can set up any crime and then spend as long as it takes cajoling and coercing you to get involved, and as soon as you do you are nicked and have no defence. It's a naughty trick but one used by police and customs on a regular basis. What the police wanted Scarface to do was organize a few jobs and take some men on them who could then be nicked. Scarface, starting to relish his new role as a double agent, was eager to do it.

Camberwell Jimmy had just finished serving a twelve-year sentence for armed robbery, and for the sake of his family was trying his best to go straight. He took a dead-end job as a manual labourer, determined not to go back to jail. He was looking forward to his first Christmas out with his wife and children but was worried about finances when he was approached by his old jail mate Scarface. Scarface had a proposition for Jimmy. He had set up the robbery of a security van and needed a couple of likely bods to help him do it. He told Jimmy that one of the guards was in on the job and that as soon as it went off he would send money bags worth £1.3 million out on to the pavement for them to scoop up. Jimmy was sorely tempted but told Scarface that he would have to pass as he had only been out of prison for a month and, if he got caught again, he would be looking at twenty years. But Scarface was very persuasive, telling Jimmy that, with the guard on their side, the risk was negligible. Then he threw in the sweetener. 'Imagine your kids' faces on Christmas morning when they see the presents you'll be able to buy them! I bet that would make up for all the ones you've missed.' Jimmy was hooked and agreed to do the robbery. He suggested the Beard as their third man. Scarface agreed and told him he'd be in touch.

Scarface's Flying Squad handlers picked out a security-van job in a place they could easily organize an ambush and gave the details to Scarface, who passed them on to Jimmy and the Beard, of course, minus any mention of Old Bill involvement. On the morning of the robbery, a week before Christmas, Scarface picked up Jimmy and the Beard and supplied them with guns. They had been given to Scarface by the police and had been doctored by their firearms experts so that, while they looked the part, they would not fire. The van pulled into its spot, and when the crew jumped into action, there was an immediate cry of 'Armed police!' and they were surrounded. The police ordered the robbers to drop their guns and put their hands in the air and, though Scarface and the Beard did so immediately, Jimmy, seeing the bleak and barren landscape of many more years away from his family stretching before him, threw down his gun and legged it. The police chased him on foot for almost a mile before one copper who had driven ahead and lain in ambush brought him down with a baseball bat to the shins.

When he was marched back to the robbery site Jimmy was shocked to see Scarface sitting on the bonnet of a police car smoking one of his trademark cigars and laughing and joking with the cops. It was a devastating blow as Jimmy had considered Scarface a real friend and one of the few men in the world he never believed would betray him. Jimmy couldn't even speak, he was so gutted. He and the Beard went into prison on remand and, realizing that the word would soon be out on Scarface's *volte face*, the police raided the homes of several other robbers Scarface had given them the word on. They had enough evidence from Scarface to put these men away for a very long time and the cops were buzzing.

Only one man escaped the police swoop, and he was the youngest and newest member of an east London robbery crew that had been hitting it big. Dex, only twenty-three but already with a reputation as a good earner and a staunch geezer, was at his girlfriend's house when the putsch happened, and when he heard he bought a fake passport and ID and headed for Spain. Meanwhile, in England, several of the capital's top armed robbers found themselves remanded in custody, and the subject of most of their conversations was Scarface, and what they should do about him. None of them was short of a few quid, so they all decided to throw some money into a kitty and get Scarface wiped out before he could come to court and give evidence at any of their trials. Without Scarface standing in the box and pointing the accusing finger, the police cases would fall apart. The boys came up with a figure of £50,000 in cash for anyone who could make Scarface go away, permanently.

In the normal course of events you can hire a hitman for

as little as five grand, but for that price they'll leave the body on the street and probably give you up as soon as they get their own collar felt. The Scarface Cartel wanted a foreigner, one of the ex-special forces professionals who ply their trade on the Continent and are experts in making people vanish. And that was why they were offering such a large prize. They got word out to Dex to see if he could organize things from Spain and, through some well-established criminal faces over there, he was put on to the right man for the job. The hitman was paid fifteen grand up-front, and for this he flew to England and tracked down Scarface. He eventually found him being held in a police cell in Hertfordshire living the life of Riley – which was the name he was being held under. The hitman reported that the job would be difficult but not impossible, as Scarface sometimes left his cell to go drinking and shopping in town with two plainclothes police officers. The Cartel told the mercenary to go ahead with the hit in his own time, but obviously before the first trial date.

Having Dex in Spain was very handy for the Cartel as it made it easy for them to get things moving and he was great at sorting things out. But then things started to go Pete Tong – the prison authorities captured a stiff, an illegal letter, being smuggled out by one of the Cartel on a visit and handed it over to the police. It contained a contact telephone number for Dex at his hotel in Spain. Working closely with the Spanish cops, the Flying Squad traced the number and flew two officers over to arrest Dex. In order to cut any red tape and delays in procedure they proposed getting the Guardia Civil to nick him for passport and ID irregularities. Once he was in custody he could be deported in the Flying Squad's company. The two pasty-faced London cozzers flew off to Spain to do the business.

Dex had some of the staff of the hotel onside – he knew the value of flashing a bit of cash – and when the cops turned up asking what room he was in, the desk clerk buzzed his room and told him that the bizzies were on their way up. Dex was on the fourth floor but had already tested an emergency escape route – climbing down the side of the hotel building using the window-sills and balconies. He grabbed his essentials, money and papers, and lowered himself over his balcony. He had reached the second floor when one of the coppers leant over, having broken into Dex's hotel room above, and threw a truncheon at him. It was a lucky shot for the copper but extremely unlucky for Dex, as it hit him on the head and he lost his grip on the building, crashing on to the road below. Dex shattered both his ankles in the fall and the paramedics had to put him out with a large dose of morphine in order to transport him.

Dex spent a week chained to his bed in a Spanish prison hospital before being loaded on to a plane with the Flying Squad men and flown back to England, where he was charged with armed robbery and remanded to the hospital wing of Wormwood Scrubs to await trial. With Dex now inside, it was hard for the Scarface Cartel to keep in touch with the hitman. Meanwhile, Scarface, as a security precaution, had been transferred to another police station in the middle of the night. The hitman flew back to Europe to await further instructions. He would need more money to bribe the English police to find out where Scarface was now being held, and it was not forthcoming. The Cartel was frustrated; they needed someone on the outside to take control of the situation and get rid of Scarface before it got too late, but the only people capable of it were in the Cartel itself and were stuck in prison.

When a criminal decides to turn supergrass on his mates the one thing the authorities insist on before any deal is made is that the criminal should give up his own crimes as well – all of them. If a supergrass works for the police and prosecution in putting others away and then an old crime he hasn't admitted to turns up, the deal is off and he can go to prison for it. The immunity a supergrass receives for his crimes covers everything except murder and treason. No amount of grassing can wipe out these two crimes. Bertie Smalls, of the Wembley Mob, was the original supergrass and the only one ever to get complete immunity from his crimes. His deal meant that he never served one day in prison for all the robberies and various other crimes he had committed. But the judge who had to formally discharge Smalls for his crimes found the task so distasteful that he strongly recommended that no such deal be done again in the future. The Director of Public Prosecutions and the Home Secretary agreed and with the Law Lords set up a list of guidelines whereby any supergrass who has been deemed a great help to the state in the prosecution and conviction of dangerous criminals should be sentenced to at least a nominal prison sentence for their own crimes so that justice can be seen to be done. The tariff for such a person was to be between five and seven years. Of course this sentence would not be served in the grim confines of a prison among the men, and friends of the men, he had betrayed, but in a 'custody suite' at certain police stations, where he would be allowed to live as normally as possible. These custody suites were so cushty that most supergrasses didn't want to leave them when their bird was done.

Now the police were to find they had a big problem with Scarface. He had, reluctantly, admitted to being involved in the armed robbery of a milk depot in which one of the workers was shot dead after putting up a struggle. What really troubled them was that they suspected Scarface had been the one who pulled the trigger. This murder could jeopardize every one of their cases and lead to all prosecutions being dropped. The wheels of the British criminal justice system ground into motion and several meetings were held between the police and prosecution. It was decided that if Scarface stuck his hand up to the manslaughter of the milk-depot worker rather than the murder, then the deal could go ahead. Even though the man had been shot at point-blank range, the prosecution was willing to accept that there had been no deliberate intention to kill and therefore it was reasonable to substitute a charge of manslaughter for murder. Presumably somebody, somewhere, thought this deal was worth it if it meant several other serious criminals would go down for their crimes.

The trials of the Scarface Cartel took up months at the Old Bailey, but Scarface himself put on some great performances and, overall, impressed the various juries. There were some memorable moments, particularly during the trial of Camberwell Jimmy and the Beard. The men's solicitors had been trying to dig up a bit of dirt on Scarface and had hired a firm of private detectives to keep an eye out. They had managed to get photographs of Scarface's beloved wife in a compromising clinch with one of his police handlers, a man he had trusted and who pretended to befriend Scarface in order to keep him sweet at court. The brief sprung the photos on Scarface in open court after having first questioned him on the issue of trust and betrayal. Scarface looked at the photos, then looked at the copper in question, who was sitting at the back of the court, and in his eyes Jimmy said he saw the old Scarface, the man who had built his reputation by stabbing and slashing other men he suspected of being traitors. The copper must have felt it too for he left the court and wasn't seen again at any of the subsequent trials. But Scarface recovered quickly and the point was lost on the jury.

During his trial, Jimmy was being escorted along a corridor under the Old Bailey one lunch-time to see his QC when, from the opposite direction and surrounded by his police handlers, came Scarface. Scarface was smoking a big cigar and laughing happily with his new cop mates and Jimmy was held against the wall by the screws until Scarface got past. Jimmy waited till Scarface was close and then asked, 'Why did you do it, mate?' It was a genuine question Jimmy really wanted an answer to. Scarface had been one of his closest friends and at one time Jimmy would have given his life for the man. Scarface stopped in his tracks and looked at Jimmy with contempt. 'I never liked you, you black cunt,' he replied casually, and blew smoke in Jimmy's face before moving on. Jimmy told me later that day that if he could have broken free he wouldn't have even had the strength to do him, he was that devastated.

Jimmy and the Beard were found guilty and sentenced to fifteen years each. Betty and the Old Boy were also found guilty at separate trials, Betty getting fifteen years and the Old Boy fourteen. Dex got twelve years. Several other men were also sentenced a total of 150 years between them. Scarface got the maximum seven-year tariff and was out in three. Betty, the worrying gossip, spread a few false rumours about the wrong man and ended up beaten to within an inch of his life at Parkhurst prison. One of the other men Scarface betrayed, a well-liked and respected south London robber who received seventeen years' imprisonment, served almost twelve years before dying in jail less than eighteen months before he was due to be released. About three years ago, it was rumoured that Scarface, under his new name, was in Norwich prison awaiting trial for armed robbery and that he was dying of cancer. I know a few people who would say that it couldn't have happened to a more deserving fella.

18. Fruitcakes and Plain Mad Bastards

Louis was a quiet, introspective man who had just served fourteen years for armed robbery and was now looking to get back into the game. He was known as a good solid worker and all-round nice guy, though the guards he terrorized and robbed during his long career would probably say different. Louis was another graduate of the most violent dispersal prison of its time, where most armed robbers ended up at some stage of their prison career if they got their collars felt in the eighties and early nineties: HMP Albany, on the Isle of Wight. (Since 1999, or thereabouts, Albany has been known as Monster Mansion II, HMP Wakefield being the original Monster Mansion, because it now houses only sex offenders and other horrible specimens.) But Louis had served his time and was now back on the street with an eye out for a lucrative bit of work to kickstart his criminal career again.

The probation service had found Louis a one-bedroom flat in a hard-to-let tower block in Bow, east London, and he sat there for a couple of days listening to the arguments of his neighbours through the paper-thin walls before deciding that the straight life had nothing for him. It was while looking down at the high street from the window of his sixth-floor hovel that Louis noticed a dark blue security van making a delivery to a bank on the opposite side of the road. Having more than a passing interest in the routines of security guards, Louis realized that his dilapidated eyrie gave him the perfect view of the van and guards. As he watched, he got to thinking how he might have stumbled across the perfect bit of work almost on his own doorstep, and noted the time and day of the delivery.

Over the next couple of weeks Louis spent a lot of time looking out of his window and noticing that the van's delivery was indeed a regular and timed occurrence. With this fact established, Louis began to formulate a plan to rob the guard. In order to carry out his plan he would need a gun, and a partner to grab the money while Louis did the business. He walked a get-away route that would cut out the need for a car: his idea was to get the money bags and then run to the end of the road, coming in on his tower block from behind. He figured he would be safely in the lift and up to the sixth floor without anyone knowing he was still in the area. His own flat would make an ideal flop. Everyone would be expecting the robbers to vacate the area as soon as possible, but nobody would know that Louis lived right above the robbery spot. He and his partner would be able to watch the aftermath of the robbery from the window and not look out of place.

Louis got in touch with one of his old contacts and was offered the use of a couple of revolvers, but there didn't seem to be anyone about who was capable of being his second man. It was just unfortunate for Louis that he was looking at a time when most of the professionals he trusted were either involved in their own projects, abroad on the fruit of their labours or stuck in shovel. His contact told him that there was one robber from the old days who was available and had been touting for work, but it was a fella called Demented Danny, a real wild man with a bad reputation for over-the-top, gratuitous violence. Louis didn't want Demented Danny on the work – the man was unstable in the extreme and could turn a simple job into a bloodbath at the drop of a hammer. So Louis thanked his contact and said he'd punt the work around, maybe in south London, 'bandit country', where he also had contacts.

The next day Louis was having a quiet drink in a villains'

boozer on the Isle of Dogs when he was approached by Demented Danny, a big smile on his crazy mooey and a won't-take-no-for-an-answer glint in his shark-like orbs. Louis had known Demented Danny since they were kids and knew how persuasive the nutter could be when he set his mind to it. Danny had heard that Louis had a bit of work lined up and he wanted in. For the next couple of hours he wore Louis down with his pleading, cajoling and veiled threats until Louis agreed to have him on the job. 'There are a couple of conditions,' Louis told him firmly. 'You do everything I say. And you don't shoot anybody.' Demented Danny agreed with a half-hearted shrug. Louis was already starting to regret his decision.

Knowing Demented Danny's penchant for letting off shots whenever the mood took him, Louis decided to take precautions. He removed the ammo from the smaller of the two revolvers; he would give it to Demented Danny on the morning of the work. He would hardly be able to cause much trouble with an empty gun, and all he really had to do was collect the cash. Demented Danny turned up at Louis's flat bright and early on the morning of the robbery and Louis outlined the plan to him. Then he handed Demented Danny the empty revolver. 'What's this?' the nutter asked. Louis shrugged. 'It's your shooter,' he said. 'I couldn't get any food for it.'

Demented Danny smiled and handed the revolver back to Louis. 'No worries,' he said, reaching into his waistband and pulling out a 9mm seventeen-shot Glock pistol. 'I brought me own.' Louis's heart sank, but it was only ten minutes away from kick-off and he just had to swallow and hope for the best.

The security van turned up right on time and the last words Louis said to Demented Danny as they were pulling their masks on were 'Remember, don't let off no shots.' Demented

Danny nodded and they slipped around the corner and across to the van just as the guard was emerging from the bank with a cash box. Louis pulled his revolver and drew down on the guard. 'Drop the –' he had time to shout before there was the sound of a gunshot from beside him. The guard clutched his shoulder and cried out, and there was another shot. Louis looked at Demented Danny in surprise. 'What the fuck . . . ?' he asked, but Demented Danny wasn't listening, he was walking purposefully towards the wounded security guard, his pistol held out at arm's length. *Bang!* There was another shot, and the guard dropped to the pavement and rolled under his own van for cover. The door of the bank opened and a man in a business suit emerged, unaware of what was going on. From fifteen feet away Demented Danny fired two shots at the man in quick succession. One of the shots went into the bank's window and left a neat hole drilled through the plate glass, and the second shot took a big splinter of wood out of the door jamb. Demented Danny was cooking with gas in the trigger-pulling stakes, but it seemed his aim wasn't worth shit, which was very lucky for all concerned.

Out in the street a woman driving a late-model BMW saw what was going on and jammed on her brakes in fear and shock. Her car screeched to a halt in the middle of the road, adjacent to the security van. Hearing the scream of the tyres, Demented Danny calmly turned his pistol in that direction and fired again. In the forensic report into the incident, which I read in HMP Albany a couple of years later, it was found that the bullet went straight through the passenger door of the car and struck the steering column before being deflected out through the roof without hitting the human target. Louis was still in shock himself. In the space of less than a minute Demented Danny had fired five live rounds and turned the high street into an east London version of the Wild West. He cursed his luck and then saw that, when the shots had started going off, the guard inside the back of the van had panicked and was dropping cash bags down the security chute in the side as fast as he could get his hands on them. There was a waist-high pile of cash bags on the road, and they were still coming out. It was as if Demented Danny's shots had hit the jackpot button on some lunatic fruit-machine.

Demented Danny had reached the pavement side of the van where the wounded guard had disappeared and he crouched down and aimed his gun under the van, fully intent on shooting the guard again, but it jammed. He stood up and tried racking the slide. Ignoring his crazy partner, Louis decided it was every man for himself now. There was no one in sight as Demented Danny had succeeded in clearing the busy shopping thorough-fare, so Louis put his own revolver back in his waistband and scooped up as many of the fallen cash bags as he could carry. Once he was loaded up he began to jog towards his planned get-away route. By now the sound of police sirens could be heard in the distance so Louis picked up his pace. He legged it around the backstreet and into his tower block, but the lift was up on the twelfth floor so he decided to use the stairs. At the fourth floor he bumped into his next-door neighbour, a friendly old man who Louis always politely bade good morning. The old man, seeming not to notice the bundle of white-cloth money bags Louis was clutching, said a cheery 'hello' as he passed. Louis let himself into his flat and, using a Stanley knife he'd bought for the purpose, he quickly slashed the bags open, checking for security devices. There were none, so he stacked the money in a walk-in wardrobe and went over to the window to see what was going on below.

Back on the street Demented Danny, having found himself with a jammed pistol, seemed to come out of his violent trance. He looked around as if seeing the street for the first time and then, with a puzzled frown, he legged it. He completely forgot about the money, Louis and the get-away route, and headed for home. Less than a minute after he had vacated the area, the police arrived, in their multitudes, as you would expect after several calls of 'shots fired' on a London street in the middle of a summer's day. The police blanketed the area and spread out. Around the corner in the courtyard of the tower block they started stopping people and asking them if they had seen anyone in a hurry. By now the descriptions were of two gunmen, one tall and white and one short and black. A couple of armed police pulled Louis's neighbour and asked him if anyone had passed him in the last few minutes. 'Only my next-door neighbour,' he replied, 'and he did seem in a bit of a hurry.' The police asked the man to describe his neighbour and, when he told them that he was a short black man who had been sweating profusely and carrying something, the cops surrounded the tower block.

Up on the sixth floor Louis was panicking. He had looked out of his back window and seen dozens of armed police taking up residence in the courtyard and knew they were on to him somehow. There was nowhere he could go, so he decided to hide in the flat. He climbed into the airing cupboard and squeezed behind the water boiler, but not before leaving the two revolvers and a stack of banknotes out in plain view in the empty living room. He also opened his front door and left it swinging wide. His hope was that the police would think he had been in the flat but that he had panicked and gone elsewhere. From his hiding place he watched through a crack in the door and hugged his stack of stolen money.

The police approached the flat cautiously, sending a police dog in first. The dog went wild when it caught the scent of the two abandoned guns but missed Louis in his airing cupboard. The cops shouted for whoever was in the flat to come out, but Louis never moved a muscle. Eventually the cops deemed it safe enough to enter, but they came like a search-and-destroy team; kicking open every door and leaving no corner unsearched. They found the guns and the bait money, and they also found Louis.

The security guard had been shot twice, once in the shoulder and once in the hand but neither wound was life-threatening and he was released from hospital after a week. The man who had exited the bank in the middle of the firestorm needed treatment for a head injury which occurred when he was struck by a wood splinter from the shot that hit the door jamb behind him, and several people, including the woman in the BMW and the guard in the back of the security van, had to be treated for shock. At first the police thought that Louis had also been firing, and it was only after they had taken all the witness statements and the two revolvers had been tested for gunshot residue that they accepted he had not fired. It didn't really matter because the robbery was a joint enterprise, which meant that Louis was just as guilty as Demented Danny. Louis was charged with three attempted murders, armed robbery of £79,000, which was the amount he managed to get back to his flat, attempted robbery of £1,435,000, which is the amount that ended up on the road next to the van, possession of firearms with intent, and having a firearm in a public place with intent. He was remanded into custody as a category A prisoner.

Demented Danny, lucky fuck that he was, made it out of the area with no problems. As Louis was being charged later that evening, Demented Danny was snorting coke and drinking cheap champagne out of a whore's slipper in celebration of his escape. Of course he couldn't help boasting about it, and two weeks later he was pulled in by Old Bill for questioning. By now there was no gun, no clothing and no gunshot residue on his body. He was put on an identity parade, but he'd had his hair cut and shaved off his beard and no one picked him out as the gunman. Louis, in true underworld tradition, refused to name his partner, even though he knew he was risking a few extra years on top of his sentence. So Demented Danny walked. Louis pleaded guilty to everything except the three attempted murders. Whilst the judge accepted that he had not actually pulled the trigger, he noted that Louis had refused to name the man who had. But he sentenced Louis to only sixteen years so he must have taken pity on him. Louis remained restricted as a category A prisoner for eight years of his sentence and was sent back to Albany, where I met him and heard his story.

Demented Danny was eventually captured on another robbery during which he also started shooting, and was jailed for eighteen years. His problem was that, once he entered a stressful situation with a loaded firearm in his hand, he just went into some sort of fug and acted on instinct. He never really planned to hurt anyone, he was just . . . demented.

Having one mad bastard on your firm can be dangerous enough but when the whole crew are crazy as shithouse rats there's bound to be trouble. One such lunatic gang was made up of five Jamaican yardies led by a fella called Tasty. Tasty's mob was not only certifiable but there was also hardly a brain cell between the lot of them. They had access to massive firepower, no lack of bottle, unlimited ammunition, but they still insisted on robbing post offices five-handed. Sometimes there were so many of them stuffed into a sub-PO that they could barely turn around without poking each other in the eye with a gun. But this gang of melts was almost single-handedly responsible for allowing the Flying Squad to be given access to modern firearms and more of them. And for that they deserve at least a mention.

Up until October 1988 the standard-issue weapon for the Metropolitan Police certified firearms officers was the Smith & Wesson, Model 10, a five-shot revolver of .38 calibre. They also had a few Mossberg twelve-gauge pump-action shotguns, but it was only the specialist firearms squad, then known as PT17, who had access to the real modern stuff like sub-machine guns, sniper's rifles and assault rifles. If the likes of the Flying Squad were going on a job that might turn hairy they had to request that PT17 come along too, like older, better-armed brothers who would look after them. This was a bit embarrassing for the Flying Squad, who dealt only with armed crime and every day of the week, but the top brass didn't even want to consider the cost of rearming the Flying Squad with modern automatic or semi-automatic weapons, let alone risk upsetting the public's perception of the jolly British bobby armed only with his trusty truncheon. So, in some ways, Tasty's crew was a bit of a godsend to the Flying Squad.

Maybe it was because they didn't nick any really big prizes – £15,000 shared between five doesn't go very far – or their natural West Indian exuberance, but Tasty's boys started getting a bit out of their prams and took to firing shots on their work. This made them top priority, as it really was only a matter of time before they killed someone. The Squad had a few leads on them, and then one morning they received a hot tip that the crew was about to hit a post office in west London. Unfortunately, PT17 were not available on such short notice so the Squad decided to go it alone and set up a quick ambush around the post office. They set up with no bother and didn't have long to wait before Tasty himself, leading his quartet of fuckwits, arrived and entered the building. There was the sound of shots being fired and the Squad got ready to take the crew down. As the robbers exited the PO and saw themselves covered by a force superior in numbers if not in firepower, their bottle went and they threw their guns down and surren-dered. All except Tasty, that is. Tasty was never going to be taken alive by no 'bloodclaat Babylon bwoy', so he set off running, firing his 9mm Browning automatic behind him as he ran.

How no one was killed that day is almost beyond comprehension. The Squad did put six bullets into Tasty but, with the coke fuelling him, he didn't go down. Despite his wounds he carried on running and firing his gun off indiscriminately. He only went down when a copper stepped from a shop doorway directly in his path and laid a baseball bat, which the Flying Squad also carried in their weapons kit, across his canister. Tasty went down and stayed down until Old Bill had disarmed him. He made a surprisingly quick recovery from his wounds and in prison his party piece was showing off the holes the police bullets had made in his torso. Tasty's crew was up at Knightsbridge Crown Court on the same day as me and Crazy Dave were getting weighed off, and we had a good chat with them in the cells. They got between nine and seventeen years, with Tasty copping the seventeen-stretch.

The Flying Squad used the Tasty case as a prime example of why they should be better armed. Here was a dangerously violent armed man, and he was still running and firing with six police .38 slugs in his body. This proved beyond a shadow of a doubt that the squad needed better firearms. The last time I was arrested by the Squad, in 1998, ten years after the Tasty case, they were armed with 9mm Glock nineteen-shot semi-automatic pistols and Heckler & Koch sub-machine guns. Knowing how seriously the Squad takes its gung-ho reputation, I wouldn't be surprised if they still think a little bit fondly of the lunatic who was responsible for allowing them to get their hands on the big guns at last.

There have been several cases of criminals managing to shoot themselves with their own firearms, but very few where they have actually been shot by their intended victims. Budgie was a fella I met on the exercise yard at Wormwood Scrubs in the eighties, and he had a horrific gunshot wound in his shoulder and an interesting story to tell. He and a mate of his had been the recipients of a bit of good fortune which had benefited quite a few London robbers back in the days when *Miami Vice* suits, the jacket sleeves rolled up, and hair flicks were considered the height of fashion. A shipment of brand-spanking-new Remington riot guns, which were rumoured to have been diverted from a National Guard armoury in California, USA, and bound either for the IRA or for the UVF, depending on who was telling you the tale, somehow ended up in the hands of criminals in London. The gross of guns, in pristine manufacturer's condition, along with thousands of rounds of ammunition, were soon being sold at £500 a pop to anyone who fancied a go and had the relevant ackers. I actually bought one myself and thought it well worth the money. The guns were twelve-bore pump-action five-shot shotguns but small enough for concealment as they had a folding stock – perfect for armed robbery. Budgie and his pal bought one each and went to work.

Budgie and Bilbo, which I will call his mate, as he turned out to be a bit of a hobbit, which is not a good thing in criminal parlance, hit a couple of targets and did OK. Then Bilbo suggested that they rob a double-glazing firm where he used to work before hearing the call of the pavement. He claimed there was a safe in the main office and that sometimes there was as much as fifty grand in it. Now, I know that double-glazing is pretty expensive, but I would have smelled a spoofer if someone told me there was fifty large in the safe of a company that sold windows and probably did most of its business in cheques. But Budgie trusted his pal and thought the job was worth a shot. So it was game-on and happy days.

The two blaggers rolled up to the window firm in their get-away motor and, wearing ski-masks and clutching their Californian riot guns, they entered the building. There were twelve people working there and the two gathered them all together at gunpoint. Budgie kept them covered while Bilbo took the manager into his office to open the safe. The manager wasn't going to put up any resistance: the six grand that was in the safe wasn't his personal money and it was fully insured. So he got to work with his key. But in his haste he forgot to switch the safe-alarm off and as soon as he swung the door open there was a loud wailing that filled the building and seemed to bounce from every surface. Bilbo, momentarily surprised, clubbed the manager with the butt of his gun and then grabbed the money bag and legged it from the office.

In the outer office with the rest of the staff, Budgie was surprised by the alarm and even more surprised when Bilbo came running out at speed, straight past him and down the stairs into the street. The original plan had been to lock all the staff in the office after they got the loot so as to aid their get-away, but Bilbo, driven by greed, just wanted to get away with the money and assumed that Budgie would take his cue and follow on. Budgie started to get a bit nervous – the alarm was still going and it didn't look as though Bilbo was coming back. He thought he heard something behind him, and when he took the gun off the staff, one of them, a middle-aged man who fancied himself as a bit of a hero, knocked the riot gun from Budgie's hands and dived on it. Instead of having it on his toes, Budgie stood in front of the man and demanded it back. The man, confident now that he had the gun in his hands, pointed it at Budgie and shouted, 'Back off, you bastard!' But Budgie wanted his shotgun back and put his hand out. The man pulled the trigger.

Budgie later told me that being shot at almost point-blank range was like being hit with a giant club hammer. The load hit him in the left shoulder just below his neck and drove him back three or four steps with the force of it. He felt no pain but looked down at his shoulder and saw smoke coming from the wound where the red-hot lead had impacted. It was lucky he had been standing so close to the gun when it went off, as the riot gun was designed to spread its shot over a large area, and if he'd been another couple of feet away the shot would have widened out and taken half his head off. As it was, he noticed the white, jagged end of his collar bone poking out of the blackened smoking hole where his shoulder used to be and this panicked him. Budgie had no idea where he was going but he ran. Down the steps and out on to the street, where he was just in time to see Bilbo speeding away in the get-away motor. Bilbo didn't even stop for his wounded pal and just drove off with the money.

You would think that any civilian who had just turned the tables on an armed man and shot his first human being, close up and dirty, might need, at the very least, a sit-down and a cup of hot, sweet, milky tea, but this fella had got a taste for it and wanted another go. He ran after Budgie and caught up with him where he was staggering, dazed and bleeding, along the street. The man ran in front of him, pointed the gun at Budgie's head and pulled the trigger. Nothing happened and the man realized he hadn't racked the slide to eject the spent cartridge, which he now did. In his eagerness to reload the gun and get another shot off, he jammed a cartridge in the breech. Budgie lost consciousness and slipped to the ground as the man continued struggling to try and load the gun, cursing as he did. It was lucky for Budgie that the police arrived when they did, because as sure as hell is warm, if that citizen had managed to reload he would have executed Budgie on the spot.

Budgie had extensive surgery, which managed to save some movement in his left arm, but they couldn't get all the pellets out. Several witnesses who had seen the man's attempt to shoot Budgie the second time out on the street came forward, and Budgie's legal team, as well as all the jailhouse lawyers in the Scrubs, advised him to press counter-charges on the citizen for attempted murder. But Budgie was old school and realized that by going armed he had to accept the shit with the cream. No one had forced him to go robbing and he wouldn't start playing the sympathy vote now that he was caught bang-to-rights. He refused to get the man charged and pleaded guilty to armed robbery and possession of a firearm. He was sentenced to fourteen years' imprisonment, but I often wondered how he really felt when he saw the man who had tried to kill him standing in court with a smile on his face as the judge commended him for his 'remarkable bravery' and awarded him £500 out of public funds. I think Budgie got well and truly rumped. Bilbo was never nicked for the windows job but not long afterwards he was shot to death in a nightclub after stepping on the wrong yardie's toes. Budgie did his bit of sparrow quietly and went straight from then on. There's a moral here somewhere, but I'm fucked it I know what it is.

Starsky was a well-respected blagger out of Peckham who ended up shot by the police, not once but twice. At it for years and very successful at the game, Starsky was well known by all the London robbers, which meant he was also well known to the Flying Squad. Starsky's main game was robbing security-vans' pony-bags, but he was willing to have a pop at anything with a prize involved. One day in 1988 Starsky and his crew drew down on a security guard who was carrying a couple of bags, and all hell broke loose. They didn't know that Old Bill had had them under obbo for quite a while and had been waiting for just such an opportunity as this to get them off the streets for a good long stretch. Starsky, not fancying a decade or so of lumpy porridge and hard bed, decided to have it on his toes. A police marksman shot him in the left leg and put paid to his running days for good.

Due to legal shenanigans by the prosecution, there was doubt thrown up at the subsequent trial, and Starsky walked on a technicality. Then he thought, well if there was no robbery according to the law, Old Bill have shot me for nothing, so he got himself a good brief and sued the police for crippling him. After the usual legal dance-steps the police decided to settle out of court and Starsky got a nice lump sum. In fact, it was more than he would have got from the robbery, had there been one, which the law decreed there hadn't. So Starsky invested this bit of dough and for the next few years he did very nicely, thank you.

In the nineties, things started to go pear-shaped for Starsky when a few of his investments lost money, and this was when he made the mistake of going back to crime. Along with an enigmatic Colombian gunman who had made south London his home and a couple of likely amateurs who were willing and possibly able, Starsky went to work robbing pony-bags again. But the police had not forgotten about Starsky, and when they heard he was back at it they planned another ambush. This time Starsky was shot in the other leg, and he swears it was done while he was unarmed, under arrest, and lying face down on the street. The Colombian was shot ten times as he drew down on a security guard but, miraculously, he survived. Both Starsky and the Colombian pleaded not guilty, but this time there were no legal technicalities. They were found guilty and sentenced to twenty years each. Both men are still hobbling around the prison system at the time of writing.

If you carry loaded guns on to the streets, then don't be surprised if bad things happen to you. Life is not a Hollywood movie, and don't make the mistake of thinking it is.

19. The Faces

The Player was the robber's robber, the epitome of what being a blagger in the eighties and onwards was all about: a Bermondsey boy who worked his way up through the ranks from petty thief and Millwall football hooligan to become one of the most respected money-getters in the business. I first met the Player in Rochester Borstal in the seventies, and even then he had a reputation as a solid bloke who, if you were his pal, would back you to the hilt. He had an old head on young shoulders, and even when we were kids the values he espoused harked back to an earlier era of British crime: never grass, don't talk to Old Bill or screws, never let your pals down and never take a liberty with anyone weaker than yourself. By sticking to this code, the Player knew he could never go far wrong, and he was right. In the late seventies, after leaving Borstal, the Player was recruited by a top professional team of robbers who recognized his worth and were happy to have this relative youngster in their crew. At that time the big money was in security vans, and several methods had been devised for getting into these cash-laden tin-cans on wheels. One little firm known as the Chainsaw Gang used to stop the vans by pretending to be police officers and then use diesel-powered chainsaws to cut through the skin of the van to get to the money inside. This method was very successful for a while, until the security firms got wise and started to reinforce their vehicles. After that, the time it was taking to cut through to the cash meant that the police were alerted and able to get to the scene before the work was done. But the Chainsaw Gang had some very nice touches before the game changed. Another crew would hijack a small crane and ram the jib through the rear doors of the van. And if you think that might be dangerous for the guard inside the van, then think about this – at the same time, French robbers were using armour-piercing rockets fired from a portable launcher to do the same job and killing all the guards as a matter of course. They don't fuck about, your Continentals.

The Player got into the big-money leagues on the ground floor and had all the trappings of wealth from a relatively young age, but he was smarter than the average bear and willing to think outside the box even in moments of extreme danger. Perhaps the best story about the Player is one from his early days on the pavement, which illustrates exactly why he is held in such high regard in the underworld. It was around 1981 and the Player, along with a very heavy robbery crew, was in the process of relieving a security van of its load in Dulwich, south-east London, when Old Bill ambushed them. The cops had been on to this crew for a while and had been patiently lying in wait for this day. Their aim was to take one of the most successful robbery gangs off the streets for a very long time. Either that, or shoot them dead if they put up a fight. The Metropolitan Police have shot dead, or wounded, more armed robbers on the streets of London than they have terrorists in the last twenty years, and that's a fact. Armed, unarmed, at it or just sitting in a stolen car, it's all the same to some police officers, and if you are known as an armed robber they will shoot you first and ask questions when the gunsmoke clears. Armed robbery is a high-risk business and you have to take the rough with the smooth. The Player's crew knew this, so when crowds of police with itchy trigger-fingers started popping up right in the middle of the work, the gang did as they were ordered and laid their guns down and held their hands high. All except the Player.

The Player was young and full of confidence and there

was no way he was going meekly to a fifteen- or twenty-year sentence. He tucked his revolver into the waistband of his jeans deliberately and legged it. He was fit as a butcher's dog and left the shocked Old Bill in his dust. This had never happened before. Everyone knew the drill: when Old Bill shouted 'Armed police!', that meant nobody was to move, let alone have it on their toes. The Player was very lucky he didn't just end up with a ring of .38s in his back as he disappeared fast into the distance. Old Bill could do nothing but give chase through the residential streets of Dulwich and try and arrest this fleet-footed blagger. As the Player got around the first corner and out of sight of the out-of-shape pursuing cozzers he saw a lorry waiting at a road junction, so he launched his revolver on to the back of it. As he ran on, he was pleased to see the lorry take off, along with his firearm. Next he pulled off his ski-mask and stuffed it down a drain; then his gloves, one at a time, were launched into two separate gardens. By now the unfit Flying Squad officers were still chasing him but did not yet have him in sight. Around the next corner he took off his jacket and threw it into a bin. Just in time, as the armed and puffing coppers came around the corner and caught sight of the Player once more. The Player knew he was going to be caught – it was inevitable, as the police would be in their vehicles by now and on his trail – but he had a stroke of genius. He put on a burst of speed and ducked around another corner, but this time he ran up the garden path of the nearest house and kicked the front door open. He ran into the front room, where a man and woman had just sat down in front of the telly with their lunch. They stared, open-mouthed, as the Player rushed across the room and grabbed their television set, yanking the wires out of the wall and hurrying from the room with it.

As the Player came through the shattered front door with the television set in his arms, he found himself surrounded by sweating, out-of-breath policemen pointing guns at him.

'Armed police, get your hands up!' they shouted. The Player dropped the TV and did as he was told. He was immediately arrested for armed robbery and searched, but no gun was found. Once the Player was safely cuffed, ensconced in a police car and being conveyed to the station, the police started searching for his gun. They went back over the route along which they had chased him but he had been out of sight for a while and the cops weren't sure exactly where he had been. They did find one leather glove in a garden, but these were the days before DNA was a forensic tool in the armoury of the police force, so it wasn't much cop as evidence. By now the Player's gun was probably half-way up the M1, and his mask was likely swirling around the sewage system on its way to Southend. The jacket the Player had been wearing was never found either. The police were not that bothered about the loss of evidence – with the exception of the gun, obviously – as they had plenty of surveillance photos of the Player in conversation with the rest of the crew in the run-up to the robbery and they also had a camera clicking away on any ambush as standard operating procedure. The Player was remanded in custody with his mates, charged with attempted robbery of £2 million in cash.

He hired one of the best young up-and-coming briefs to handle his case at the Old Bailey, and by the time he got to trial he had a list of pertinent questions for his mouthpiece to ask. It was a wonder the police hadn't colluded with each other and got their stories straight, or maybe they were just that rarest of creatures – police officers who were honest and truthful. Under oath, the officers admitted that they had lost sight of the robber they were chasing on several occasions. Then they had to admit that they had arrested the Player almost a mile from the scene of the robbery and that he had been leaving domestic premises with a television set he had just stolen. And that he had no gun or mask, and that his upper garments were a different colour and style to that shown in the photographs of the robbers taken at the scene. By now the police must have had more than half a clue where this defence was heading, but there was nothing they could do about it.

In his closing speech to the jury the Player's brief asked how the police could say that his client was taking part in a £2 million security-van robbery when it was quite plain that he was a mile away from the scene committing a burglary that netted him a television set. He pointed out that just because his client had been photographed with a robbery gang some days before they committed a robbery, it did not make him guilty of that robbery. He was a criminal, he admitted that, but a petty, unsophisticated burglar who happened to be friendly with some robbers, not a professional armed robber. The brief then pointed to the photos taken at the scene just before the police sprang their ambush and particularly to the armed, masked, gloved robber in the bright yellow puffer-jacket whom the police claimed was his client. He then read the witness statements of the couple whose television set had been stolen and their description of the thief as 'bareheaded and wearing a black T-shirt'. His client had also, by the police's own admission, been gloveless and unarmed at the time of his arrest. It was a brilliant defence and very eloquently put.

The security-van crew were all found guilty of armed robbery and possession of firearms, except the Player. There was enough doubt in the mind of the jury to acquit, though they did recommend that he be charged with burglary, which he was. The robbery team received sentences ranging from seventeen to twenty-two years. The Player pleaded guilty to aggravated burglary and was sentenced to five years' imprisonment. The Player served his time and went on to bigger things. In the late eighties he was convicted of stopping and robbing a security van in Kent while disguised as a police officer, for which he got seventeen years' imprisonment.

The Hammer is east London's equivalent of the Player, an ex-West Ham football thug who rose through the criminal ranks to become a top-notch armed robber. The Hammer is a true hard-man in that he is skilled in boxing, kick-boxing and other martial arts as well as being a street fighter. He is also a fitness fanatic and gets withdrawal symptoms if he can't get to the gym to train at least once a day. I was in Albany with the Hammer in the early nineties and then spent a bit of time in Highdown with him in 2002. I was down from HMP Whitemoor for my accumulated visits and the Hammer was on remand for conspiracy to rob and possession of a firearm, having been nicked at a motorway service station by the NCS, Britain's answer to the American FBI. It wasn't really surprising that the Hammer was on the National Crime Squad's most-wanted list as his record reads like a bad novel, overly long and with plenty of predictable bits. When I first met him in Albany he was in for an armed robbery that had gone very wrong. This is what happened.

The Hammer was approached by a mate of his who offered him a nice bit of work robbing the takings of a very successful nightclub in the East End. The job looked like a piece of piss, and the Hammer agreed to give it a shot. The robbery was planned for 2.30 a.m., when the club should have been just about ready for locking up, with only a couple of bouncers and the manager left in the gaff, but unknown to the Hammer and his pal, there was a birthday party in that night and they had an extension. The Hammer and his oppo parked their car around the back and made their way into the club by way of a fire door that had been sabotaged that afternoon so as not to shut properly. Masked, and with pistols at the ready, the duo made their way along deserted corridors to the office. They found the manager there counting the evening's take, with the safe conveniently open. While his pal cuffed the manager, the Hammer went to round up the bouncers, the idea being that, if they left everyone trussed up, the alarm probably wouldn't be raised until morning when the cleaners came in and found them.

The Hammer was as game as a brace of rabid pit-bulls and able to fight his own weight in kung-fu Chinamen, but when he entered the main part of the club and was confronted with five hundred pissed-up birthday revellers, even he decided it was time to take a back seat. The trouble was that some of the crowd had seen his mask and pistol and, thinking it was a hit, they began to panic and run about. In seconds there were people lying all over the dance floor, their fellow party-goers trampling them underfoot in their hurry to vacate the premises. The bouncers, six instead of two because of the party, as big as houses but with barely an independent thought between them, ran after the Hammer as he slipped back to the office to warn his pal. The club was in the centre of town and when sixty phone calls about a masked man with a gun running loose in the nightclub jammed the police switchboard, the wailing sirens would not be far behind.

The Hammer's pal had the money bagged and the manager secured and was ready to go when the Hammer came into the office closely followed by a herd of bouncers. The Hammer turned to face them, and one grabbed hold of the barrel of his snub-nose .38 revolver. The Hammer pulled the trigger and blew part of the bouncer's thumb off. In anger at having been forced to fire his gun on what was supposed to have been an easy job, the Hammer then shot the man three more times, once in the stomach, once in the arm and once in the hand. Things were going wrong very quickly, and the Hammer meant business. He had no intention of going back to prison for anyone, and if that meant shooting everyone who got in his way, then he was well up for it. Unfortunately, when the Hammer started shooting it had panicked his mate into firing off his own .38, and the bullet had ricocheted back at him and severed an artery in his arm. The Hammer's pal was now bleeding to death. The Hammer, never one to leave anyone in the shit, pocketed his mate's gun and then hoisted him over his shoulders and began to jog through the club.

Outside on the street, a large crowd had gathered, some of whom had been inside the club, when the Hammer, a gun in each hand and his bleeding and unconscious partner on his shoulders, burst through the doors. The Hammer ordered everyone to move back and pointed his .38s for emphasis. He was a nightmare sight, eyes bulging in his mask and soaked from head to foot in his mate's arterial blood. The Hammer went jogging up a hill towards the car park where the get-away motor was parked. It was now that all the training he had put in at the gym came in handy, as he was carrying the dead weight of a fourteen-stone man on his shoulders. Reaching the top of the hill, he looked back and saw about twenty police cars arriving, but he kept going. As he reached the get-away car and lowered his mate to the floor in order to get the door open, a police car screeched up to him and a cozzer jumped out.

The cop must have thought he'd just give it the old Dixon of Dock Green bollocks – you know, 'Give me the gun, lad. If you don't, it will look bad for you in court' – but the Hammer was in no humour for negotiations or bad scripts. He grabbed the copper and put the barrel of one of his .38s to his neck. He turned to the rest of the cops who were coming up on him and ordered them to stay back. They did. The Hammer pushed the cop back into his patrol car and then lifted his shot pal up and threw him into the back. The Hammer then climbed into the front passenger seat and put the gun to the cop's head. 'Drive!' the Hammer shouted, and off they went. The patrol car raced through the streets at 70 mph, closely pursued by a posse of police cars. The Hammer didn't want company on his get-away, so he ordered the cop to get on his radio and tell the pursuing units to back off. The cop, as you would, did as he was told. With that the Hammer's gun went off again and blew out the driver's window, missing the cozzer's head by a fraction. It hadn't been deliberate, the Hammer had just been gripping the trigger too tightly. By now the cop in the car was absolutely shitting himself.

The Hammer, seeing that the other patrol cars had fallen well back, ordered the driver to take a few backstreets and pull up near a darkened alley-way. He got out of the now blood-soaked patrol car and told the copper to get his mate out of the back and carry him. They set off down the alley. The Hammer knew he had to find another car, and quick. The trio came to a house with a car parked in the drive, and the Hammer ordered the cop to put his pal on the ground, knock on the door and ask for the car keys. The door was opened by a man in just his vest and pants, having been got out of bed, and the cop demanded his car keys for 'police business'. The man, seeing the blood all down the cop's shirt and the masked man holding two .38s right behind him, picked up the keys from the hall table and handed them over, but the Hammer, deciding that two hostages might be better than one, told the man to get out of the house and into the car. With the copper driving and the Hammer's mate and the car-owner in the back seat, the Hammer kept watch from the front passenger seat, guns at the ready. Soon the fugitives had left London behind and were speeding through the wilds of Essex towards Chigwell. At one stage the Hammer noticed they were being shadowed by a police helicopter and that a patrol car with no lights on was behind them. He ordered the hijacked car to halt and got out and fired a shot at the following car as a warning.

The hijacked car was reaching speeds of 100 mph, but everywhere they turned there seemed to be police cars waiting. Eventually, as the car came round a bend near Epping Forest, the tyres lost traction and they skidded into a bridge stanchion. The car was a complete write-off, and the copper and the other hostage took this opportunity to scramble out and run off into the darkness. The Hammer was beyond caring. This was turning into a long night and he would be glad to see the back of it. He pulled his pal out of the back seat and laid him on the road. A patrol car turned up and the Hammer ran towards it waving his guns and roaring until it reversed away at speed. The Hammer noticed the lights were still on in a Chinese restaurant near by and began banging on the door until it was opened by the proprietor and his girlfriend. After a few quick words, emphasized with a bit of gun-pointing, it was established that the man had a car and it was parked outside. The Hammer told the man that he was now the latest designated driver and got him to load his wounded pal in the back. The Chinese man's girlfriend wanted to come to, as she was worried about her man. But the Hammer, in typical chivalrous style, would not even contemplate taking a female hostage, so he promised that he wouldn't hurt the man and left the girl behind.

By now the Hammer's pal had regained consciousness and, looking around, realized that they were only a couple of miles from one of his friend's houses. The Hammer knew that his pal desperately needed hospital treatment and ordered the Chinese man to drive to the safe house. The police had not gone away all this time, but fearing a large body count if they got too close, they kept their distance and just observed. The Hammer knew he couldn't allow the police to see which house his pal was going into, so he asked the hostage to stop the car and took him back along the road at gunpoint to distract the police while the wounded man crawled out of the car and into his pal's house. Once he was safely inside, unnoticed by the police, the Hammer took his hostage back to the car and forced him to drive on. Having got his pal to safety, the order of the night was now to escape himself. Up ahead, the Hammer saw a stand of trees and, behind, a couple of armed-response vehicles. He knew he would be an easy target for a police sharpshooter as long as he stayed in the car, so he ordered the hostage to pull over and legged it into the trees, leaving his hostage behind unharmed.

The Hammer had thought that the stand of trees was the start of deep woods where he might lose his police pursuers, but beyond the trees was a wide potato field. He ran out into the middle of it as the police hung back and got flashlights. Working fast, the Hammer dug a quick hole in the muddy earth and dived into it. It was pitch-black in the field and he pulled earth and potato plants back over himself until he was buried in the ground, with only a small hole near his face through which he could breathe and see a bit of the night sky. The police swamped the field, marching up and down with dogs, lights and firearms at the ready, but it had started raining heavily and they found nothing. At one stage a copper stood right on the Hammer's leg, but he resisted the urge to start blasting and the copper moved on. For eight hours the Hammer stayed in his hole while the police searched the field and the pig farm beyond.

With the sun high in the sky, at least four hours since the Hammer had seen or heard any police presence, he judged it safe to come out of hiding. Covered in blood and mud, he must have looked a terrible sight rising from his hole in that field. He saw no one near the trees and road, and his heart began to sing. He had escaped! After everything that had happened the night before, he had made it to freedom! His joy was short-lived. He heard a sound from behind him and turned in the direction of the pig farm. The armed coppers were lined up in ranks of twenty, and they all had the Hammer in their sights. He sighed wearily. There was nothing to do but drop his guns and stick his hands up.

Luckily, despite all the shots that were fired, no one died that night, though the bouncer who had been shot first required forty-eight pints of blood and the surgeon who operated on him was compelled to add to his witness statement, 'He is extremely lucky to have survived such a vicious attack.' The Hammer's pal survived and disappeared into the wide blue yonder, never having been identified for the night's work. The Hammer himself appeared at the Old Bailey charged with assault with intent to rob, possession of firearms with intent, using a firearm to resist arrest, assault with intent to resist arrest (twice), and kidnapping (three times) – he was sentenced to twenty-four years in prison. No matter what ordinary straight-going civilians may think of the violence and mayhem the Hammer meted out that night, in the criminal world he is highly respected. He refused to leave his wounded friend behind despite his own difficulties.

The College Boy is another well-respected east London face. I have never met him personally, but I have been in the same prisons as him, know some of the people that he knows, and I have corresponded with him regularly since his release. The College Boy is now going straight, and that's a relief not only to his family but to the security firms and financial institutions of the capital. He's now written two very good books and become a bit of a media star, but there was a time when the only place you would see his face was on wanted posters and *Crimewatch UK*.

Originally from Canning Town, an area with a reputation for wildness so fearsome even the pit-bulls go around in pairs, the College Boy was seduced by the easy money and easier lifestyle of serious armed crime at a very early age. After various youthful indiscretions which saw him end up in Borstal and then prison, the College Boy decided that incarceration was not really for him and that if he ever went down for a long one, then escape would be his only option. Just like the Player, he was recruited and tutored by older villains who saw in him the makings of a top robber. The College Boy was a deft practitioner of the pony-bag robbery and could ride a powerful motorbike like a pro, which was handy for zipping in and out of the narrow streets of the City of London. He worked with various partners and had it right off on a regular basis during the late seventies and early eighties.

In 1984 the College Boy was jailed for fifteen years for a bank robbery that had netted £20,000 and immediately started planning an escape from prison. He was sent to Parkhurst, where he got heavily into the two things – other than escape – that interested him: sport and education. It was through his quest for further education that he was eventually able to see a way out of his predicament and back to his family. In those days an emphasis was put on educating prisoners as part of the rehabilitative process. (This was pre-Michael Howard, who slashed prison education budgets by 60 per cent and advocated more time locked in cells as a way of reducing the re-offending rates.) The College Boy had a yearning for learning, as his nickname implies, but he had even more of a yearning for freedom. He applied to go to HMP Maidstone on transfer in order to take advantage of its reputation for providing good educational courses but, in reality, what he wanted to take advantage of was its possibilities of escape.

The College Boy, once he knew the date of his transfer from the Isle of Wight, got in touch with his confederates outside and organized for them to come and break him off the van. A prison pal of his, whom I shall call the Gimp, had inveigled his way on to the van and was in on the coup. The

Gimp was part of a professional burglary team, also out of the East End, and was a personable kind of man, full of good humour and great for rousing the spirits of those faced with many long years behind the high grey walls of HMP. Most people liked the Gimp, and when I was later to spend almost three years on the same spur as him in HMP Whitemoor, I looked forward to his daily japes as a way of forgetting my eight life sentences plus eighty years in concurrents, for at least part of the day. The Gimp was at that time serving eight years, and it would be another poke in the eye to Old Bill to have him out.

On 20 November 1984 the College Boy, handcuffed to the Gimp and escorted by five screws, was loaded on to a prison transport. Meanwhile, on the M25 two stolen BMWs with three occupants were waiting. As the van turned on to the A217, one of the stolen beemers sped up to the front of the van and crashed into it side-on, causing it to swerve on to the verge. The second beemer rolled in behind the van, blocking any escape route by the van driver, and two men alighted, one with a pair of bolt-croppers and the other with a pick handle. The man with the pick handle shattered the windscreen of the prison transport and ordered the driver to hand the keys to the back of the van. Inside, the College Boy got into a bit of a struggle with the screws, who tried to grab hold of him, but a more sensible senior officer, seeing the futility of such actions, ordered the screws to step back. It was the best thing to do because any team who were serious enough to stop a prison transport were certainly serious enough to cause some damage to anyone who might try to stop them. Within less than a minute, the College Boy and the Gimp were in the back of a speeding BMW having their cuffs cut off with the bolt-croppers. And then it was back to London and a safe house.

The College Boy liked the Gimp, who was a good crack in

prison, but now that they were out he became a bit of a burden. He seemed incapable of thinking for himself and tended to ask a lot of stupid questions, embarrassing the College Boy in front of his pals, who were very serious people. The escape made front-page headlines, and it was the *News of the World* that gave the College Boy his nickname. In the following months every major armed robbery in the capital was laid at his door by the media, who speculated that the reason for the escape was to free him to take part in specialist jobs. Why they couldn't just accept that human beings find incarceration for long periods abhorrent and will naturally try to escape is obvious: it wouldn't make a good headline. But being on the run is an expensive business and soon the College Boy did have to go back to work, and against his better judgement, he took the Gimp along.

In June 1986, nineteen months after escaping from the prison van, the College Boy and the Gimp, riding tandem on a Yamaha 1100cc motorbike, set off to rob a security van. At Kensal Rise, west London, they spotted a guard doing a bank run and decided to have a crack at it. The College Boy was armed with a Smith & Wesson .38 revolver and the Gimp had a little .22 pistol. The duo took the guards easily and within a minute were back on their motorbike with £35,000 in cash. But as they got around two hundred yards from the scene of the robbery and were about to power out of sight, a have-a-go-hero who had witnessed the robbery crashed his Ford Granada straight into the motorbike. The College Boy was thrown through the air and completely shattered his right leg on impact with the road. Another have-a-go in a gas van pulled up and, seeing one robber completely incapacitated, tackled the Gimp. The Gimp, with his little .22, shot the man three times but was eventually brought down by the wounded gas fitter and held until the police arrived.

The College Boy's armed-robbery career was over. It took

months of operations and then recuperation in prison hospitals before he was able to walk again. He pleaded guilty to armed robbery and prison escape and was sentenced to a further sixteen years' imprisonment. The Gimp pleaded not guilty and in 1987, while in HMP Gartree awaiting trial, he escaped with another prisoner: a hijacked helicopter landed on the exercise field and whisked them away. But that's a whole other story, which has been well documented in other books . . .

In 2003 Terry 'the College Boy' Smith released his autobiography, and when I reviewed the book for a prison newspaper and questioned his labelling of the Gimp as a police informer, he wrote to me and explained his reasoning, which was sound and logical. He has since written a novel in which he explains everything. Terry and I are still in touch and he has managed to leave his life of crime behind him and start a new career as an author and TV pundit. I'm pleased for him: getting out of the criminal life is a long, hard process at which many career criminals fail. Terry is an inspiration to me and others like me who wish to emulate his success in the straight world. As for the Gimp, well, the less said about him the better.

20. The Final Round-Up

As you may have noticed from the preceding chapters, armed robbery, no matter how carefully planned, can be a very unpredictable business. I have been involved in over a hundred raids and know to my cost that whatever you are capable of imagining can go wrong will go wrong. Sometimes it is a small and funny thing, but other times it is something massive which can leave the robber with a couple of decades of incarceration to ponder on it. We all make mistakes, and I often think that my biggest was setting out on a life of crime in the first place, but that is something I cannot change. I was a career criminal for nearly thirty years, and an armed robber for most of that time, so I had my own share of blunders. The worst was probably the last robbery I ever committed, on a bank on Streatham High Road. First, I forgot to pull my mask down on entry, so I exposed my face to the CCTV cameras and was on a loser right from the start. Then I accepted a bunch of £50 notes which quite obviously contained an exploding dye-pack, a cardinal sin for a bank robber with my experience. I was almost at the get-away car when the dye-pack exploded inside my coat, setting both me and the money alight and covering me in red dye as well. With a twenty-foot cloud of red smoke right above my head, you wouldn't have to be much of a detective to spot the robber. This incident, if nothing else, should have told me I'd been too long in the game and that maybe it was time to hang up the mask and gun and retire, but it took an Old Bailey judge to do that for me. But even my dye-pack blunder pales into insignificance next to a bloke I met in HMP Dartmoor who, after robbing a bank in Preston, stuffed the bag of money down the front of his trousers. When his dye-pack went off he not only ended up nicked but he also suffered third-degree burns on his family jewels. It makes me wince just thinking about it. I have recently come to the conclusion that, contrary to popular misconception, there are no criminal masterminds, there are just criminals who get lucky for a while. And then there are those who are unlucky.

Johnny the Jug was a West End face from the seventies whose previous convictions read like an old British black-and-white gangster-film script; he had been done for crimes which now belong firmly in a different era, an era in which criminals always wore hats and overcoats, and shouted things like, 'You'll never take me alive, copper!' to the bobbies pursuing them in old Wolsey cars with bells on the roof instead of sirens. Johnny had been convicted of smash-and-grab on a jewellery shop, hijacking a lorry-load of furs, warehouse breaking and living off immoral earnings. In fact, I would not be surprised if he'd also been done for 'being a footpad and person of low birth and morals'. It's not that Johnny was that old, just fifteen years older than me, but he grew up in a different time, when hijacking furs and smash-and-grab were still viable. You try hijacking a fur lorry nowadays – if you can find one – and people think you're an animal-rights protester. Anyway, Johnny had reached the ripe old age of forty-nine without resorting to armed robbery and decided he'd quite like to give it a try. He teamed up with a bloke called Smasher he'd met when they shared a cell together for nine months in HMP Wandsworth, and they went to work like the pair of rookie robbers they so obviously were.

Johnny was a lovely fella and in no way cut out to be a blagger, but he was fresh out of jail and on his uppers and in need of some quick cash. He was mooching around the West End when he bumped into his old cell mate lurking in Soho.

They had always got on OK and they went for a cup of tea to renew their acquaintance. Both men expressed how broke they were and started talking about various ways in which they might get their hands on a few shekels. Smasher said he knew of a building society in Crouch End which would be pretty easy to rob if they had the bottle. Johnny liked the sound of this, as it would be straight cash with no middle man to pay off, but they needed guns. Johnny had been a pretty fair hoister in his younger days and, though his hands were now a bit shaky, he decided he could give it one more for the old gipper. They walked up to Regent Street and into Hamley's. Amid the stereotypical toys for stereotypical children they found a couple of realistic-looking plastic pistols, and Johnny quickly skyed them before making a nonchalant exit from the store. Next they needed masks or something to cover their faces, and Smasher nipped into a charity shop and stole a cardigan that was on a rack by the door. They ripped the sleeves from the garment and had a sleeve-mask each. The boys were ready to rock 'n' roll.

The gruesome twosome bunked the tubes over to Crouch End and took a look at their potential target. There was only one cashier behind the counter and no customers at all in the branch. Johnny had psyched himself up so much on the journey over that he wanted to get in there and get on with it – but this was where Smasher lost his bottle. Having suggested the job in the first place, he was now not so sure that it was a good idea and stood dithering on the pavement. Johnny knew that he had no other option, and that if he didn't go ahead with the robbery he would be sleeping on the streets that night, so he went ahead without Smasher. As he came through the door of the building society he pulled his sleeve-mask over his face realizing as he did so that he had forgotten to cut holes in it. The material was pretty thick and he could see vague shapes through the weft, but it was also hard to breathe.

So, wheezing like an asthmatic and bumping into things, he made it to the jump with his toy pistol. 'Give me the money!' he demanded, in a voice muffled by the thick material obstructing his airways. But the cashier knew the drill even if she couldn't understand the words and put a wad on the counter. Johnny took three goes at grabbing it before he actually got it into his hand. He turned around to run from the building and didn't see the decorative rope across the queuing section, which caught his shins and sent him crashing to the carpet. The money and gun flew out of his hand and just then the door opened and a customer, a young man, walked in. Johnny knew there was someone there, though he couldn't quite make out who, so he reached for what he thought was his gun but turned out to be no more than a stain on the carpet. In frustration he ripped his mask off and, now able to breathe and see again, crawled quickly across the carpet and picked his gun up.

The young man who had walked in on this pantomime could do nothing but stare at the strange sight before him. Once Johnny had the plastic gun back in his hand he ordered the young man to 'Hit the deck!' The man explained that he had a bad leg and couldn't actually get down without causing himself quite a bit of pain. So Johnny revised his order and told the man to go and stand by the counter and make no false moves. The young man and the cashier looked at each other and shrugged as Johnny got down on his hands and knees and crawled around gathering up the scattered loot. Finally Johnny had all the money in his hands. Then Smasher burst into the building society, waving his plastic pistol, wearing his sleeve mask and demanding the return of his pal. Smasher had thought Johnny was taking too long and might be in trouble, especially after he saw the young man go in. So, taking his courage in both hands, he decided to rescue Johnny. Unfortunately, when he burst through the door he managed to run straight into Johnny, who was on his way out. Smasher's head made contact with Johnny's nose and he managed to break it. Johnny cried out in agony and dropped the gun and money again. He was bleeding profusely and cursing Smasher, but he got himself together long enough to pick up the money once more and drag the mask-blinded Smasher from the premises.

Somehow Johnny and Smasher made their get-away with just over £600. Twenty minutes later they were sitting in a greasy spoon some miles away when the realization of what they had done hit them. Not only had Johnny probably been photographed by the CCTV cameras in the building society without his mask, but he had also left his fingerprints behind on his dropped plastic pistol. If that wasn't enough of a clue for Old Bill, he had also left plenty of his blood on the carpet. Johnny knew that it was only a matter of time before he was nicked so he decided that after the carve-up he and Smasher should go their separate ways and lie low for a while. Johnny was no grass and he knew that Smasher, who had been masked throughout, had left no evidence behind and would probably never be nicked for the job. They shared the money and said goodbye. Johnny told Smasher that if he urgently needed to see him about anything, he would be able to find him in the Lucky Horseshoe Café on Shaftesbury Avenue most days until noon. And then they parted.

It was four days later, as Johnny was playing pinball and drinking weak coffee in the Lucky Horseshoe, that the police marched in and arrested him for armed robbery. He still had £80 of the robbery money in his pocket. It turned out that Smasher was a part-time alcoholic who, when he got drink inside him, couldn't help making a complete string-vest of himself. With his share of the Crouch End robbery money he had bought a couple of bottles of brandy and after consuming them at speed had wandered around the West End shouting, singing at the top of his voice and urinating on theatre-goers. Not content with this, he had then kicked in the front windows of several shops before being jumped by a vanload of SPG. At the police station Smasher had drunkenly told any copper who would listen about how he and his pal Johnny had robbed the Crouch End building society. Eventually one of the coppers did take notice of his story and checked if there had been any robberies that day. The cop got in touch with the Flying Squad, who came to interview Smasher after he had sobered up. He admitted everything and dropped Johnny right in it.

Both men pleaded guilty to the farcical armed robbery in court. Johnny got six years and Smasher got five. It just goes to show that, no matter how ridiculous and incompetent your actions may be on the day, if you are charged with armed robbery, then you will be going to prison. And you can take that to the bank.

Lenny the Lionheart was another robber who suffered a lot of misfortune, though it must be said that he brought most of it on himself. When I first met him he was going out with the landlady of my local pub, which was a villains' hang-out, and was game for a fight but not really involved in heavy crime. Originally from Newcastle, he had settled in south London in the mid-eighties and was well known for his bravery. Lenny would act as the unofficial bouncer at his girlfriend's pub. There could be no official bouncer – that would be like a red rag to a bull to a pub full of faces – so Lenny would throw out recalcitrant and aggressive drunks and troublemakers, of which there were many. Lenny didn't care who you were or what your reputation was, he would offer a straightener to anyone, and though he wasn't the best fighter in the world he would certainly have a good go.

Lenny got plotted up with an ex-South African paratrooper named Zane who was in England to make his fortune having worn out his welcome in the townships of South Africa with thirteen confirmed kills to his credit. Zane knew a man who knew a man who had a post-office robbery set up and just needed a couple of willing bodies to do the donkey work, and Lenny agreed to have a go. The job was in a little Surrey town and one of the post-office employees was supposed to be in on the work. The two boys would walk into the gaff and flash their firearms before being handed a bag with £17,000 in cash in it. It sounded simple, but it turned out that there was no colluding post-office worker involved and the man who set the work up was in fact an undercover police officer. The boys walked straight into a trap. One minute they were on the threshold of the post office wearing false beards and hats and fingering the firearms under their coats in anticipation; the next they were being arrested at gunpoint by various police officers disguised as council road-menders and passers-by.

When the Flying Squad searched Lenny they found a .32 revolver, a Jif lemon containing a weak mixture of water and ammonia and two knives. Zane was carrying a sawn-off shotgun. The Flying Squad love to take photographs at the scene of every arrest they make, not only for evidence but also for their scrapbooks. But when they stood Lenny up, his hands plasti-cuffed behind him, and tried to take a picture, he became camera shy and began to struggle wildly. In the struggle he and two Flying Squad officers fell backwards through the plate-glass window of a hardware shop. Now that's a set of photos I'd like to see!

Lenny and Zane pleaded not guilty at their trial but were soon found guilty by a jury of honest men and women. Lenny was sentenced to nine years and Zane to eleven. It didn't help Zane's cause when he lied under oath and said that the shotgun had been handed to him a minute before the robbery and that he didn't know if it was loaded or not. He finished his statement by saying, 'I'm afraid I don't know anything about guns,' and smiling sweetly at the jury. He was soon forced to swallow his words when the prosecution read choice extracts from Zane's South African army record stating that not only had he been responsible for shooting dead eight rioters and five 'terrorists' in the line of duty but that he was a top marksman and so proficient in the use of firearms he had received merits for his ability to field-strip machine guns and rifles in the dark before reassembling them in seconds. The judge was probably thinking about this revelation when he gave Zane the extra two years.

The pair were sent to HMP Wandsworth after sentencing and it was there that I was to spend the next fourteen months in their company. Lenny was a bit of a fitness fanatic and never missed a gym session – the only person who could beat his time on the gruelling fitness circuit training at Wandsworth was my co-defendant at the time, Crazy Dave – so I was very surprised when I visited Lenny's cell one afternoon and found him about to indulge in a bit of heroin. He was with a well-known wing skag-head called Chalky and had the powder on the foil and the tube in his mouth when I walked in. Lenny had the minerals to look embarrassed when I caught him in this compromising position. At this time, before heroin became all-pervading within the British prison system, it was still considered bad show for 'proper' prisoners to indulge in skag. Junkies were viewed as dirty and untrustworthy by most serious criminals and getting hooked was all about losing the respect of your peers. I walked out of the cell without a word. Later I spoke to Lenny about his drug use and he became defensive. 'It's a bird killer,' he declared. 'I won't get a habit, the minute it interferes with my training schedule I'll knock it straight on the head.' I shrugged. It was his life, he knew the dangers as well as I did, and I figured it was none of my business. Though I never fully trusted him after that.

Many years went by and I lost touch with Lenny. Then, in 1998, I was out of prison on parole and doing well in the armed-robbery game. I was having my latest girlfriend around to my flat for dinner and decided at the last minute to get a couple of bottles of champagne. I pulled up outside an off-licence on London Road, West Croydon, near where I was living, and went inside and made my purchases. As I came out of the shop I heard my name being called and looked around to see who it was. The voice was coming from a dirty bundle of rags wrapped in a sleeping-bag on the pavement. Staring at the grimy, sore-encrusted face staring from out of the sleeping-bag, I finally recognized Lenny, though a much thinner and haggard-looking Lenny to the one I had last seen in Wandsworth prison. At first, when I recognized him, I thought he must be working a disguise and was waiting for a security-van delivery to rob or something. Brilliant! I thought, and almost said it out loud. But it was no disguise. Lenny explained that he had got seriously hooked on heroin during his years in prison, and when he got out he had tried crack cocaine in the hope of weaning himself off his habit. Instead, he had become addicted to both and was now living on the streets and begging for a living, too weak and wasted even to go thieving. I listened to Lenny's story and then slipped him the few quid I was carrying. He was more than grateful for this and suggested that we get together for a drink some time and talk about the old days. I nodded and told him that I had to be off. As I walked back to my car I suddenly had a thought. I turned back to him. 'Here, Lenny,' I said. 'Are you still training?' He gave me a wry smile, and I knew he was remembering that day in his cell at Wandsworth.

Shotgun Johnny, who I mentioned earlier in this book, also had his own bit of bad luck, back when he worked with a partner. One day, he robbed a main branch post office and in his hurry to vacate the gaff took the dye-packs along with him for sorting out in the car.

Dye-packs are very attractive to the robber because, in the heat of a robbery, they look just like a stack of large-denomination banknotes, usually £50s. They work on a radio signal, which means that, if they get too far from the home signal, inside the bank, the charge will detonate. The red dye is indelible, and you may as well burn your robbery clothing lest it become incriminating evidence at a later date. It will come off human skin but only after repeated scrubbing with a stiff nailbrush and a solution of washing-powder and white spirit. In my local you could usually recognize those who'd had a bit of a shit day at work by the red-raw patches on their skin from the scrubbing. The money can be washed in a bath with the same solution of washing-powder and white spirit. You leave it in the solution for a day and eventually most of the dye will lift from the notes and float to the top. Each note then has to be rinsed and hung up to dry, though I used to iron them to make them crisp again. You can never get all the dye off the notes, and they often retain a pink tinge, which is not so bad as long as you do not try to pass too many in the same place. The worst thing is that the exploding pack also burns the notes. I once had to get rid of £8,500 because of burnt edges, a dead giveaway to any vigilant shopkeeper. I managed it, but it took me three weeks of going to several different boroughs of London.

Shotgun Johnny knew he was carrying at least three dye-packs in his freshly stolen load but time was of the essence as he'd just left the post-office ceiling over the carpet and his get-away driver was getting a bit antsy. Sitting in the passenger seat, Johnny told the nervous driver to hold his horses as he went through the bag and tossed out the dye-packs that were unexploded because they were still in range of their home signal. He pressed the button and the electric window of the car began to close as Johnny told the driver it was now safe to go. Then he heard a warning fizzing sound from the bag on his lap and realized that there was a fourth dye-pack in there. By now the driver had his foot down and was tooling down the high street, so Johnny reached into the bag and found the UXB. He launched it out of the window, but it hit the glass and bounced back inside the car, straight into the driver's lap. At the same time the speeding car reached the optimum distance away from the home signal in the post office and the dye-pack exploded. Now, these things are not like Christmas crackers: think three bonfire-night bangers tied tightly together and then imagine that exploding in your lap while you are driving at about 70 mph. The resulting explosion set light to the driver's jeans and instantly filled the speeding car with red smoke thicker than a police blanket. The driver swerved across a road he couldn't see and bounced off four parked cars before shooting through a busy junction against the lights and flow of traffic. Shotgun Johnny jabbed the control button that would lower the electric windows but decided they were moving too slowly, pulled his shotgun out and blasted the back screen of the motor.

Of course the driver couldn't see Shotgun Johnny through the smoke, and even if he had been able to he was too busy screaming and trying to put out the fire that was eating through his jeans. So when he registered the sound of the shotgun blast he thought that the police must have been shooting at them from the roadside, and this put him into even more of a panic, if such a thing was possible. He jammed the brakes on but found that movement of his leg increased the fiery pain in his lap, so he threw the handbrake on. The car went skidding in a 360-degree turn and hit the kerb before coming to rest. By now, with all the windows open and the back screen shot out, the smoke was beginning to disperse. Johnny leant over and jammed the money bag into the driver's lap, extinguishing the last of the flames. The driver was moaning in pain, his hands also burnt where he had tried batting the flames out with his fingers. Johnny quickly took stock. He was OK, they still had the money, the car was cleared of smoke – happy days. 'Let's go,' he ordered the driver. The man didn't really want to go anywhere except to a major burns unit in the nearest hospital but Johnny prodded him with the barrel of his gun and he started the car up once again. Hitting the kerb had punctured the front nearside tyre and the car went limping away.

Shotgun Johnny and his driver got away on the day but the driver was never to work with Johnny again. When they dumped the get-away car the driver could hardly walk and the whole front of his jeans had been burnt away, revealing seared and dyed genitals. It took the poor geezer almost five months of bed-rest and TLC from his girlfriend before he felt any way right in the trouser department again. A year later, when Shotgun Johnny was under arrest for a separate matter, the cops questioned him about the post-office job. They said that after forensic examination of the dumped get-away car they were going to put out an APB for someone who was walking like John Wayne and with a pair of glow-in-the-dark bollocks. Johnny offered to drop his strides but Old Bill didn't want to get an inferiority complex so declined the offer. But that incident was how it became mooted in the underworld that working with Shotgun Johnny was very bad luck.

Epilogue

The days of the bread-and-butter armed raider are numbered now. The professional walk-in bank robbers have all but gone the way of the dinosaurs due to increased bank security and because there is hardly any money in it any more. Electronic steel shutters that snap shut at the touch of a button, clearer high-definition CCTV footage, invisible dye sprays that show up only under infrared light, electronic doors and lockable till-drawers have all contributed to the demise of the spec robber. Nowadays you would have to brave more devices and traps than Indiana Jones just to get your hands on a lousy bit of till-money. It's just not worth the candle for career criminals to rob banks now. That's left to desperate junkies with fake guns and slightly off-key pensioners who need money for the gas meter. The professional robbers are all at the high end of the market now, doing 'tiger' kidnappings, such as the one pioneered by Deadly Dave. Up in that criminal stratosphere the rewards are massive, millions of pounds, but so are the risks of ending up with thirty-year sentences wrapped around you.

Sentencing for armed robbery has grown steadily more draconian over the last forty years. When the Great Train Robbers received a thirty-stretch each in 1964, the country took a collective gasp at the severity of the sentence for men who had basically stolen a vast amount of money using only pick handles. At that time the length of the average life sentence, given for murder or manslaughter, was only seven years. Questions were even asked in Parliament as to whether these men could survive such a long period in prison. In 2000 a couple of my mates, Charlie and Frannie, received thirty years each for attempted robbery on a security van in which a guard was shot in the hand. Nobody batted an eyelid. These days you can count yourself lucky if you get less than fifteen years for robbing a post office with a cap gun. Life has become the average tariff for armed robbery. For eight armed robberies, in which no shots were fired and no one was physically hurt. I was sentenced to eight life sentences plus eighty years in concurrent sentences. When you compare that to, say, Jeremy Bamber, who murdered his whole family, including two children, and only got five life sentences, you may begin to see the unevenness in sentencing in this country. But, it has to be said, if I was big and bad enough to walk around with a loaded firearm robbing people, then I can hardly start whingeing if the system chooses to whop it up me!

As I said in my preface, armed robbery is a serious and dangerous crime, and it is not only physical injuries that are inflicted on its victims. In most cases it causes a deep psychological trauma that can be worse than any physical wound or scar. And as the men in this book found to their cost, it causes a ripple effect that reaches their own families and children. Having to grow up with a father in jail sometimes scars the next generation and turns them on to the wrong path. I know, because it happened to one of my sons. And be assured, if you are stupid enough to take up armed robbery as a career, you will be going to prison. It's odds-on.

Razor Smith
Ex-armed robber
September 2006

Glossary

Agg	aggravation, trouble
At it	engaged in crime, usually armed robbery
Big One (the)	a robbery that will net enough money to retire on
Blag	a robbery
Blagger	armed robber
Bottle	courage
Brahmer (Brahma)	top-notch, the best (from Brahma, Hindu god who created the universe. Brought into London slang by servicemen returning from India in the Victorian era)
Bread-and-butter robber	career criminal who robs every week but never the Big One
Bubble	Information, to inform, an informer
Bye	'give him a bye'; to pass unquestioned
Category A, + AA + AAA	prisoner whose escape would jeopardize the safety of the police, Government and society as a whole
Change-over car	the second car in a get-away. Less hot than the first
Corey	security guards (from Securicor)
Div	a mug or fool
Gipper	'for the old gipper'; give your best (from the 1940s film *The Gipper* in which Ronald Reagan stars as an American football coach who inspires his team

with his dying words, 'Get out there and win one for the old Gipper!')

Greybar Hotel	prison
Happy bag	bag that contains the robber's kit, fire-arms, etc; also used to carry money
Hoisting	shoplifting (hoister: shoplifter)
Jump	counter area of a bank
Kiting	passing dud cheques (kiter: one who passes dud cheques)
Louisville slugger	baseball bat
Make one	commit robbery or escape from prison
Melt	an idiot with no bottle
Minerals	'to have the minerals'; to have courage and determination
Mooey	face or features
Nause	to mess up or ruin
Nostrils	double-barrelled sawn-off shotgun
Obbo	'under obbo'; observation
Oppo	friend or crime partner
Pony-bag	security cash bag insured for up to £25,000
Ready-eye	ambush set up by the Flying Squad
Recce	reconnoitre
Screw	prison officer
Shovel	prison (Cockney rhyming slang: shovel and pick: nick)
Spec	speculation; no particular target in mind
Stone ginger	certainty (racing slang)
Stretch	time spent in prison
String-vest	pest (Cockney rhyming slang)
TDA	Taking and Driving Away; old criminal charge for car theft, now known as TWOC, or Twocking, Taking Without Owner's Consent

Tom	'loved a bit of tom'; jewellery (Cockney rhyming slang: tomfoolery)
Ton-box	security cash box insured for up to £100,000
Two-bob	no good; not worth very much
Two-of-toast	best friends or crime partners, always together
Work	armed robbery